Feminist Criticism:
Theory and Practice

THEORY/CULTURE 8

General editors: Linda Hutcheon and Paul Perron

Feminist Criticism: Theory and Practice

Edited by Susan Sellers

University of Toronto Press
Toronto   Buffalo

Contents

Acknowledgements

The editor gratefully acknowledges the help of Sue Roe in commissioning essays for this collection.

Susan Sellers

Introduction

'In the beginning, feminist criticism was simple and polemical', writes Rebecca O'Rourke. Discussing the impact of Kate Millett's *Sexual Politics*, published in America in 1970, O'Rourke examines the links between the women's movement of the 1960s and 1970s and the feminist critique of literature.[1] Spearheaded by a spate of American publications in the wake of Millett's attack,[2] the canons of English and American literature were ransacked for their patriarchal and misogynist assumptions as well as for any positive representations of women they afforded. Recognition of the way male bias had privileged certain writers, themes and genres[3] initiated a search for a *female* literary tradition in works such as Ellen Moers' *Literary Women: The great writers* and Elaine Showalter's *A Literature of Their Own: British women novelists from Brontë to Lessing*. Drawing on the collective and individual interests of women's groups and the socio-historical and biographical foundation of literary study in American academia, this 'first wave' of feminist criticism was marked by its personal and empirical emphases.[4]

At approximately the same time,[5] European feminism, dominated for most American and British feminists by developments in France,[6] was evolving in a quite other direction.[7] Deriving from different political, intellectual and social traditions,[8] psychoanalyst Luce Irigaray challenged the innately masculine account of identity given by Western metaphysics,[9] whilst linguist and critic Julia Kristeva and writer Hélène Cixous cited the literary text as the locus for revolutionary change.[10]

The position of British feminist criticism within this divison is interesting. The work of British critic Cora Kaplan paralleled French insistence on language, ideology and the formation of the writing/reading self to question the notion, implicit in much early American feminist writing, that literature is direct representation, whilst employing Marxist analysis to foreground the material differences that exist between women-as-subjects.[11] One of the problems with Millett's critique in *Sexual Politics*, as Angela Leighton points out,[12] is that her reading views characters as if they are real people without acknowledging their textual creation or the role of the reader's response. French feminism has prompted investigation into the nature of

1

representation and desire, whilst the sociopolitical roots of Anglo-American feminism have maintained the connection between theoretical accounts of woman as linguistic and literary construct and actual women's lives.

The essays in this collection illustrate the current preoccupations and practices of thirteen British feminist critics.[13] Spanning a range of genres and a broad chronology of writings in English, the readings outline the individual positions of their author(s) through the detailed study of a text.

For her reading of Mary Shelley's *The Last Man*, Jane Aaron adopts a combination of socio-historical-material, poststructural-linguistic and psychoanalytically informed approaches.[14] She argues that to apprehend the complex patterns of gender in Shelley's novel we need to recognise the material and ideological pressures on nineteenth-century middle-class English-women – including the way these constraints impinge on the individual unconscious – and hence are figured in the narrative and language of *The Last Man*. Only by comprehending the precarious position for women of Shelley's class and interests, Aaron suggests, can we understand her refusal to be a spokesperson for the radical cause, and, by attending to the way her situation is figured in her writing, heed the message of her work.

Aaron demonstrates how through its narrative and metaphorical forms *The Last Man* indicts the polarisation of male and female roles brought about in Britain during the early years of the nineteenth century through industrialisation. This condemnation, together with the images of disease and war which pervade *The Last Man*, are reflected in Linda Williams's reading of Henry Miller's *Tropic of Cancer*. To Linda Williams, the sex war Miller wages is not the outcome of any personal enmity between men and women, but the result of the opposing positions historically reserved for the two sexes. Like Jane Aaron, Williams argues that to read productively we need to draw on feminist research into the historical and material causes of gender as well as psychoanalytic and linguistic-literary theories. She suggests that Freud's account of the death drive illuminates the war between males and females in *Tropic of Cancer*, surfacing this as the protagonist's – 'Miller's' – desire for *self* annihilation rather than any conventional striving for masculine mastery. Williams stresses that this preoccupation with *self* dissolution is embodied in the literary context of the struggle: Miller's attack is also an attack on the ways such a self is enshrined in traditional narratives. Early feminist critiques of Miller – such as Kate Millett's assault in *Sexual Politics* – Williams writes, overlooked this dimension, and so failed to confront the questions or possibilities raised by *Tropic of Cancer* and hence, ultimately, to read it. Extending the lexicon of warfare, Williams concludes that feminist reading cannot proceed from a predetermined and therefore potentially blind position but must, as in a guerrilla operation, employ the weapons and defences of the other against itself to engender a criticism in practice.

A number of the issues broached by Linda Williams, such as the problem of identification for women readers and the tensions between conscious – politically 'correct' – intention and unconscious desire, are developed in Ann Thompson's reading of Shakespeare's *The Tempest*. Thompson argues that early forms of Anglo-American feminist criticism, such as that focusing on 'images of women', necessarily draw a blank when confronted with texts like *The Tempest* from which females are largely excluded. Like Jane Aaron, she believes a more fruitful aim is to read so as to reveal how a particular ideology of gender functions within a text, thereby highlighting the hold that ideology may have on us. Utilising the frameworks of historical and political analysis, psychoanalysis and contemporary literary theory Thompson shows how, despite the virtual absence of women characters from *The Tempest*, woman as a subject – including the various themes associated with her – is abundantly figured in the play. She surveys the body of Shakespeare scholarship to suggest that the single application of a critical strategy privileges, distorts or obliterates elements of the text; whilst a knowledge of the politics of seventeeth-century England may foreground the colonialist underpinnings of Prospero's endeavour, and psychoanalytic studies of the absent mother disclose flaws in the patriarchal island order, neither reading, she stresses, fully engages with the complexities of Shakespeare's play.

Thompson completes her essay with a warning against the dangers of attempting to establish a fixed position for reading. Although as a feminist and a woman it is possible to gain pleasure from probing the fault lines in Prospero's patrimony, approaching the play as a white British reader, Thompson writes, the pleasures are differently aligned. Her reminder as to how the axes of nationality, race, class, education, age and sexuality intersect with our status as women is explored in Rebecca O'Rourke's reading of Jeanette Winterson's *Oranges Are Not the Only Fruit*. O'Rourke suggests that one of the contributions of feminist criticism has been its acceptance of the provisional nature of reading: not only is each reading shaped by the frameworks we employ and our own changing predilections and prejudices, but, she stresses, our understanding is governed by the context and purposes for which reading occurs. Like Ann Thompson, she argues that our interpretation is informed by the judgements of others, whether these are the 'official' views of the academy and media or the unofficial opinions of friends. Deploring the recent tendency amongst feminist critics to adopt fashionable theoretical models for reading, O'Rourke proposes the image of a circle – composed of a number of elements – across which the reader is free to move as interests and circumstances dictate.

Ann Thompson stresses that one of the problems with psychoanalytic readings of *The Tempest* is that they require us to focus as much on what the text does not say as on what it actually says. Reflecting on the figure of the absent mother may prove instrumental in unmasking the play's obsession with the father, but, Thompson writes, such readings exist only by default and create difficulties when staging the play. Her anxiety concerning the implications of concentrating on the not-said of a text is paralleled in Janet Todd's essay on Jane Austen. Todd argues that Austen poses problems for feminist readers despite attempts to claim her for the feminist cause. She describes how Sandra Gilbert and Susan Gubar's seminal reading in *The Madwoman in the Attic: The woman writer and the nineteeth-century literary imagination*, which instates Austen as a would-be revolutionary, depends on locating an indictment in what Austen omits. Todd believes such readings have prevented feminists from hearing what it is Austen does say. Like Linda Williams, she suggests that feminist criticism must engage with the challenges and contradictions posed by writers and their work. To read Austen effectively, Todd writes, requires a knowledge of her historical and social context as well as its *literary* traditions. She stresses that only by situating Austen within the cult of the eighteenth-century novel of sensibility can we apprehend her attack on the unreal premisses of the genre, and so discern her true radicalism.

One of the issues broached in Rebecca O'Rourke's reading of *Oranges Are Not the Only Fruit* is how far the novel can be considered a lesbian text. This question opens Paulina Palmer's study of Antonia White's *Frost in May*. Palmer suggests that whatever status White's novel is accorded, a lesbian feminist reading offers productive routes into the text. White's indirect style, for instance, can be fruitfully contextualised within the taboo against female relationships in Britain in the inter-war period. According to Janet Todd, one of the difficulties with the English novel of sensibility is its treatment of femininity as if it is unchanging, a perception Austen ruthlessly attacked. Palmer similarly insists that sexual identity must be viewed through the lenses of culture and history, though she also warns of the potential obliteration of a women's and lesbian continuum as a consequence of such a view. She concludes her essay with a plea for a feminist criticism in which both positions can be accommodated.

Palmer's investigation of the changing material and ideological conditions of gender and the need for a continuity of women's and lesbian writing is developed in Rebecca Ferguson's reading of Toni Morrison's novel *Beloved*.

Ferguson suggests that continuity is vital to black – and particularly black women – writers. Although black writing in America has drawn freely on the formal experiments of postmodernism, Ferguson stresses that the postmodern preoccupation with the *dis*continuity of history, language and identity creates problems for black writers: blacks and whites have had reason to forget black history, and the official exclusion of blacks from language and any autonomous sense of identity have been powerful instruments in black repression. Employing historical and cultural analysis in conjunction with poststructural and psychoanalytic theory, Ferguson examines how the themes of history, language and individual and collective identity are embodied in Morrison's novel, as both enabling and preventing progress in the specific context of black experience.

A key concern of Ferguson's reading of *Beloved* is the difficulty that confronts Morrison in attempting to express what has been repressed. A major component in this is the relationship between Sethe and her two daughters. In her study of H.D.'s *Helen in Egypt*, Claire Buck pursues this area of the suppressed mother–daughter bond. Adopting the psychoanalytic and philosophical writings of Luce Irigaray, Buck details how, within Western patriarchal culture, women are denied access to the maternal origin. Like Paulina Palmer, she addresses the division between essentialist and constructionist views of gender to suggest that the roots of Irigaray's thesis lie in her recognition of the role of fantasy in psychic reality, rather than any notion of an unchanging biology. Buck considers how, for Irigaray, this area of fantasy is ringed in by the existing social order: our perceptions of ourselves and others are informed by fantasies, themselves the mirrors of our history and culture. In *Helen in Egypt*, Buck suggests, the narrator rewrites the founding phallic story to open a potential space for *feminine* expression and desire, thereby offering the reader an other, utopian vision of the configurations of sexual differences.

H.D.'s motivation in choosing a *masculine* narrative voice for the poem, Buck writes, can be linked to this difficulty in giving expression to the feminine within the monoculture of Western patriarchy. By employing a masculine narrator and view, and through this means disclosing the attendant annihilation of a daughter's relation to *her* m/other, Buck argues that H.D. deciphers the fabrications of male myth, and ghosts an alternative for both sexes. This issue of gender and narrative voice is the theme of Lynne Pearce's reading of John Clare's *Child Harold*. Like Janet Todd, Pearce stresses that the literary context is intrinsic to our understanding of the poem. She demonstrates how *Child Harold* embodies the tenets and forms of the romantic love tradition by adopting a masculine subject and feminine love-object. This awareness of the gender politics of the poem, Pearce explains, alters the results of her previous readings which had failed to investigate the sexual dynamic of Clare's address. Like Linda Williams and Ann Thompson, she believes such conventions create difficulties for women readers, forcing us either into the position of surrogate male or the schizophrenia of a double identification with masculine subject *and* feminine object: both places, Pearce writes, marginalise our status as women.

Whilst Lynne Pearce acknowledges the importance of feminist critique of male writers within an establishment which continues to privilege men, she questions the ultimate political value of such activity, and her plea for greater engagement by feminist critics with women's writing is echoed in Elaine Hobby's reading of the seventeenth-century radical Hester Biddle. Hobby opens her essay by describing how, as a postgraduate student, she was told that there were no women writers in the seventeenth century. This statement initiated her research into women's writing during the English Civil War. Hobby argues that whilst her retelling of this incident has highlighted some details and obliterated others, the story does have a grounding in fact, and she refuses the current tendency amongst critics to dismiss history as an amalgamation of recorders' and readers' biases. She stresses the role of a historical perspective in reading even though the information available to us may be inaccurate and alter as fresh evidence comes to light, an approach she combines with theoretical accounts of the relationship between texts and ideologies. Her reading of Hester Biddle's pamphlet 'Woe to thee, city of Oxford', which she reproduces here, exemplifies this conjunction of historical, intertextual and Marxist strategies and challenges the assumption that only certain types of text merit literary study.

In their joint reading of the *Assembly of Ladies*, Ruth Evans and Lesley Johnson similarly apply material and theoretical frameworks to situate the late fifteenth-century poem within its historical, ideological and cultural contexts. The *Assembly of Ladies* nevertheless raises a problem for feminists in that the name – and hence the sex – of its author remains unknown. Dismissing critics' attempts to determine the author's sex, Evans and Johnson shift the focus for meaning to within the text itself. Using a combination of empirical and poststructural strategies, they highlight both the fantasised scenario for the poem, which could not have existed under the codes of medieval law, and the comparative rarity of a female narrator within the tradition of courtly love verse, to disclose the impossible constructions imposed on femininity during the late Middle Ages as well as the poem's resistance to these.

Like a number of the critics writing here, Evans and Johnson argue for a conjunction of material and theoretical approaches allied to a 'close' reading of the text itself. This insistence is echoed in Penny Boumelha's essay on George Meredith's *Diana of the Crossways*. To Evans and Johnson, the cracks beneath the seemingly innocent picture of a privileged society at play in the *Assembly of Ladies* are both real – reflecting the tensions within medieval society – and symbolic/literary, a distinction Boumelha continues in her analysis of the *textual* composition of Meredith's Diana. Boumelha suggests that Meredith's task in *Diana of the Crossways* – that of writing a woman – has to be seen in terms of the literary arena of the undertaking. In her study of *Helen in Egypt*, Claire Buck considers the difficulties that confront a writer attempting to express a woman who will not be the mirror of man, and Boumelha similarly insists that Meredith's project needs to be viewed in the light of this dilemma. The novelist's failure to create in Diana 'a woman of the future' who will be both *a* woman and species representative, Boumelha argues, can be attributed as much to the patterns and forms of the realist novel – itself a reflection of nineteenth-century views on women – as to the absence of any alternative, real-life models.

In her reading of Mary Shelley's *The Last Man*, Jane Aaron suggests that gender is the product of material and ideological influences. We are women and men not only as a consequence of the rules that govern our external conduct, but also as a result of how we repeat, internalise and resist the *stories* of who we are. Unravelling these configurations in the literary text is a fruitful enterprise for feminists, requiring a corresponding amalgam of reading approaches if we are to apprehend the various threads of our sexual and textual identities. The essays in this collection both individually and together illustrate such an endeavour, offering productive routes into the literary text as well as to how we may read ourselves.

NOTES

1. Although feminist criticism in America and Britain did not begin with the publication of *Sexual Politics*, it can be argued that the book's wide circulation – *Sexual Politics* became an international bestseller reprinted three times in the first four years of its appearance in Britain alone – represents the first general acknowledgement of the issues involved. See Virginia Woolf, *A Room of One's Own* (1928; Harmondsworth: Penguin, 1963), for an earlier, pioneering work of feminist criticism.
2. See the bibliography for details of texts by American feminist critics published at this time.
3. Annette Kolodny's *The Lay of the Land: Metaphor as experience and history in American life and letters* (North Carolina: North Carolina University Press, 1975) and Judith Fetterley's *The Resisting Reader: A feminist approach to American fiction* (Bloomington: Indiana University Press, 1978) are good examples of this attack on malestream criticism.
4. Janet Todd's *Feminist Literary History* (Oxford: Polity Press, 1988) gives a useful overview

of the developments of American and British feminist criticism – including their relations to French theory – during this time.

5. Hélène Cixous first published in 1967 (her thesis *L'Exil de James Joyce ou l'art du remplacement* was published in 1969, Paris: Grasset), and Luce Irigaray's *Speculum de l'autre femme*, Paris: Minuit, Julia Kristeva's *La Révolution du langage poétique*, Paris: Seuil and Annie Leclerc's *Parole de femme*, Paris: Grasset were all published in 1974.

6. The publication of translated extracts by French feminists such as Hélène Cixous, Xavière Gauthier, Luce Irigaray, Julia Kristeva, Annie Leclerc and Monique Wittig in *New French Feminisms: An anthology*, edited by Elaine Marks and Isabelle de Courtivron (Amherst, Mass.: University of Massachusetts Press, 1980; Hemel Hempstead: Harvester Wheatsheaf, 1981) helped to crystallise this perception.

7. In order to highlight the *differences* between American and French concerns, I have omitted here all reference to those works, such as Mary Daly's *Beyond God The Father: Towards a philosophy of women's liberation* (Boston: Beacon, 1973) and *Gyn/Ecology* (Boston: Beacon, 1979), Adrienne Rich's *Of Woman Born: Motherhood as experience and institution* (New York: Norton, 1976) and Beatrice Didier's *L'Écriture-femme* (Paris: Presses Universitaires de France, 1981), which cross the lines of this divide.

8. As stressed in Note 7 above, I have deliberately omitted reference to the more socio-politically based French feminist campaigns and publications. There are now a number of anthologies available in English which serve to correct this initial privileging of the more 'theoretical' writers of French feminism. See, as examples, Claire Duchen (ed.) *French Connections: Voices from the women's movement in France* (London: Routledge, 1987), and the translated article 'Protofeminism and Antifeminism' by Christine Delphy, in Toril Moi (ed.) *French Feminist Thought: A reader* (Oxford: Blackwell, 1987). My own study *Language and Sexual Difference: Feminist writing in France* (Macmillan: Basingstoke, 1991), whilst it focuses on the theoretical debate, seeks to extend the now standard triptych of Cixous/ Irigaray/Kristeva to include a wider range of theorists and writers. Claire Duchen's *Feminism in France: From May 68 to Mitterand* (London: Routledge, 1986) offers an accessible account for English readers of the development of the women's movement in France. It can be argued that the infamous court case, brought by a leading member of the *Mouvement de Libération des Femmes* for possession of the movement's name, exacerbated the split between intellectual and campaigning interests.

9. See Luce Irigaray, *Speculum of the Other Woman* (1974), trans. Gillian C. Gill (Ithaca, NY: Cornell University Press, 1985).

10. See Julia Kristeva, *Revolution in Poetic Language* (1974), trans. Margaret Waller (New York: Columbia University Press, 1984) and Hélène Cixous, *The Newly Born Woman* (with C. Clément, 1975), trans. Betsy Wing (Manchester: Manchester University Press, 1986).

11. See, as an example of Cora Kaplan's work, 'Pandora's Box: subjectivity, class and sexuality in socialist feminist criticism', in *Making A Difference: Feminist literary criticism*, ed. Gayle Greene and Coppélia Kahn (London: Methuen, 1985), pp. 146–76. See the bibliography for details of more recent American feminist critical publications. Collections such as Nancy Miller's (ed.) *The Poetics of Gender* (New York: Columbia University Press, 1980) demonstrate contemporary American feminist engagement with theoretical questions. Miller's 'Preface' also points to the renewed interest in issues of class, race and postcolonialism evidenced in much current American feminist research.

12. Angela Leighton, 'Feminist literary theory: an introduction', Occasional Paper 8, University of Hull English Department Erasmus programme 'Women's studies in literature', 1989.

13. I am using the term 'British' to denote critics working within what can be broadly labelled a British tradition, rather than in any narrow sense of current place of work. I am indebted to the British-based 'Network' of women in higher education for providing, through their members' register, details of feminist interests and research. This register was the starting-point for commissioning the contributions to this volume.

14. The essays are not grouped according to the chronological or genre formats so often the hallmark of malestream criticism. I am grateful to Isobel Armstrong for suggesting the current division between those contributions most concerned with strategies for *reading* gender and those which primarily address the *written* construction of gender within the text.

Jane Aaron

The Return of the Repressed: Reading Mary Shelley's *The Last Man*

I

In her widowed later years, isolated, in financial difficulties and painfully sensitive to Victorian England's disapproval of the romantic improprieties of her youth, Mary Shelley professed herself to be in agreement with her society's conventional view of women. 'My belief is . . . that the sex of our material mechanism makes us quite different creatures [from men] – better though weaker but wanting in the higher grades of intellect', she wrote in 1835.[1] By this date Shelley had already established herself as a noteworthy figure in the literary circles of her time; five of her novels had already been published, along with a number of short stories and a volume of travel writing, and she was soon to produce a sixth novel, an annotated edition of her husband's poetry, another account of her travels and a series of biographical essays on eminent European thinkers and writers. Given the range and quality of her productive output, it hardly seems surprising that those amongst her contemporaries who deplored the denigration of woman looked to her as a spokesperson in their defence. Her half-sister, Claire Clairmont, wrote to her vehemently, charging her with this task:

> If you would but know your own value you could give the men a most immense drubbing! You could write upon metaphysics, politics, jurisprudence, astronomy, mathematics – all those highest subjects which they taunt us with being incapable of treating, and surpass them; and what a consolation it would be, when they begin some of their prosy, lying, but plausible attacks upon female inferiority, to stop their mouths in a moment with your name.[2]

But for Mary Shelley the prospect of being the focus of such public attention was anathema: 'There is nothing I shrink from more fearfully than publicity', she confesses to Edward Trelawney in 1829, and goes on to tell him that, far from taking pride in her intellectual and creative abilities, she believes her 'chief merit' to be 'a love of that privacy which no woman can emerge from without regret'.[3] It is her consciousness of herself as a woman

9

that makes her reluctant to enter the public arena; she defends her withdrawal as being in accord with the expected characteristics of the female role. Given her close familial connections with radicalism and early feminism (as the daughter of Mary Wollstonecraft and William Godwin, and the wife of Percy Bysshe Shelley), she could not, however, easily dismiss the expectations others had of her. An entry in her journals for 21 October 1838 attempts a defensive rationalisation of her position:

> In the first place, with regard to 'the good cause' – the cause of the advancement of freedom and knowledge, of the rights of women, &c. – I am not a person of opinions. . . . I do not feel that I could say aught to support the cause efficiently; besides that, on some topics (especially with regard to my own sex), I am far from making up my mind. I believe we are sent here to educate ourselves, and that self-denial, and disappointment, and self-control, are a part of our education; that it is not by taking away all restraining law that our improvement is to be achieved; and, though many things need great amendment, I can by no means go so far as my friends would have me.[4]

Shelley's insistence on quiescent self-restraint was indeed an outcome of the female education she and her contemporaries had received. One of the chief merits of a late twentieth-century *feminist* education, however, whether or not we were 'sent here' to acquire it, is that it allows us to decode and understand the social and psychological pressures that lie behind Shelley's anxious, self-distorting need to conform with the sequestration of women in the private sphere. What is more, I believe that an investigation of the effects of gender discrimination in earlier epochs can aid us in the understanding of contemporary structures, and the processes by which they came to be; perceiving how a repressive system exerts its grip upon the individual subject can free us and enable us to bring analytic clarity and energy to the task of righting the 'many things' which still 'need great amendment' in present-day society. The Romantic era, my chosen area of specialisation, constitutes a fruitful field for such an investigation since it was a period in which attitudes and beliefs with regard to gender, as to other aspects of social control, were in a state of radical flux. Mary Shelley's life spanned a period of transition from the proto-feminism associated with pro-French revolutionary radicalism in England in the 1790s to the strongly polarised gender system characteristic of the Victorian period, a loss of ground in feminist terms from which it may be said we have still not yet fully recovered.

At this point I imagine a reader wondering why, if such be my concerns, I'm not reading and teaching social history rather than literature. But a literary text, given that its figurative use of language can reveal the effects of ideological indoctrination upon the unconscious as well as conscious mind, in some respects provides a richer page for feminist analysis than document-ary material. At the same time, close textual scrutiny, still the mainstay of literary teaching, sensitises us to variances and nuances in the tones and styles of writing generally; variances which may be at odds with the professed beliefs or purposes of the writer. The interaction of tensions affecting the nineteenth-century woman writer, who must to some extent accommodate herself to the prevailing dogma in order to achieve publication, and yet whose very act of inscription announces her defiance of its strictures, can only fully be appreciated by bringing into critical play a variety of the available methodological approaches. As feminist theorists are currently stressing, a consideration of the functions of gender in writing, or indeed in the history of human society generally, requires a combination of both socio-historical and psychoanalytic approaches in order to achieve anything like an adequate appreciation of the complexities involved.[5] On the one hand, the particular functioning of gender difference in a text cannot be adequately assessed without exploring its ideological relation to the prevalent attitudes in the society which informed it. But, on the other, a purely materialistic investigation of the determining pressures upon individual formation limits itself, when it comes to an analysis of gendered power relations, if it fails to appreciate the manner in which the unconscious, as much as the conscious mind, is constructed by socioeconomic, as well as sexual–familial pressures. A psychoanalytically informed deconstruction of the ambivalences at play in language can provide a demystifying route into the experience of gender, and of power relations generally, in a given subject. In the reading which follows, I first explore the changing pattern of gender formation at work during Shelley's time, and then move on, through textual analysis informed by psychoanalytic theory, to investigate what it gives rise to in her texts.

II

The publication of Leonore Davidoff and Catherine Hall's *Family Fortunes: Men and women of the English middle class 1780–1850* has substantially added to our understanding of the gender formations characteristic of middle-class society in nineteenth-century England, and their effects. During the early years of the century, the woman's world was more and more limited to a domestic sphere set apart from the man's world of work and business. The old eighteenth-century way of life, in which work and leisure had both taken place within the home and involved the combined activities of all members of the family, rapidly disappeared as economic changes in the structure of an increasingly industrialised society brought about a division of material production from domestic life, and, consequently, a new polarisation of social roles. According to Davidoff and Hall, this developing segregation had become entrenched by the 1830s: 'it was recognised that men would be preoccupied with business and domesticity had become the "woman's sphere" rather than . . . a way of living for both men and women.'[6] In her book *The Proper Lady and the Woman Writer*, Mary Poovey, discussing the same polarisation, argues that it was strengthened and in part brought about by the need to retain a sacrosanct area of personal relationship within increasingly impersonalised methods of production: 'as competition and confrontation replaced the old paternalistic alliances of responsibilities and dependence, women . . . as exemplars of paternalistic virtues . . . were being asked to preserve the remnants of the old society within the private sphere of the home.'[7] The years bridging the eighteenth and nineteenth centuries saw a great increase in the publication of popular conduct-books for women, designed to advise a newly literate female readership as to the mores and behaviour patterns they needed to adopt in order to achieve the status of 'Angel in the house'. Hannah More, for example, in her influential *Strictures on the Modern System of Female Education* (1799), exhorts women to impose upon themselves patterns of habitual restraint and deference to the male, and to instil in their daughters self-mistrust and conformity to patriarchal authority:

> They should be lead to distrust their own judgement; they should learn not to murmur at expostulation; they should be accustomed to expect and endure opposition. . . . It is of the last importance to their happiness even in this life that they should early acquire a submissive temper and a forbearing spirit.[8]

There are obvious similarities here between More's stress upon the necessary self-discipline of women and Mary Shelley's emphasis on the importance of female self-denial in her 1838 journal entry, quoted above. An earlier text, whose influence may be detected in both More's and Shelley's writings, appears to be Rousseau's *Émile*; parts of the *Strictures* read practically as translations of Rousseau's advice on how to bring up daughters, and we know from her journals that Shelley was reading *Émile* in 1822.[9] The first part of *Émile*, on the education of boys, is entirely in accord with the radical doctrines, preaching the need to free men from the chains imposed by socialisation, with which Rousseau's name is generally associated. But when he turns to the question of girls' education in the second part of his treatise, it becomes clear that when Rousseau speaks of men as 'born free, but everywhere in chains', and of the need to free them from those chains, he is specifically thinking of men, of males, and not including women within the category. On the contrary, according to him, the very system of human reproduction entails upon women a necessary and life-long restraint; he bases his nostrums on female education upon what he sees as the necessary role of women during the sexual act:

> In the union of the sexes each alike contributes to the common end, but in different ways. . . . The man should be strong and active; the woman should be weak and passive; the one must have both the power and the will; it is enough that the other should offer little resistance. . . . If woman is made to please and to be in subjection to man, she ought to make herself pleasing in his eyes and not provoke him to anger . . . Girls . . . should early be accustomed to restraint. . . . They must be trained to bear the yoke from the first, so that they may not feel it, to master their own caprices and to submit themselves to the will of others.[10]

Mary Shelley's mother, in her *Vindication of the Rights of Women*, had argued strongly against such debilitating theories; Mary's friends expected her too to demonstrate their iniquity. But Mary's personal writings, her letters and journals, show her, rather, to have interiorised the notion that biological differences create inherent psychological differences, that the female is through her biology necessarily inferior to the male in intellect, although the perpetual patterns of self-restraint with which she has been inculcated may make her morally his superior. She accepts for her own estimation of herself the sexist ideology prevalent during her period. Yet her self-denial brought with it its own pain, as she explains in a journal entry:

> To hang back, as I do, brings a penalty. . . . To be something great and good was the precept given me by my Father: Shelley reiterated it. Alone and poor, I could only be something by joining a party; and there was much in me – the woman's love of looking up, and being guided, and being willing to do anything if any one supported and brought me forward – which would have made me a good partisan. But Shelley died and I was alone. . . . My total friendlessness, my horror of pushing, and inability to put myself forward unless led, cherished and supported, – all this has sunk me in a state of loneliness no other human being ever before, I believe endured . . . If I write the above, it is that those who love me may hereafter know that I am not all to blame, nor merit the heavy accusations cast on me for not putting myself forward. I *cannot* do that; it is against my nature. As well cast me from a precipice and rail at me for not flying.[11]

A debilitating consciousness of what it is to be a woman restricts her: it is 'the woman's love of being guided', the woman's 'horror of pushing' and of 'putting myself forward' which holds her back.

And yet, for all her painful interiorisation of her society's sexual ideology, Mary Shelley did in fact write and publish extensively, at a time when merely to publish was in itself a subversive act when performed by a woman, an act frequently disguised by anonymity or pseudonym; for a woman to write threatened the common assumption of female passivity, and broke the bonds of propriety which inculcated female silence. For all the vehemence with which she expresses her belief in the narrow feminine role, and for all her desire to stay within its confines, Mary did act contrary to her self-restraining principles. She may have done so with reluctance, but nevertheless the existence of her writings indicates to us a degree of inner resistance to the doctrines she was espousing, a contradiction within the self between the limitations of the female role she had accepted and her own manifest capacity to surmount them. The loneliness which she frequently laments in her journals is in part the consequence of this contradiction; she is caught between two conflicting worlds. Her radical inheritance, and her position as a woman writer, along with the history of her elopement at the age of 16 with the married Shelley, meant that she was not always easily acceptable amongst the conventional circles of upper- and middle-class society; she hardly had the required image of propriety. But her impulse to protect herself with the mantle of prescribed femininity makes her fearful of alignment with the few radical figures still voicing objections to the status quo during her time. On the one hand, she experiences herself as seen by others as representative of the monster figure of radicalism and the monstrous impropriety of the woman writer; on the other, she has taken upon herself, she has internalised, the limitations of her period's prescribed feminine role, which, from our present-day perspective, and that of Mary Shelley's own more radical acquaintance, in itself appears monstrous. Thus divided, she seeks to hide herself from the public gaze which has imposed such self-distortions upon her.

Feminist critics of Shelley's work have argued that in her fictional writing she did seek to give expression to her feelings at thus being made to experience herself as monstrous. Many of her fictional texts explore the pain and destruction entailed when an individual feels forced to interiorise a derogatory and limiting view of him – or her – self. In *Frankenstein* (1818) the monster, in his narrative, presents himself as initially well-disposed towards others, for all his repellent appearance. His biological oddity appears so alarming to all the humans he encounters, however, that they attribute monstrosity to his psychological self, and fearfully reject him on sight. Eventually, he vengefully determines to adopt their view of him, and become, in his actions as well as his appearance, the monster they believe him to be. Sandra M. Gilbert and Susan Gubar, in their seminal work on nineteenth-century women writers, *The Madwoman in the Attic*, point to the ways in which the monster's situation can be compared to that of women in nineteeth-century society.[12] The monster desires to play a full part in social affairs, but is prevented from doing so, as women are, by his society's conviction that his biological difference must entail a psychological difference.

Frankenstein's monster, though, is in a position to see himself as having been created, or constructed, as a monster; he may interiorise a sense of himself as monstrous but he can pin the blame for his deficiencies upon his creator Frankenstein. Thus he dodges the intensity of guilt associated with an acquired sense of monstrosity which cripples the life of the central character in the next novel Mary Shelley wrote, *Mathilda*. *Mathilda*, like *Frankenstein*, is about the suffering caused by irresponsible parenting; unlike the Monster, though, Mathilda is loved by her progenitor not too little but too well. Her widowed father confesses to his 16-year-old daughter his incestuous passion for her, and although he is driven by guilt to commit suicide rather than act on his desires, his daughter, for the rest of her brief life, feels constrained to take upon herself to a marked degree the sin and the guilt of his illicit desires. Merely the knowledge of having innocently aroused such a passion is enough to make her monstrous to herself. She chooses complete social isolation as the only way to protect the world from her own hideousness. Her experience seems too poisonous to divulge it to others; she only tells her tale in writing, in the narrative we read, when she knows herself to be dying of consumption. In the account she gives of herself in the final pages of her narrative, however, she does indicate some understanding of the processes of introjection, of how she has irrationally taken upon herself the guilt and shame of incest. After her father's confession, Mathilda writes,

> I believed myself to be polluted by the unnatural love I had inspired, and that I was a creature cursed and set apart by nature. I thought that like another Cain, I had a mark set on my forehead to shew mankind that there was a barrier between me and they [sic]. . . . there it lay a gloomy mark to tell the world that there was that within my soul that no silence could render sufficiently obscure. Why when fate drove me to become this outcast from human feeling; this monster with whom none might mingle in converse and love; why had she not from that fatal and most accursed moment, shrouded me in thick mists and placed real darkness between me and my fellows so that I might never more be seen? [sic] and as I passed, like a murky cloud loaded with blight, they might only perceive me by the cold chill I should cast upon them; telling them, how truly, that something unholy was near? . . . I verily believe that if the near prospect of death did not dull and soften my bitter [fe]elings, if for a few months

longer I had continued to live as I then lived, strong in body but my soul corrupted to its core by a deadly cancer . . . I should have become mad, and should have fancied myself a living pestilence: so horrible to my own solitary thoughts did this form, this voice, and all this wretched self appear; for had it not been the source of a guilt that wants a name?[13]

Mathilda's account vividly suggests how the victim of sexual assault can see herself as tarnished by the deed, and imagine herself guilty of collusion with it, merely because her physical presence became its target. Mathilda cannot, like Frankenstein's monster, locate the guilt firmly where it belongs, upon the shoulders of her father; she still loves him, and feels bound to him. Instead she turns her destructive anger upon herself, and welcomes her own death. Her narrative as a whole, had it been available, would perhaps have helped previous generations to become aware of the psychological conse-quences for the assaulted child of incest and child abuse, factors which we are only painfully beginning to understand today. But *Mathilda* was never published during Mary Shelley's lifetime, and did not appear in print until the middle of this century, and even then only in the relatively obscure form of an academic edition from an American University press, now out of print. Mary appears to have felt some anxiety about the scandalous nature of its subject-matter; she sent the manuscript to her own father, William Godwin, asking him to act as arbitrator as to whether or not it should appear in print. Given its topic, this does seem something of a mistake – practically the equivalent, say, of Salman Rushdie sending the manuscript of *The Satanic Verses* to Ayatollah Khomeini for him to see it through the presses. Godwin, who by 1820, when he received the manuscript, had for many years left behind him the more radical allegiances of his young manhood, was disturbed by the tale. He found its subject-matter, he said, 'disgusting and detestable', and was unprepared to see it published.[14] Mary's frequent requests to him either to revise and publish the book, or to return it to her, went unanswered; the novel was left hidden amongst his papers, and deposited at his death, along with a vast mass of Shelley's manuscripts, in the Bodleian library, where it lay unpublished until Elizabeth Nitchie edited it. An early version of the story, called *The Fields of Fancy*, has still not been published. *Mathilda's* textual history seems to constitute a repetition of the incrimination of the victim which Mary describes in the book: the tale itself is seen as 'disgusting and detestable', and the hidden realities of exploitation and suffering which it intends to surface remain unread.

III

A few years later, however, in 1826, Mary did publish another novel, *The Last Man*, which, in a covert and subversive way, takes its revenge upon a patriarchal system dependent upon the repression of female lives and female self-expression. An early example of the science fiction genre, the novel opens in the year 2073; nevertheless, Mary Shelley cannot imagine that even at this future date the relation of the sexes to one another will have fundamentally changed. In *The Last Man*, women are still restricted to domesticity, and cut off from all action in the public domain, as they were at the beginning of the nineteenth century. But in this novel, unlike *Mathilda*, she does allow some of her female characters to express their anger at the limitations of their lives. Perdita, for example, when deserted by her husband Raymond, responds with bitterness to the inequalities in gender relations:

> He, she thought, can be great and happy without me. Would that I also had a career! Would that I could freight some untried bark with all my hopes, energies and desires, and launch it forth into the ocean of life – bound for some attainable point, with ambition or pleasure at the helm! But adverse winds detain me on shore; like Ulysses, I sit at the water's edge and weep.[15]

Perdita's association of her own frustrations with those of the classical male hero, Ulysses, presses home the point that women have the same desires for adventure and achievement as men, and suffer similarly when thwarted.

Later in the text, however, disaster strikes this still deeply patriarchal twenty-first century: an irresistible and deadly Plague sweeps across the world, wiping out, with tremendous rapidity, whole populations. Throughout the novel, this monster, the Plague, is personified as female, and referred to as 'she'. It is as though Mathilda's image of herself as a 'living pestilence' has taken physical form, and set itself to wreak a fearful vengeance on the society which created it: the femaleness of the Plague seems to indicate its function as a destructive and vengeful 'return of the repressed' in Freudian terms. In classic Freudian psychoanalysis disabling physical symptoms, which have no apparent physiological cause, are interpreted as signs and indicators of frustrated drives and desires unconsciously repressed by the psyche, in its attempts to conform with the demands of socialisation. The Plague in *The Last Man* appears to symbolise the eruption of pent-up female discontents, no longer affecting only the interior psychological balance of the individual, but exteriorised, on a vast scale, to threaten the continuity of the human race as a whole. At first, England girds up its manly loins to resist this affliction. Lionel, the novel's narrator, proclaims:

> 'If manly courage and resistance can save us, we will be saved. We will fight the enemy to the last. Plague shall not find us a ready prey; we will dispute every inch of ground; and, by methodical and inflexible laws, pile invincible barriers to the progress of our foe. Perhaps in no part of the world has she met with so systematic and determined an opposition.' (p. 178)

All men are called upon to take action to resist the foe. Another character, Adrian, who because of his contemplative and sensitive personality had not hitherto found it possible to take a public role in this macho society, now emerges as a leading light, a Florence Nightingale figure:

> 'I am now going to undertake an office fitted for me. I cannot intrigue, or work a tortuous path through the labyrinth of men's vices and passions; but I can bring patience, and sympathy, and such aid as art affords, to the bed of disease; I can raise from earth the miserable orphan, and awaken to new hope the shut heart of the mourner.' (p. 179)

His sister Idris, the narrator's wife, at first, like her brother, wishes to put her energies to work to help the afflicted. But she is prevented from doing so; women, in her society, are not even allowed to take up the Florence Nightingale role:

> Maternal affection had not rendered Idris selfish; at the beginning of our calamity she had, with thoughtless enthusiasm, devoted herself to the care of the sick and helpless. I checked her; and she submitted to my rule. I told her how the fear of her danger palsied my exertions, how the knowledge of her safety strung my nerves to endurance. I shewed her the dangers which her children incurred during her absence; and she at length agreed not to go beyond the inclosure of the forest. . . . After watching over and providing for their safety, her second care was to hide from me her anguish and tears. Each night I returned to the Castle, and found there repose and love awaiting me. (p. 199)

There is no indication that Shelley is writing with conscious irony here; from her narrator's point of view, it is of the utmost importance that, even in the face of the Plague, the polarisation of gender roles be maintained, and an Englishman's home remain his castle. But though no authorial voice intervenes, the text's plot, with a sweeping energy like that of the Plague itself, soon makes it abundantly clear that, in this disintegrating society, such polarisation can spell nothing but destruction, for both women and men. As the Plague wreaks its havoc, making a mockery of all their manly inflexible resistance, Adrian yet gains a new lease of life from his more active role, and seems 'born anew'; but Idris's stifled energies begin to consume her inwardly:

She was uncomplaining; but the very soul of fear had taken its seat in her heart. . . . she compared this gnawing of sleepless expectation of evil, to the vulture that fed on the heart of Prometheus; under the influence of this eternal excitement, and of the interminable struggles she endured to combat and conceal it, she felt, she said, as if all the wheels and springs of the animal machine worked at double rate, and were fast consuming themselves. (p. 219)

The 'over active life within her . . . deprived her limbs of strength' (p. 231). Again, frustrated womanhood is compared to the classical male heroes: Idris is another modern Prometheus, bound by the inflexible rules of her society to the rock of passivity, and its internal torments. The energies of half the race have not been released to combat the crisis; the frustration of that energy has created an enemy within, consuming the psychological substance of the repressed, even as the Plague consumes them physically.

The Plague sweeps on, destroying the narrative's characters one by one, until at the close only Lionel, the narrator, is left behind, as the 'last man', to tell the tale of the desolation. Lamenting dead humanity, he presents its lost civilisations as having been, as indeed the text shows they were, an entirely male construction:

Farewell to the giant powers of man, – to knowledge that could pilot the deep-drawing bark through the opposing waters of shoreless ocean, – to science that directed the balloon through the pathless air, – to the power that could put a barrier to mighty waters, and set in motion wheels, and beams, and vast machinery, that could divide rocks of granite or marble, and make the mountains plain! . . . O farewell! . . . It is all over now. . . . Unsupported and weak, let him wander through fields where the unreaped corn stands in barren plenty, th[r]ough copses planted by his fathers, through towns built for his use. . . . Thou, England, wert the triumph of man! . . . Thy manly hearts are still; thy tale of power and liberty at its close! . . . The species of man must perish; the noble proportion of his godlike limbs; his mind, the throned king of these; must perish . . . Will the earth still keep her place among the planets . . . will beasts pasture, birds fly, and fishes swim, when man, the lord, possessor, perceiver, and recorder of all these things has passed away, as though he had never been? (pp. 233, 234, 235, 300–1)

Women have had no place in this civilisation; it has obliterated the significance of their contribution, or repressed their energies entirely. A female plague wreaks ultimate vengeance on a male world, which had assumed in its pitiful arrogance that it could control and possess its environment. The earth, like the Plague, is personified as female, and the female has now been released to live in her own right again: of course the earth will keep her place amongst the planets when the Last Man is gone. Although the women characters in *The Last Man*, trapped in their domestic roles, unable to find sufficient consolidated strength to break through and assert themselves, are wiped out along with their menfolk, the female principle – which had not been included within this civilisation's frame of things – is released to live on, uncontrolled and unpossessed. In Mary Shelley's own society, too, women were excluded by an enforced passivity from bringing the values of love and relation – left to them to maintain in the domestic sphere – into the public domain. When this monstrous figure of female passivity and the repression of energy is internalised, as it was to some extent in Mary Shelley's own case, the result is isolation and crippling anxiety for the individual, and the loss to both men and women of those silenced voices and unpublished texts, which might have brought them to a more balanced and less destructive understanding of their relation to the world, and to one another. But underneath the surface acquiescence of texts such as Mary Shelley's we may read the signs of a return of the repressed, cataclysmically freeing itself from its chains.

NOTES

1. *The Letters of Mary Wollstonecraft Shelley*, ed. Betty T. Bennett (2 vols; Baltimore and London: Johns Hopkins University Press, 1983), ii, p. 246.
2. Florence A. Marshall, *The Life and Letters of Mary Wollstonecraft Shelley* (2 vols; London: Richard Bentley & Son, 1889), i, pp. 226–7.
3. *Letters*, ed. Bennett, ii, p. 72.
4. *Mary Shelley's Journals*, ed. Frederick L. Jones (Norman, Okl.: University of Oklahoma Press, 1947), p. 204.
5. See, for example, Rosalind Coward and John Ellis, *Language and Materialism: Developments in semiology and the theory of the subject* (London: Routledge, 1977), pp. 1–11; Cora Kaplan, 'Pandora's Box: subjectivity, class and sexuality in socialist feminist criticism', in Gayle Greene and Coppélia Kahn (eds) *Making a Difference: Feminist literary criticism* (London: Methuen, 1985), pp. 146–76; and Joan Kelly, 'The doubled vision of feminist theory', in Judith L. Newton, Mary P. Ryan and Judith R. Walkowitz (eds) *Sex and Class in Women's History* (London: Routledge, 1983), pp. 259–70.
6. Leonore Davidoff and Catherine Hall, *Family Fortunes: Men and women of the English middle class 1780–1850* (London: Hutchinson, 1987), p. 181.
7. Mary Poovey, *The Proper Lady and the Woman Writer: Ideology as style in the works of Mary Wollstonecraft, Mary Shelley, and Jane Austen* (Chicago and London: University of Chicago Press, 1984), p. xv.
8. Hannah More, *Strictures on the Modern System of Female Education* (2 vols; London: T. Cadell & W. Davies, 1799), ii, pp. 142–3.
9. *Journals*, ed. Jones, p. 64.
10. Jean-Jacques Rousseau, *Émile, or Education*, trans. Barbara Foxley (London: Dent, 1911), pp. 322 and 332.
11. *Journals*, ed. Jones, pp. 205–6.
12. Sandra M. Gilbert and Susan Gubar, *The Madwoman in the Attic: The woman writer and the nineteeth-century literary imagination* (New Haven and London: Yale University Press, 1979), pp. 213–47.

13. Mary Wollstonecraft Shelley, *Mathilda*, ed. Elizabeth Nitchie (Chapel Hill: University of North Carolina Press, 1959), pp. 71–2.
14. Frederick L. Jones (ed.), *Maria Gisborne and Edward E. Williams, Shelley's Friends: Their journals and letters* (Norman, Okla.: University of Oklahoma Press, 1951), p. 44. For an account of the textual history of *Mathilda*, in which this reference is given, see Anne K. Mellor, *Mary Shelley: Her life, her fiction, her monsters* (London: Routledge, 1988), p. 255.
15. Mary Shelley, *The Last Man* (London: Hogarth Press, 1985), p. 117. Subsequent references in this essay to *The Last Man* are from this edition.

Linda R. Williams

Critical Warfare and Henry Miller's *Tropic of Cancer*

This is not a book. This is libel, slander, defamation of character.

Henry Miller, *Tropic of Cancer*[1]

It is a moral plague, a leprosy of the mind, whose evil stench hits you in the face the moment you open a book of his.

L. Yakovley on Miller[2]

What he really wants to do is shit on her.

Kate Millett on Miller[3]

Tropic of Cancer is Henry Miller's polemic of anti-humanism. It is an attempt to write 'The last book',[4] an affirmation of extremity in the forms of transgression, disease and violence. For the Miller of *Tropic of Cancer* life is war, with Paris as its theatre. Men and women fight each other on the sexual battlefield of its pages, with a violence which makes the impossibility of impartial reading explicit: if we read the book at all, it is hard not to take sides. Want, sexual warfare, and a lack of sentiment about humanity interconnect in the cravings of the selves which populate *Tropic of Cancer*, and Miller's exploration of the savage and exploitative battles or contracts between men and women has made him an obvious target for feminists. The novel's grim opening movement – 'toward the prison of death. There is no escape' – is a kind of perverse come-on to those of us who would not be deemed faint-hearted readers. Thus Miller begins his attempt to show a world revealing itself 'for the mad slaughterhouse that it is',[5] in which desire becomes ultimately the desire for annihilation, a nirvana in which the hero screams exultantly '"*I am inhuman!*"'[6] It is a book which wants to be literally 'beastly', setting itself an extreme aesthetic agenda which aims to violate the coherence and the ethical priorities of the conscious self. Miller's universe is apocalyptic: 'The age demands violence',[7] and sex prowls on the volcano's edge.

Much of the novel's reputation for offensiveness can be put down to the moral perspectives of the left and right at the time of its first attempted publication (its actual American publication was delayed until 1961); the judgments against sexual explicitness and language would not be so clearly made now, and *Cancer* retains little of the power to shock it held for the Judge who tried it for obscenity at a failed attempted publication in 1951: 'If this be importable literature, then the dignity of the human person and the stability of the family unit, which are the cornerstones of our systems of society, are lost to us.'[8] To be deemed dangerous is, however, exactly the critical response Miller sought; in *Tropic of Capricorn* he wrote 'I look at people murderously', and his novels invite readers to look back with critical knives at the ready. In the first section of this essay I hope to show that Miller defines the terrain of sexual warfare on his own terms, terms which are not fully challenged by early feminist critique in its hostile engagements with him, before suggesting how other readings might combat this problem. Miller delights in outrage, but outrageousness is ever more difficult. Perhaps the only reader who would now not disappoint him in this is the feminist critic.

Feminist outrage at Henry Miller has characteristically engaged with him according to that familiar dialectic of shocking fiction countered by shocked critical response. This is not difficult. *Tropic of Cancer* tries very hard to be nasty, embracing in its frenzy of violation an ambitious range of objects. Miller promises us a novel which is 'a prolonged insult, a gob of spit in the face of Art, a kick in the pants to God, Man, Destiny, Time, Love, Beauty . . . what you will'.[9] However, this anti-metaphysic is not pointed enough for Miller, and he proceeds to mark out more specifically the recipient of the text's outpourings, an implied reader who will submit to a readerly 'libel, slander and defamation of character' in receipt of the text. The ideal forms insulted above soon become pin-pointed as a 'you': 'I will sing while you croak, I will dance over your dirty corpse.' Who, then, is this 'you' which the novel invokes in order to trample on? Who is created as listener only to become a corpse?

It is to you, Tania, that I am singing.

The 'you' that croaks and is buried, and the 'you' that listens, is of course a woman. But she is woman as reader, as muse and inspiration, as Miller's necessary victim and – as a key inhabitant of the 'mad slaughterhouse' – the mediator of his desired annihilation. Through a deathly sexual communion which *uses* Tania, Miller touches 'his own' non-existence. She is the 'dirty corpse' but also the Tania who does not die, who returns and recurs as an obscure object of desire throughout the novel, one of the vilified recipients of Miller's heinous aphorisms. For whilst this Tania is the object of one of

Miller's most notorious streams of violent intentions ("'I will send you home
to your Sylvester with an ache in your belly and your womb turned inside
out. . . . I shoot hot bolts into you. . . . I will bite into your clitoris and
spit out two franc pieces'"),[10] she is also something quite other. The tension
between the violent 'intentions' of the 'I' which rants so purposefully here,
and his desire for a Tania who offers him a 'chaotic' self-subversion, is a key
area which I will explore. "'You, Tania, are my chaos'", Miller writes, in
tandem with the key statement,

> Chaos is the score upon which reality is written.[11]

How, then, can feminist criticism respond to such an impossible network of
identifications?

The link between sexuality and death in Miller connects explicitly with
Freud's theory of the death drive. Miller admits in *The World of Sex* that he
cannot write about one without calling upon the other:

> Sex and death: I notice how frequently I couple them. . . . For the poet, the
> final ecstasy does not lead into the daylight of God, but into the nocturnal
> darkness of passion. Sometimes life itself takes over, writes its own poem of
> ecstasy, signed 'Death'.[12]

Whilst the Romantic force of this eulogy to the erotics of annihilation is
characteristic of Miller, the coupling of Eros and Thanatos is not of course
unique. Miller's lack of originality is of little interest to me, however; what
is more important is the way in which sexual violence, aggression and
submission come together in his corpus, and the implications of this for
feminism. My concern here is to show how that plexus in *Tropic of Cancer*
can unlock and illustrate questions which still nag feminist criticism and
theory; indeed, the poetics of sexuality and violence which Miller struggles
to activate impinges on territory occupied not only by feminism, but also by
psychoanalysis and military science. Miller offers a key articulation of the
kind of desire made explicit in Freud's last topography, in which the sexual
model of libido is subordinated to that of the death drive. What happens
when feminism, late Freud and strategic theory come together in relation to
Miller's *Tropic of Cancer* is the subject of this essay.

MILLER'S SEXUAL WARFARE

> Men and women come together like broods of vultures over a stinking carcass, to mate and fly apart again. . . . A huge intestinal apparatus with a nose for dead meat. *Forward!* Forward without pity, without compassion, without love, without forgiveness. Ask no quarter and give none! More battleships, more poison gas, more high explosives! More gonococci! More streptococci! More bombing machines![13]

Henry Miller writes his way into the front line of the sex war, declaring that peace is only possible on the other side of conflict. If *Tropic of Cancer* as a whole is the war in which Miller tries 'fighting with ink' (to borrow his phrase about D.H. Lawrence),[14] its sexual passages are the individual battles or bouts. As I will explore when I look at the disruptions in Miller's language, this inky battle is not fought to enshrine a sexist self in writing, but to fend off the 'self', ostensibly made coherent by grand narratives. Miller – for the hero of *Tropic of Cancer* is called 'Henry Miller' – goes to Paris like a war correspondent going straight to the front line; but he is not an innocent reporter. Paris invades him and makes him participate, intoxicating like a poison or addiction; he is a delirious but willing victim infiltrated by 'her' contagion or drug. Some of Miller's most passionate writing is reserved for Paris, which he is both inside of and, in reading her, 'other than'; she is a city which 'attracts the tortured, the hallucinated, the great maniacs of love'.[15] But the city's importance lies in its openness to the conflicts which obsess Miller – it is his vision of a city which says Yes to everything, and as such it is both dubiously feminised and acts as an externalisation of the affirmative Freudian unconscious. At another point Paris is the maternal incubator of reality: 'Paris is the cradle of artificial births'.[16] The whole novel is then enacted within the body of a voracious woman, for 'Paris is like a whore':[17] 'From a distance she seems ravishing, you can't wait until you have her in your arms. And five minutes later you feel empty, disgusted with yourself. You feel tricked.'

This five-minute fuck is elsewhere in the novel likened to an exhausted military operation:

> It's like a state of war: the moment the condition is precipitated nobody thinks about anything but peace, about getting it over with. And yet nobody has the courage to lay down his arms, to say, 'I'm fed up with it. . . . I'm through.'[18]

Sex between a prostitute and her client is like taking up arms, when both agree on a price and begin to fulfil the contract from positions of enmity. It is important to recognise the complex way in which *Cancer*'s metaphorics of warfare work; the opposition is not simply that of hatred between men and women, who hardly engage on an emotional level but instead lock themselves into a pattern of opposition already historically marked out for them. In *Cancer* prostitutes are mercenaries, paid to 'fight', so that sex-as-contract is simultaneously sex-as-battle, and winning is getting one's money's worth or getting the contract fulfilled. The individual encounter between whore and customer thus becomes a microcosm of wider human relations for Miller; the whore's space, the woman herself, is the city scaled down and intensified. Miller is keen to emphasise that this particular state of war is not passionate or *personally* aggressive; both opponents are forced to engage not because of individual desire or human feeling but because of their conflicting roles. Whore and client are the foot soldiers of the sex war, whose own egoistic priorities are irrelevant. Whilst it is often said that Miller's women do not have their own identities and are seldom even named ('"Imagine that! Asking me if I loved her. I didn't even know her name. I never know their names"'),[19] in Miller's world personal characteristics are ruthlessly subjected, either to the ecstatic experience of loss which I will explore later ('"Sometimes I get so lost in my reveries that I can't remember the name of the cunt or where I picked her up"'),[20] or to the roles which history has acribed men and women and which render them simply active servants of the war (in this sense Miller's men can be equally nameless, like '"that cute little prick who drives me bats about his rich cunt"').[21]

In the whore's world the exchange of money becomes 'the primal cause of things'[22] which opens hostilities, and thus three forms of exchange, of sex and bodies, of money, and of violence, are conflated: '"she's got her mind set on the fifteen francs and if I don't want to fight about it she's going to make me fight."' The sexual contract between prostitute and client signifies a declaration and acceptance of war, which silences any pacific voice of reason. They are locked in a tunnel-vision of the inevitability of conflict:

> rather than listen to one's own voice, rather than walk out on the primal cause, one surrenders to the situation, one goes on butchering and butchering and the more cowardly one feels the more heroically does he behave, until a day when the bottom drops out and suddenly all the guns are silenced and the stretcher-bearers pick up the maimed and bleeding heroes and pin medals on their chest.

Whilst Miller's mind might be 'on the peace treaty all the time', he must nevertheless proceed in the knowedge that the armistice can only come when the battle is over.

Simply because of the explicitness with which Miller shows the violence of sex and gender relations in their unfeeling extremity, *Tropic of Cancer* is an important novel for feminist criticism. What happens between the whore and her customer makes Miller's attitude to war more explicit than his attitude to sex, even if it does both at the same time. Her bed is the theatre of war, and a space within which the public/private division explicitly breaks down; it is a microcosm of Paris as 'an artificial stage, a revolving stage that permits the spectator to glimpse all phases of the conflict'.[23] Making love with a whore can be synonymous with waging war in a frenzy of territorialism against those who have come before. The man who fucks her 'fights like a thousand devils . . . to wipe out that regiment that has marched between her legs'.[24] It is 'a fight in the dark, a fight single-handed against the army that rushed the gates, the army that walked over her, trampled her, that left her with such a devouring hunger that not even a Rudolph Valentino could appease.' Here again there is no question of love; it is an impersonal engagement which subordinates sexuality to the death drive, and Miller never even bothers to tell us who won. She is trampled but she also devours. And just as individual personality is immaterial to the conflict, there is never any question that 'pure' sexual desire – Freudian Eros, or libido in the form of a life instinct – has led to this.

In order to explore more fully this loveless engagement, I want to look at the way in which Miller's sexual writing can be seen as a literary encounter with the death drive. The callous tone of *Cancer* comes from its blithe disregard for the humanism of self-respect; bodily drives and the active role one fulfils, neither of which one necessarily *chooses*, are more important and determining. In his sado-masochistic world personal bodies are political in the sense that they are cannon-fodder in a conflict which they do not control and which subordinates personal identity to the exigencies of sexual warfare. What is important for a feminist reading of Miller is not, however, the position he occupies in relation to this struggle, but rather his obsession with it in the first place. A feminist understanding of the 'origins' of this war require, for me, a detour via Freud's late analysis of 'devouring hunger'. If there is any 'truth' in Miller's representation, it emerges from the way he brings together his disturbing vision of desire with a strong image of the exploitative manner in which men and women relate to each other. This is a representation which requires an equally complex feminist response – one which can incorporate not only the wealth of feminist work on the social and historical bases of hostile gender relations but which also makes use of the more controversial aspects of psychoanalytic theory. Encountering a disturbing vision of desire like Miller's, which embraces sadism, masochism and the desire to 'let go' of the self, requires a theory which disturbs any notion that libido is a healthy, humanistic life-instinct.

Miller articulates sexuality through the metaphorics of warfare because it allows him to bring together the violent and violating forms of sexual desire which are given a particular power within the historical framework which enlists men and women against each other. Existent conventional patterns of gender enmity are energised by and enter into a grim alliance with sado-masochistic violation. The materially fixed gender relations upon which Miller's sexual warfare is mapped is combined with a celebration of desire which violates or disregards the self, painfully and sadistically or, as I shall explore, ecstatically. These apparently *separate* forms of desire – first, to enter erotically into a painful scenario, and second, a desire which seeks nirvana as the 'zero-point' of self – are what Freud attempted to explain *together*, as two forms of the same drive, in the theory of the death drive, developed in his work during the First World War, introduced most fully in *Beyond the Pleasure Principle* (1920), and then maintained as the basic structure of his theory of the instincts. What we have seen so far on Miller's battlefield is the first kind of desire – the sado-masochistic desire for pain, restraint or simply the battle for domination; what I shall explore next is the second kind of desire – the desire to abolish subjective unities and to enter the blissful extinction evoked by the nirvana principle. The death drive becomes the exemplary instinct for Freud; desire is the desire for non-self, a state of equilibrium, or, more radically, the desire to take the self back to its 'original' inorganic state of zero tension. Only this ultimate trajectory could explain to Freud the sexual expressions of sadism and masochism, as elaborate or warped forms of the desire to return. Despite its obvious importance in the analysis of the sexual power-relations with which feminism is concerned, the death drive has proved to be one of Freud's most controversial theories and has been largely ignored by feminists interested in psychoanalysis, except by those explicitly concerned with the taboo areas of feminine masochism and dangerous pleasures.

Bringing historical constructions and the form of desire explained by the death drive together in this way needs to be worked through more fully. Whilst feminism has used psychoanalysis productively, and has showed the political gaps at certain moments in the history of psychoanalysis, the discussion which occurs in later Freud of sadism, masochism and the transgression of egoistic boundaries has not been extensively linked to the needs of feminism. *Tropic of Cancer* requires this link to be made. Whilst any discussion of the violence of heterosexual sex is interesting to feminism, what is at stake in the literalisation of the sex war in *Tropic of Cancer* is more disturbing and less clear than has been acknowledged. Miller is exploring an at times confused conflation of the history of gender conflict and a form of desire closer to the death drive than to straightforwardly sexual models of libido.

Miller is clear, then, that sex is war when men and women come together – the fact that the woman is being paid only clarifies what exists for him implicitly in all cross-gender encounters. When Freud explores the warfare of sexuality, however, he does so via a series of discussions of sadism and masochism, forms of erotic violation which Miller enthusiastically indulges. Nevertheless it is not only, or even primarily, Miller's women who want to be violated. For instance Mona (the long-time love of several Miller novels) recognises that Miller's masochism matches her understanding of Strindberg's, who she reads voraciously, delighting in an image of *masculine* desire which meets her sadism:

> I can see her looking up from her book after reading a *delicious* passage, and, with tears of laughter in her eyes, saying to me: 'You're just as mad as he was . . . you *want* to be punished!' What a delight that must be to the sadist when she discovers her own proper masochist! When she bites herself, as it were, to test the sharpness of her teeth. In those days, when I first knew her, she was saturated with Strindberg. That wild carnival of maggots which he revelled in, that eternal duel of the sexes, that spiderish ferocity which had endeared him to the sodden oafs of the northland, it was that which had brought us together.[25]

The obvious point to be made about this is that it reverses the sado-masochistic model so familiar to our culture; it is more often Miller's *men* 'who cannot resist the desire to get into a cage with wild beasts and be mangled'.[26] Here it is Mona, like the original Wanda in Sacher-Masoch's *Venus in Furs*,[27] who finds in Miller her masochist; she is the sadistic lover and reader. At another point in *Cancer* Miller's (male) friend Van Norden talks about sex in this curiously masochistic way:

> 'I get so goddamned mad at myself that I could kill myself . . . and in a way, that's what I do every time I have an orgasm. For one second like I obliterate myself. There's not even one me then . . . there's nothing . . . not even the cunt. It's like receiving communion.'
> 'But what is it you want of a woman, then?' I demand.
> '. . . I want to be able to surrender myself to a woman,' he blurts out. 'I want her to take me out of myself. But to do that, she's got to be better than I am. . . .'[28]

This takes up the idea of orgasm as a 'little death' but twists it in the service of an expression of masculine masochism, a male character's manifest desire to submit to an experience of absence, at the same time as his submission to a woman. Thus the point when Van Norden says in the middle of this discussion, '"There's something perverse about women . . . they're all masochists at heart"', has to be read as a moment of audacious self-irony.

What is surely more important for feminism here is the way Miller finds himself – perhaps despite himself – asking his own version of Freud's famous question, which becomes 'What does the *man* want?' This is not at all obvious; the composite image of masculine desire formed across the whole of *Tropic of Cancer* is bizarrely diverse. Miller is exploring forms of masculine sexuality which incorporate the ostensibly feminine desire for submission, as well as a variety of experiences of self-loss towards which masochism can form a pathway.

This exploration is important for feminism because as a representation or fantasy of masculine sexuality it challenges what Jessica Benjamin calls the 'major tendency in feminism [to construct] the problem of domination as a drama of female vulnerability victimized by male aggression'.[29] It is a 'tendency' in readings of misogynous literature which is exemplified by Kate Millett.

DEFENSIVE FEMINISM

Miller's talent for irritating everyone does not fail him in his encounter with Kate Millett. She takes the bait and fights back venomously in her highly combative reading of Miller in *Sexual Politics*, which exemplifies an early moment of feminist criticism. Millett's work on Miller became a model for feminist readings of violently sexual 'masculine' writing. She fights back, but she fights on Miller's terms, and all too often reads like a repetition of Miller; her extensive quotes and enraged comments would hardly be destructive of a writer already so keen to offend. In Millett one senses that Miller found his perfect reader, one who offers back revitalised images of 'gender relations according to Miller' which have been freshly charged with the energy of feminism. Miller may have met his match, but the battle continued to rage on the terms he set up.

A more effective feminist strategy, for me, would be one which either rewrites the rules of 'conventional' hostile encounter – the strike and counter-strike which occurs in the open from clearly opposite sides – or a kind of critical guerrilla operation which uses the 'arms' of the text against it to show how the text capitulates and contradicts itself. The latter strategy is perhaps most appropriate to a text like *Cancer* which offers such a contradictory range of masculine images. Whilst these responses may seem bizarrely violent ways to read books, violence is already present in Miller's writing, and in a whole history of feminist critical responses to the literature of misogyny. Reading Miller is often a painful experience, and if we read through the lens of identification with a character of the female sex, we are put in the position of the nameless 'cunts' and whores Millett defends, when defence is unnecessary: Miller's women can surely look after themselves. What, then, would an effective strategy of engagement be? Miller revels in the voracious desire both to consume and to be violated which is taken to extremes in his representations of masculine and feminine sexuality. Crucial questions of identity are raised when the masculine 'I' of *Tropic of Cancer* repeatedly calls for his own sexually engineered non-existence. But what for Miller is a positive 'impersonality' for Kate Millett is a necessarily negative dehumanisation: 'The perfect Miller "fuck" is a biological event between organs, its hallmark – its utter impersonality.'[30] Any desire to explore psychic and sexual splitting is in Millett's language 'a pathological fear of having to deal with another, and complete human personality'.[31] Her priorities are integrative and holistic, prescribing the humanisation of erotica against Miller's 'cheap dream of endlessly fucking impersonal matter . . . a childish fantasy of power untroubled by the reality of persons or the complexity of dealing with fellow human beings'.[32]

Thus the grotesqueness of Miller for some women readers, taken at face value, easily provokes engaged repulsion – Millett's combative response – if not a bizarre masochistic identification, which casts the text in the role of sadist who inflicts a painful experience on the reader. Miller's obsession with warfare, conflict and disease imagery (the enemy within) on a metaphoric and a narrative level, provokes Millett to set up his corpus as an enemy. But Miller fights dirty, inconsistently and apparently unsystematically, so that ascribing a motive or model to his attack is difficult. Disturbed by one who characterises himself as a murderous and 'roving cultural desperado'[33] ('Blow it to hell! Kill, kill, kill! . . .' he writes in *Capricorn*), Millett is poked into indignant defensiveness.

What happens when someone marks out another as their enemy? Despite the pleas of some pacific women, feminism has had to affirm the act of taking sides and recognising the need for strategies. Kate Millett is right to deploy a criticism of conflict with reference to Miller, both because this is what Miller invites and because we often use a military lexicon when we discuss criticism (strategies, defences, engagements, etc.). But what is at stake in the notion of a feminist critical *strategy*? Feminism engages with the sex war on the page in its critical writing and in the academy, and it does so through deploying the language and tools of a number of military strategies. At its strongest, feminist literary criticism is not applied feminist theory, which would approach texts through a pre-ordained perspective, practising secondarily what it theorises first. If we are to take terms like 'critical strategy' at all seriously, it is necessary to make critical militarism explicit. Both the practice of playing on the contradictions of a political force until it capitulates, and the practice of meeting the opposing force straight on in conventional terms, armed with a coherent strategy, are military operations. Attacking the text head-on with a critical strategy developed prior to a knowledge of that text produces responses which perhaps inadequately meet the 'enemy' threat since they lack a tactical understanding of its form. This conventional attack/defence approach is much less appropriate to reading than are the operations of guerrilla or 'people's war'. Military theorist Carl von Clausewitz, writing in his seminal 1832 text *On War*, characterises a 'people's army' as a diffuse, subversive and non-totalising force which overturns the balance of power not by 'cracking the nut' but, having ascertained the nature of the terrain of encounter and the form which the enemy force takes, by deploying a strategy based on the strength of dispersal, unpredictability and difference, not like a conventional 'platoon of soldiers . . . [who] cling together like a herd of cattle and generally follow their noses'.[34] The flexibility of this approach is important, and it requires a knowledge of the other which is like reading, but reading as reconnaissance. Constructing one's enemy at his strongest point requires the space to imagine, listen to, and 'know' him, and precludes the existence of combative theories constructed prior to the event – theory is engendered in practice. Projecting thought beyond the enemy lines is a powerful exercise in reading. The success of a guerrilla war is described by Clausewitz in these terms: 'The flames will spread like a brush fire, until they reach the area on which the enemy is based, threatening his lines of communication and his very existence.'[35]

If one has already set up a text as a threatening or aggressive force, this would surely be the desired result – a reading which sets the text on fire, and allows that fire to destroy the text as culturally important if it is not strong enough to survive the attack. At its most dextrous, feminist criticism listens to the other voices of writing, finding sources of power – points at which literature becomes something other than it seems – as well as showing how texts position themselves politically. Feminist criticism deals most effectively with violently misogynous writing when it opens up paradoxes where the text promises certainty, when it shows inconsistencies beneath a ruthless logic, and finds fault-lines in monoliths. There is something far more satisfying in showing how a piece of sexist writing trips over its own doubts and, in its ideological capacity, self-destructs, than in meeting that writing head-on with a pre-formed theory, often deploying the opponent's rules of engagement, and battling it out at the risk of losing. A more subversive strategy acts 'Like smouldering embers, it consumes the basic foundations of the enemy forces . . . a general conflagration closes in on the enemy'.[36] A feminist reading of Miller is, then, more complex and more successful if it kindles the doubts already inherent in *Cancer* – a novel so obsessed with disease as an internal other, the cancer of its title – causing the text to burn itself out or capitulate to the gnawing enemy within.

PORNOGRAPHY AND THE OFFENSIVE

When a feminist reads a writer like Henry Miller she engages in a kind of critical warfare. Oppositional feminism like Millett's holds Miller up as the exemplary fiction of misogyny, a fit enemy for feminist critique to pit itself against. Miller is 'offensive' to some feminists because he is seen to go on the offensive against women in his writing: he offers an example of Klaus Theweleit's dictum in *Male Fantasies*: 'the erotic woman is the terrain of warfare.'[37] However, we need to distinguish between what happens when women such as Millett find Miller 'offensive', and the moral castigation of Miller's obscenity which underpinned the debate about whether he should be published,[38] in order to avoid once more evoking that uneasy and paradoxical alliance of feminism and the Right which has occurred in recent debates on pornography.[39] This is a question which has been opened up particularly strongly since the early 1980s, and two critical anthologies, the Barnard collection *Pleasure and Danger* and Snitow, Stansell and Thompson's *Desire: The politics of sexuality*[40] contain especially important feminist work carried out recently on the question of dangerous pleasures, showing Millett's early position clearly in relief. The difference between Millett on Miller and, say, Alice Echols or Muriel Dimen on more recent anti-porn feminist positions represents a crucial historical move. Echols discusses feminism's emphasis on forms of 'politically-correct sex'[41] which would prohibit not only pornography but sexual fantasy *per se*. Dimen succinctly writes: 'When the radical becomes correct, it becomes conservative',[42] although whether this makes Miller's rampant *incorrectness* radical is another question.

The cultural feminisms Echols discusses would consign Miller to the censor's bonfire not only for his violence but also for his exploration of psychological aberration, and for his insistence on the politically difficult notion that sexual desire and conscious intent do not always work together:

the danger of desire is that what I want is not necessarily good for me, and I might want it more if it isn't. The alternative propounded not only by Millett but more recently by writers such as Susan Griffin, Andrea Dworkin and Adrienne Rich is an idealised notion of 'loving and being loved by women in mutuality and integrity',[43] a 'love' which is consciously ordained, simultaneously enforcing psychic coherence and prohibiting fantasy: '"Integrity", their answer to patriarchy's dangerous dualism, entails the transformation of all aspects of our lives into one seamless, unambiguous reflection of our politics. Such a view assumes that we can and should be held accountable for our desires.' Echols's question, 'How has it come to pass that some lesbians are in the forefront of a movement which has resurrected terms like "sexual deviance" and "perversion" . . .?'[44] opens up an incisive discussion of the alliance between forms of lesbian cultural feminism and the New Right. But in pin-pointing the polemic against porn as also a fear of fantasy, she moves the debate one stage on: 'in advocating sexual repression as a solution to violence against women, cultural feminisms resort to mobilizing women around their fears rather than their visions.'[45] Jessica Benjamin in her excellent volume *The Bonds of Love*, which uses late Freud in its analysis of sadism and masochism, puts it this way: 'a theory or a politics that cannot cope with contradiction, that denies the irrational, that tries to sanitize the erotic, fantastic components of human life cannot visualise an authentic end to domination but only vacate the field.'[46]

Benjamin's whole book is written with a Hegelian vision of 'an authentic end to domination' as its goal, taken through a thorough analysis of contradiction. Any approach to Miller which cannot cope with his insistence on irrational sex and dehumanised bodies, or which would sanitise his erotics, as conventional Miller criticism has done, into a transcendence of bodies and disease in a wholesome and integrative experience of self-liberation,[47] is obviously a non-starter. However there is no straightforward reason why what Gore Vidal calls 'Miller's hydraulic approach to sex and his dogged use of four-letter words'[48] should a priori be offensive to feminists. The problem is rather what misogynous machinery runs on Miller's hydraulic power. For Millett this is clear; her Miller is a 'brutalised adolescent'[49] whose 'formula is rather simple': 'you meet her, cheat her into letting you have "a piece of ass", and then take off. Miller's hunt is a primitive find, fuck, and forget.' Miller is indeed a gift to Millett, since his insistence on sex as an inhuman and dissolute experience, and on women as cunts, acts as a perfect foil for Millett's plea for wholesome sexual relations, for women's right to integrated subjectivity. She eloquently develops her position as the negative of Miller's and D. H. Lawrence's misogynies:

> Lawrence had turned back the feminist claims to human recognition and a fuller
> social participation by distorting them into a vegetative passivity calling itself
> fulfilment. His success prepared the way for Miller's escalation to open contempt.
> Lawrence had still to deal with persons; Miller already feels free to speak of
> objects. Miller simply converts woman to 'cunt' – thing, commodity, matter.[50]

Henry Miller was notoriously sexist, and thus if one is interested only in producing a chamber of sexist horrors he is a soft if eager target. When Millett identifies Miller as enemy she unwittingly allows him to choose the weapons. Taking on his lexicon of warfare she fights his game rather than her own. But it is one thing for feminism to engage with misogyny on *its* terms, and quite another when feminism appropriates those terms as armaments – fighting *with* its terms. When Millett identifies with Miller's representations of femininity she prosecutes him for winning a sex war for which he has written the strategic rules of engagement. For Millett Miller is something of a case history: an example to diagnose, the articulation of the offensive position: 'Miller does have something highly important to tell us; his virulent sexism is beyond question an honest contribution to social and psychological understanding which we can hardly afford to ignore' (p. 313). This is the nearest Millett gets to defeating Miller, using his corpus in service of the project of *Sexual Politics*. But this is also the point at which she ceases to read him; not only is the essay about to end, but here he becomes important only as a piece of pathological evidence. This leaves feminist criticism in a position of impasse which is hard to break. Once the terrain of engagement has been set up as either attack or defence, Millett's defensiveness means that in the end she ceases to read.

Vincent Pecora offers a clarification of critique which is less defensive than Millet's and thus offers a powerful purchase on the text: 'The objective of critique is then to read a specific narrative . . . as if it were *the* narrative a contradictory social order told to itself to make sense of its own inconsistencies.'[51] I have said that the key 'experience' for Miller is the desire to escape into a nirvana space of inhumanity; he paradoxically *wants* his 'lines of communication' to be consumed and inflamed. But not, presumably, by feminist flames: the means of destruction has to be of his own choosing. My task is then to read Miller's desire for annihilation, which I shall now look at briefly, as a theory of his self-inconsistency, first as a possibility of anti-humanist and perhaps 'feminine' disruption, and secondly as possibly a means of closet-reintegration – the absurdity of a masculinity beyond death.

THE WRITING MACHINE

> The man watching the clock was shackled and gagged; inside him were a thousand different beings tugging for release. . . . My only recourse – I no longer had a choice – was to lose my identity. In other words, flee from myself.[52]

Millett has identified Miller's writing as murderous, but its misogyny is not on any obvious level taken to the point of death – the male 'I' fucks an awful lot of women, but they are not fucked to death. On the other hand Miller's 'own' desire for annihilation, or the erasure of personal identity, is a form of ecstatic self-violation which Millett ignores. Whilst sex and violence might be inextricable, death in Miller is more likely to be an exultant male suicide than murder; 'vast relief' comes with violence to the self not to woman as other. What obsesses Miller is what has been characterised as a feminine state of openness, and an inability to identify with any conventional image of humanity. His 'I' wants to be *not* an 'I', in a novel which is about want.

What I am interested in is how Miller desires to *lose* in the sex war he fights. His desire becomes, despite itself, not the desire for victory over the enemy, but the desire for an experience of emptiness, the annihilation of restrictive economies, and an affirmation of a position which, according to the rules he is working with, is uncannily feminine; he is blamed for stripping women of their identities, but then reclaims this loss as his own in a struggle to lose himself. His concern is to plunge into a state of radical self-loss, an experience of 'letting go' which at one point he calls the Absolute. His openness to suffering is a craving for orgasmic negation, the emptiness of the 'spent', suffering as literally 'allowing' – being open to anything. The novel is written on the knife-edge of loss; on one side Miller wanders the streets in 'the splendour of those miserable days . . . a bewildered, poverty-stricken individual who haunted the streets like a ghost at a banquet',[53] whilst on the other this loss turns inside out into an ecstatic experience of egolessness which comes close to the writing of *jouissance*. By risking feeling loss painfully, he gains access to its freedom and weightlessness, unencumbered by the spirit of gravity.

Millett discusses Miller's euphemistic use of 'spending', but prefers to concentrate on its contractual aspect rather than the fact that it affirms a state in which he is in possession of nothing, reaching out to a point as near as possible to his own non-existence. Miller has nothing, and nothing to lose: 'I am the one who was lost in the crowd.'[54] This is indeed part of a longer project, picked up again in his essay 'My life as an echo': 'My ideal is to become thoroughly anonymous – a Mr What's-his-name . . . I am at my best when nobody knows me, nobody recognises me.'[55] 'I' is, of course, still present here, paradoxically calling for its own extinction; it is a paradox incorporated into his statement 'I am inhuman', where the 'I' militates against its proclaimed inhumanity. Miller is primarily exploring desire as that which *wants nothing*, which is directed toward radical self-destruction. Nothing, therefore, is quite tangibly attractive: 'No appointments, no invitations for dinner, no program, no dough. The golden period, when I had not a single friend.'[56] Austere as this may sound, this is no stoical sensual deprivation but Miller's road of excess, driving him towards his culminative affirmation of dehumanised sex.

In his famous essay 'The Brooklyn Bridge' Miller shows the characteristic mechanism of transgression which inverts an opposition – here emptiness and possession, or loss and gain – in an attempt to fracture that whole economy, gouging a gap into which he can jump, a point at which he is neither lost nor found: 'in the city I am aware of . . . the labyrinth. To be lost in a strange city is the greatest joy I know; to become oriented is to lose everything.'[57] By throwing away one's egoistic compass one can find one's way to a labyrinth of 'joy' inaccessible to the psychically 'oriented'. The moment one *recognises* – boundaries, pathways, identities and landmarks – one 'loses everything'. At this point, Miller wants not to map out enemy territory so as to wage war more effectively, but to jump into its strangeness – 'the city is crime personified, insanity personified' – so that sides are forgotten. The experience of poverty in a strange city is valuable in the way that it estranges self from self, and facilitates desire as loss of self:

> It was only in moments of extreme anguish that I took to the bridge, when, as we say, it seemed that all was lost. Time and again all was lost, irrevocably so. The bridge was the harpy of death, the strange winged creature without an eye which held me suspended between two shores.

Suspended between two shores, he is unfixed and positioned over a flow rather than stasis – as he tells us in his eulogy to movement in *Cancer*, 'I love everything that flows.' But this is a *repeated* experience of all being lost, one which recurrently fulfils his anonymous ideal. Death never comes to the textual Miller as an absolute end; rather it is an interruption of identity which manages to return. This uncanny 'Time and again' sensation is what gives the self its discontinuity, and it is what gives *Cancer* its formal fragmentation. Here is perhaps another example of a male writer producing *écriture féminine*, for *Cancer*, like its central 'I', is discontinuous; it slips into repeated narrative deaths so that its identity as a 'whole' novel is problematic.

It jumps across time with no warning, allowing half-notions to spread like a disease, expanding into streams of elements (Miller's famous raving lists). At the risk of turning Miller into a postmodernist, his surreal collage of disparate sexual landscapes can be understood as being engendered by an 'esthetic of interruption which structures contemporary consciousness'[58] in the terms used by Sylvere Lotringer in *Pure War*:

> it's the death of intimacy. All the reflection of these last years on an exploded, 'schizophrenic' model of subjectivity corresponds to the great esthetic of the collage. The ego is not continuous, it's made up of a series of little deaths and partial identities which don't come back together, or which only manage to come back together by paying the price of anxiety and repression.[59]

Tropic of Cancer is a montage of bodies and cheap hotel rooms, of formal disruptions and narrative gaps partly created by Miller's aphoristic style (Lotringer again: 'It's . . . by interruptions that writing is worked on. . . . aphorisms . . . are interruptions of thought.')[60] Formal disunity emphasises the 'I' as a possible source of coherence, but it is here that Miller would defy our need for an old-fashioned great narrative most, when the 'I' itself insists on slipping away, apparently at will. But then 'he' comes back, denying even the certainty of absolute disappearance.

Clearly, then, this 'blissful' experience is an important moment for Miller, but that does not make it in itself important for feminism. And what has become of his gendered vision? One simple answer is that the interruption of identity which Miller slips into in this reverie is, negatively speaking, a self-violation – a turn-about in the fortunes of war, when the 'I' transgresses the terms of gendered combat and turns upon himself – and, positively, a 'feminine' gap, both of which render a monolithic feminist critique problematic. Miller is one site upon which we can question the priorities of feminism when confronting what at first seems to be a straightforwardly misogynous text.

In his notes on D. H. Lawrence, written in his Paris Notebooks at the same time as he was writing *Tropic of Cancer*, Miller conflates his 'aesthetics of death' with sexual warfare:

> [With t]he great sexual interpretation of all things . . . comes the silent admission. . . . that death can not be averted. It can only be glorified. It gets *aestheticized*. And men forget too, that in this final period which Lawrence represents *woman must fight man* desperately.[61]

For Miller the desperate fight comes at the same moment as the aestheticisation of death; political conflict is part of the historical 'final period' – as the moment of *Cancer's* writing is apocalyptically identified – which is more important for Miller because it is also the moment at which loss or ecstasy is given an artistic rather than a religious or ethical importance. This is the key to what the 'I' says he is doing in writing 'The last book': the prioritisation of an ostensibly unlimited artistic self-overcoming over political battles: the 'complete release' which Clausewitz calls 'Going to extremes', and which can only come when the limits of political expediency are abandoned. This is what Virilio terms 'an infernal tendency'

> heading toward an extreme where no one will control anything. There, Clausewitz says something fundamental: 'Politics prevents complete release.' It's because war is political that there is not complete release. If war weren't political, this release would reach total destruction.[62]

In attempting to abandon the political limits of social morality and, apparently, the imperatives of the reality principle, Miller-as-'writing machine' desires this extreme point of release.

What is at stake in the loss or interruption Miller deifies is not simply subjective sensation, or the radical lack of it. This final moment of annihilation takes Miller to the space of writing, and at this point the moral response of certain feminisms comes into its most direct confrontation with Miller's aesthetic, for when he becomes 'a writing machine' he casts off everything except irresponsibility. 'The last book' is the death of him: 'I have simplified everything. . . . I am throwing away all my sous. What need have I for money? I am a writing machine. The last screw has been added. The thing flows. Between me and the machine there is no estrangement. I am the machine.'[63] Once the machine is turned on it is inhuman; the body it uses dies as a human being, the book it produces is written 'anonymously',[64] and Tania, who has humanly invested in him, is destroyed too: 'She knows there is something germinating inside me which will destroy her.'[65] So when *Tropic of Cancer* plays out its conflict between artistic production and personal ethics, it sets up an extreme agenda which separates inhuman artists from ethical humans:

> Side by side with the human race there runs another race of beings, the inhuman ones, the race of artists who, goaded by unknown impulses . . . turn . . . everything upside down, their feet always moving in blood and tears, their hands always empty, always clutching and grasping for the beyond, for the god out of reach: slaying everything within reach in order to quiet the monster that gnaws at their vitals.[66]

The morality of personal relations which so concerns Millett is subordinated to the needs and desires of the writing machine. This is clearly a problem for a feminist criticism which in its political readings has been most concerned with ethical fair play. *Tropic of Cancer* is important to this discussion not because it actually *is* 'The last book', but because it keeps returning to the question of the amoral psychic and sexual conditions which would engender such a book. When feminism subordinates writing to morality the call for politically correct sex becomes a call for politically correct art. This is not a priority I am happy to echo. At the end of a long and violent meditation on a girl's 'dark, unstitched wound' Miller has a vision of 'The story of art whose roots lie in massacre'.[67] It is this image which *Cancer* celebrates. Whilst many feminisms have confronted and analysed massacre, the writing which violence produces cannot be understood through a blindly ethical perspective. To borrow again from Lotringer, *Tropic of Cancer* is a text written in 'the discourse of war': 'It's a whole politics of writing. It's not an organised discourse of war, even less a discourse *on* war, it's a discourse at war. Writing in a state of emergency.'[68]

NOTES

1. Henry Miller, *Tropic of Cancer* (London: Granada, 1984), p. 10.
2. L. Yakovley, 'Henry Miller' in *Henry Miller Between Heaven and Hell*, ed. Emil White (Big Sur, Cal.: White Press, 1961), p. 33 (first published in *Soviet Literature*, 1950).
3. Kate Millett, *Sexual Politics* (1969; London: Virago, 1981), p. 309.
4. Miller, *Tropic of Cancer*, p. 33.
5. *ibid.*, p. 186.
6. *ibid.*, p. 255.
7. *ibid.*, p. 19.
8. Louis Goodman, 'District Judge of the US, Louis Goodman on the "Tropics"' (17 September 1951), in *Henry Miller Between Heaven and Hell*, ed. White, p. 8.
9. Miller, *Tropic of Cancer*, p. 10.
10. *ibid.*, p. 13.
11. *ibid.*, p. 10.
12. Henry Miller, *The World of Sex* (1940; London: Calder and Boyars, 1970), p. 105.
13. Miller, *Tropic of Cancer*, p. 268.
14. Henry Miller, *Notes on 'Aaron's Rod' and Other Notes on Lawrence from the Paris Notebooks*, ed. Seamus Cooney (Santa Barbara: Black Sparrow Press, 1980), p. 30.
15. Miller, *Tropic of Cancer*, p. 186.
16. *ibid.*, p. 35.
17. *ibid.*, p. 211.
18. *ibid.*, p. 146.
19. *ibid.*, p. 107.
20. *ibid.*, p. 134.
21. *ibid.*, p. 106.
22. *ibid.*, p. 147 – subsequent discussion refers to this section.
23. *ibid.*, p. 35.
24. *ibid.*, p. 164.
25. *ibid.*, p. 185.
26. *ibid.*, p. 17.
27. Leopold von Sacher-Masoch, *Venus in Furs* (1869; London: Luxor Press, 1970).

28. Miller, *Tropic of Cancer*, p. 135.
29. Jessica Benjamin, *The Bonds of Love. Psychoanalysis, feminism, and the problem of domination* (London: Virago, 1990), p. 9.
30. Millett, *Sexual Politics*, p. 300.
31. *loc. cit.*
32. *ibid.*, p. 313.
33. Miller in a letter to a Norweigan barrister, September 1957, included in *Henry Miller Between Heaven and Hell*, ed. White, p. 13.
34. Carl von Clausewitz, *On War* (1832), ed. and trans. Michael Howard and Peter Paret (Princeton, NJ: Princeton University Press, 1989), p. 481. On similar lines Karol Stolzman 'decentres' guerrilla operations when he writes in 1844: 'Indeed, guerrilla warfare, whose centre is everywhere and whose range of activity is unlimited, is the most appropriate and effective war for a people rising in arms' (from 'Terrifying for the strongest enemy', in *The Guerrilla Reader*, ed. Walter Laqueur, London: Wildward House, 1978, p. 87).
35. Clausewitz, *On War*, p. 481.
36. *ibid.*, p. 480.
37. Klaus Theweleit, *Male Fantasies*, Vol. 1, trans. Stephen Conway (Cambridge: Polity Press, 1987), p. 50.
38. See *Henry Miller Between Heaven and Hell*, ed. White, which contains Goodman and Yakovley's contributions cited above as well as Miller's self-defence.
39. The support of some feminists for various censorship campaigns, which are also supported by right-wing campaigners, in the cause of 'rehumanising' representations of the female body, has been widely documented; Alice Echols argues that American cultural feminism at times sounds unnervingly like US New Right campaigner Phyllis Schlafly in its 'equation of sexual freedom with irresponsibility, selfishness and dehumanisation [which] has, in fact, already been used by the New Right in its struggle against feminism, abortion and gay rights' (in 'The taming of the id: feminist sexual politics, 1968–83', in *Pleasure and Danger: Exploring female sexuality*, ed. Carole S. Vance, London: Routledge 1984, p. 63).
40. Vance's volume *Pleasure and Danger* contains papers collected from the 1982 conference at Barnard College, New York, hence its widespread citation as the 'Barnard anthology'. See also *Desire: The politics of sexuality*, ed. by Ann Snitow, Christine Stansell and Sharon Thompson (London: Virago, 1983).
41. Echols, *Pleasure and Danger*, p. 62.
42. Muriel Dimen, 'Politically correct? Politically incorrect?', in *Pleasure and Danger*, p. 141.
43. Adrienne Rich, 'Compulsory heterosexuality and lesbian existence,' quoted by Echols, p. 61.
44. *loc. cit.*
45. *ibid.*, p. 65.
46. Benjamin, *The Bonds of Love*, p. 10.
47. See, for example, essays by Lawrence Durrell, Michael Fraenkel and James Laughkin in *The Happy Rock* ed. Bern Porter (Berkeley Cal.: Bern Porter, 1945), and the humanist position taken by Lawrence Shifreen in *Henry Miller: A bibliography of secondary sources* (London: Scarecrow Press, 1979).
48. Gore Vidal, 'Women's liberation meets Miller-Mailer-Manson man', in *Collected Essays 1952–1972* (London: Heinemann, 1972), p. 198.
49. Millett, *Sexual Politics*, p. 296.
50. *ibid.*, p. 297.
51. Vincent Pecora, *Self and Form in Modern Narrative* (Baltimore: Johns Hopkins University Press, 1989), p. 92.
52. Miller, *The World of Sex*, p. 81.
53. Miller, *Tropic of Cancer*, p. 22.
54. *ibid.*, p. 252.
55. Henry Miller, 'My life as an echo' in *Selected Prose*, vol. 1 (London: MacGibbon and Kee, 1965), p. 9.
56. Miller, *Tropic of Cancer* p. 23.

57. Henry Miller, 'The Brooklyn Bridge', in *Selected Prose*, p. 59 – see this reference for all subsequent quotes.
58. Lotringer in Paul Virilio/Sylvere Lotringer, *Pure War*, trans. Mark Polizotti (New York: Semiotext(e), 1983), p. 35. This text is an exchange between Virilio and Lotringer, so I cite them independently.
59. *ibid.*, p. 38.
60. *loc. cit.*
61. Miller, *Notes on 'Aaron's Rod'*, p. 30, Miller's italics.
62. Virilio, *Pure War*, p. 48.
63. Miller, *Tropic of Cancer*, p. 34.
64. *ibid.*, pp. 29 and 33.
65. *ibid.*, p. 35.
66. *ibid.*, p. 256.
67. *ibid.*, pp. 247–9.
68. Lotringer, *Pure War*, p. 39.

Ann Thompson

'Miranda, Where's Your Sister?':
Reading Shakespeare's *The Tempest*

These are Prospero's first words in *The Tempest, or The Enchanted Island*, the adaptation of Shakespeare's play created for the most part by William Davenant, with some input from John Dryden, in 1667. They act as a clear signal to a knowing audience or reader that this is not the original. Davenant's Miranda does indeed have a younger sister, Dorinda, and the two are described in the *Dramatis Personae* as 'Daughters to Prospero, that never saw Man'. Dorinda is balanced, and ultimately partnered, by another new character, Hippolito, heir to the dukedom of Mantua, 'one that never saw Woman'. In the insistent pattern of parallels and repetitions which characterises Davenant's version, Ariel has a female consort, Milcha, and even Caliban has a twin sister named after their mother, Sycorax, whom he proposes as a bride for Trinculo.[1] This proliferation of female roles can presumably be attributed in part to the need to provide employment for actresses on the Restoration stage.

In contrast, women are notably absent from Shakespeare's *Tempest*. Miranda at one point stresses her isolation and lack of female companionship by saying 'I do not know / One of my sex, no woman's face remember, / Save from my glass, mine own' (III.i.48–50),[2] though at the beginning of the play she had claimed at least a vague recollection: 'Had I not / Four or five women once that tended me?' (I.ii.46–7). Apart from Miranda herself, the only females mentioned in the First Folio's list of the 'Names of the Actors' are Iris, Ceres, Juno and the Nymphs, all of whom are 'spirits' explicitly impersonated by Ariel and his 'fellows'. While Ariel is clearly a male spirit, he is also required to impersonate a 'nymph of the sea' (I.ii.301) and a half-female harpy (stage direction at III.ii.52), indicating a degree of ambiguity about his gender. The part has often been performed by women or by androgynous youths. Conversely, the part of Miranda would in actuality have been performed by a boy actor on Shakespeare's stage.

Miranda, in Shakespeare's play, has no sister and apparently no mother. It is odd that she does not even enquire about the fate of the latter, though she might have been prompted to do so by Prospero's reply to her question 'Sir, are not you my father?' In his only reference to his wife Prospero says 'Thy mother was a piece of virtue, and / She said thou wast my daughter' (I.ii.56–7). This is apparently all that needs to be said about her. Some fifty lines later, Miranda demonstrates that she has fully internalised the patriarchal assumption that a woman's main function is to provide a legitimate succession when asked to comment on the wickedness of Prospero's brother: 'I should sin / To think but nobly of my grandmother: / Good wombs have borne bad sons' (I.ii.117–19).

The worldly cynicism of such standard jokes was formerly thought inappropriate to the innocent Miranda and they were often omitted from performances from the late eighteenth century to the early twentieth century; Davenant's Miranda more explicitly denies that she had a mother when she remarks with a coy naïvety to Dorinda that she thinks Prospero 'found us when we both were little, and grew within the ground' (I.ii.332–3). In Shakespeare's version, Miranda's destined spouse, Ferdinand, is also motherless, and *his* sister's absence is curiously stressed: although the distance from Naples to North Africa is not enormous, Alonso insists that Claribel is 'so far from Italy removed / I ne'er again shall see her' (II.i.108–9), and Antonio expresses her remoteness even more extravagantly:

> She that is Queen of Tunis; she that dwells
> Ten leagues beyond man's life; she that from Naples
> Can have no note unless the sun were post –
> The man i'th'moon's too slow – till newborn chins
> Be rough and razorable;
>
> II.i.244–8.

Claribel had to wait until 1949 for the female poet H. D. To make her visible and give her a voice.[3] Shakespeare's Caliban has no sister and his mother, Sycorax, is long dead by the time the play's events take place. Sycorax also has a North African connection, having been banished by the Algerians who apparently spared her life because she was pregnant. Her power is at least recognised by Prospero, Ariel and Caliban, though she is vilified by the two former characters as a 'hag' and a 'foul witch'. Oddly, Shakespeare draws on the lines Ovid gave another notorious female enchantress, Medea, for Prospero's big 'conjuring' speech, 'Ye elves of hills, brooks, standing lakes, and groves' (v.i.33ff.), but Medea herself is not mentioned.

The fact that I have chosen nevertheless to discuss *The Tempest* in the context of this book may seem perverse, but my choice is a deliberate one and relates precisely to the *absence* of female characters. I want to ask what feminist criticism can do in the face of a male-authored canonical text which seems to exclude women to this extent. Much early feminist criticism consisted merely in privileging female characters and identifying with their viewpoints, especially if they could be claimed to be in any way subversive or protofeminist. This is clearly impossible in *The Tempest*: even nineteenth-century female critics, who on the whole participated enthusiastically in the trend of aggrandising and romanticising Shakespeare's heroines, could not find a great deal to say for Miranda. Anna Jameson wrote in *Shakespeare's Heroines* (first published in 1833) that in Ophelia and Miranda Shakespeare had created two beings in whom 'the feminine character appears resolved into its very elementary principles – as modesty, grace, tenderness', but added that by the same token Miranda 'resembles nothing on earth';[4] and Mrs M. L. Elliott remarked in *Shakspeare's Garden of Girls* (1885) that Miranda was too ethereal and thus tended to be more popular with male than with female readers.[5] Anyone who has taught the play recently will know that these seem very moderate views compared to the opinions of twentieth-century female students who find Miranda an extremely feeble heroine and scorn to identify with her. Perhaps, then, *The Tempest* can be used as something of a test case for discovering what else a feminist approach may offer beyond this character-based level.

Faced with a comparable problem in relation to *King Lear*, where modern readers hesitate to identify with either the stereotype of the bad woman represented by Goneril and Regan or with the stereotype of the good woman represented by Cordelia, Kathleen McLuskie writes:

> Feminist criticism need not restrict itself to privileging the woman's part or to special pleading on behalf of female characters. It can be equally well served by making a text reveal the conditions in which a particular ideology of femininity functions and by both revealing and subverting the hold which such an ideology has for readers both female and male.[6]

I shall attempt in the remainder of this essay to explore the 'ideology of femininity' at work in *The Tempest*, both through a reading of the play and through a survey of some of the most influential ways in which it is currently being reproduced in literary criticism.

Despite her small and comparatively passive role, the text claims that Miranda is nevertheless crucial to the play. Explaining the storm, Prospero tells her 'I have done nothing but in care of thee' (I.ii.16). A feminist critic might ask in what sense this is true, and whether Miranda's gender is significant: would the play have worked in the same way if Prospero had had a son? How does sexuality, and especially female sexuality, function in this narrative? Reading the play with an explicit focus on issues of gender, one is immediately struck by its obsession with themes of chastity and fertility, which occur in its figurative language as well as in its literal events. These themes are often specifically associated with female sexuality. In the first, rather startling metaphor of this kind, Gonzalo imagines the very ship which seems to founder in the opening scene as being 'as leaky as an unstanched wench' (I.i.47–8), a phrase interpreted as alluding either to a sexually aroused (insatiable) woman or to one menstruating 'without the use of absorbent padding', as the Oxford editor puts it. In his long narrative speech to Miranda in the second scene, Prospero uses a metaphor of birth to describe Antonio's treachery – 'my trust, / Like a good parent, did beget of him / A falsehood' (I.ii.93–5), and seems almost to claim that he gave a kind of second birth to Miranda in his sufferings on the voyage to the island:

> When I have decked the sea with drops full salt,
> Under my burden groaned, which raised in me
> An undergoing stomach to bear up
> Against what should ensue.
>
> I.ii.155–8.

This scene also introduces the literal contrast between the chaste Miranda and the 'earthy and abhorred' Sycorax who arrived on the island pregnant (by the devil himself, according to Prospero at I.ii.319) and there 'littered' or 'whelped' her sub-human son. It is notable that the acknowledged, if evil, power of Sycorax is effectively undermined by the bestial stupidity of her son, rather as the power of Tamora is defused in *Titus Andronicus* and that of the Queen in *Cymbeline*. As in the earlier plays, the son of the witch-like woman is a rapist (or would-be rapist); Caliban is accused of attempting to rape Miranda and he does not deny the charge:

> O ho, O ho! Would't had been done!
> Thou didst prevent me – I had peopled else
> This isle with Calibans.
>
> I.ii.348–50.

He later promises Stephano that Miranda, seen as one of the spoils of victory, will 'bring thee forth brave brood' (III.ii.103). It is perhaps not surprising therefore that Ferdinand's 'prime request' to Miranda on first seeing her is 'If you be maid or no' (I.ii.428), a topic to which he returns twenty lines later, ignoring Prospero's intervention in the dialogue.

Miranda's chastity apparently has a quasi-mystical power. She herself swears 'by my modesty, / The jewel in my dower' (III.i.53–4) and tells Ferdinand 'I am your wife if you will marry me; / If not, I'll die your maid' (III.i.83–4). Prospero warns Ferdinand in what seem to be unnecessarily harsh terms against breaking her 'virgin-knot before / All sanctimonious ceremonies' (IV.i.15–16), threatening dire consequences:

> No sweet aspersion shall the heavens let fall
> To make this contract grow; but barren hate,
> Sour-eyed disdain, and discords shall bestrew
> The union of your bed with weeds so loathly
> That you shall hate it both. Therefore take heed,
> As Hymen's lamps shall light you.
>
>   iv.i.18–23.

Ferdinand's reply is comparably graphic:

>   As I hope
> For quiet days, fair issue, and long life,
> With such love as 'tis now, the murkiest den,
> The most opportune place, the strong'st suggestion
> Our worser genius can, shall never melt
> Mine honour into lust, to take away
> The edge of that day's celebration
> When I shall think or Phoebus' steeds are foundered,
> Or night kept chained below.
>
>   iv.i.23–31.

Ostensibly reassuring, such language seems to suggest that the minds of both men are dwelling in morbid detail on the possibilities of completing Caliban's attempted violation: the image of Miranda as a rape victim interferes disturbingly with the image of Miranda as a chaste and fertile wife. The masque which Prospero organises for the entertainment of the young couple in this scene explicitly banishes lust in the form of Venus and Cupid and emphasises the blessed fertility of honourable marriage. And yet, reading as a woman, I continue to get the feeling that the play protests too much on this score.

The speakers in the masque promise rewards for premarital chastity. As Ceres sings,

> Earth's increase, foison plenty,
> Barns and garners never empty,
> Vines with clust'ring bunches growing,
> Plants with goodly burden bowing,
> Spring come to you at the farthest,
> In the very end of harvest!
>
>   iv.i.110–15.

This language echoes that of the earlier scene in whch Gonzalo speculates on what he would do, 'Had I plantation of this isle' (ii.i.141), to make nature bring forth 'all foison, all abundance' (ii.i.161), in a utopian vision which is at the same time colonialist in so far as the 'commonwealth' is subject to his royal command. Sebastian jokes that he will 'carry this island home in his pocket and give it his son for an apple', to which Antonio replies 'And sowing the kernels of it in the sea, bring forth more islands' (ii.i.88–91), similarly invoking a picture of benign exploitation and a fantasy of magical male fecundity.

The play at times takes the power of the sea to give birth, or rebirth, quite seriously: later in ii.i.249 Antonio refers to all the courtiers as 'sea-swallowed, though some cast again', a metaphor repeated by Ariel when, disguised as a harpy, he tells the 'men of sin' that Destiny 'the never-surfeited sea / Hath caused to belch up you' (iii.iii.55–6). These are both parodies of birth: birth from the mouth rather than from the uterus. A cruder version of what the body can throw forth arises at ii.ii.101–2 when Stephano sees Trinculo, hiding under Caliban's cloak, as the 'seige' or excrement of the 'mooncalf'. More seriously, in his Medea-inspired speech, Prospero claims the power to resurrect the dead: 'Graves at my command / Have waked their sleepers, oped, and let 'em forth' (v.i.48–9), though Ferdinand asserts elsewhere that it is Miranda who 'quickens what's dead' (iii.i.6). At the end of the play, after Ferdinand's apparent death 'mudded in that oozy bed' of the sea (v.i.151), he rhetorically attributes his 'second life' to Prospero (v.i.195), although it is Miranda's literal fertility which will, as Gonzalo explains, permit Prospero's 'issue' to become kings of Naples (v.i.205–6).

How, then, can a feminist interpret this pattern of references? What is going on in this text which seems, on the one hand, to deny the importance – and even in some cases the presence – of female characters, but which simultaneously attributes enormous power to female chastity and fertility? One noticeable feature of the handling of these themes is the insistence on male control: Prospero must control Miranda's sexuality before he hands her over to Ferdinand. Alonso, her father, formerly controlled Claribel's sexuality, but the play is ambivalent about his decision (a willing version of Desdemona's father Brabantio?) to 'lose' or 'loose' her to an African rather than to a European suitor (ii.i.123),[7] and she herself is said to have been 'Weighed between loathness and obedience' in the matter (ii.i.128). Men are seen as capable of controlling the fertility of nature, and Prospero even controls Ceres, the goddess of harvests, in so far as the play makes it clear that she is represented in the masque by his servant Ariel (iv.i.167). Recent criticism of The Tempest suggests two theoretical frameworks for discussing this question of control, the psychoanalytical and the political, both of which can be utilised in a feminist approach.

The traditional reading of The Tempest prevalent in the nineteenth century and earlier twentieth century interpreted Prospero's control of its events and characters as entirely benign; he was often seen as the representative of Art itself, or even identified with Shakespeare as author. Freudian and post-Freudian psychoanalytical studies of the play have undermined this view, exposing the darker side of the 'family romance' by suggesting that Prospero's control might be more problematic and that his concern with his daughter's sexuality might indicate an incestuous desire for her. In David Sundelson's essay, '"So rare a wonder'd father": Prospero's *Tempest*', the play is fraught with anxieties and uncertainties on this level which are only partially resolved by its endorsement of what he calls both Prospero's and the play's 'paternal narcissism: the prevailing sense that there is no worthiness like a father's, no accomplishment or power, and that Prospero is the father *par excellence*'.[8] Coppélia Kahn, writing on 'The providential tempest and the Shakespearean family', agrees in seeing the play as a 'fantasy of omnipotence' in which Prospero, coming from Milan to the island, 'went from child-like, self-absorbed dependency to paternal omnipotence, skipping the steps of maturation in between'. Miranda, like Marina in *Pericles* and Perdita in *The Winter's Tale*, doubles the roles of mother and daughter, uniting chastity and fertility in a non-threatening way. Yet, in so far as Kahn claims that 'Prospero's identity is based entirely on his role as father, and his family is never united or complete' – indeed he is left at the end in a state of social and sexual isolation – the 'romance' is still a narrative of imperfect wish-fulfilment representing the universally ambivalent desire we all have both to escape from our families and to continue to be nurtured by them.[9] Both these readings lay stress on the tensions that arise in the play and the sheer struggle involved in asserting the supposedly natural harmony of patriarchal control: it appears that an 'unstanched wench' constitutes a serious threat to this order.

Stephen Orgel has pointed out a danger in the tendency of psychoanalytic readings to treat the play as a case-history, either of the author or of the characters, overlooking the extent to which the reader, playing the role of analyst, is a collaborator in the resultant fantasy. He further notices that, while psychoanalysis evokes an unchanging, essential human nature, the theoretical framework does change:

> Recent psychoanalytic theory has replaced Freud's central Oedipal myth with a drama in which the loss of the seducing mother is the crucial trauma. As men, we used to want reassurance that we could successfully compete with or replace or supersede our fathers; now we want to know that our lost mothers will return. (p. 52)[10]

In consequence, his essay, called 'Prospero's wife', transfers the centre of interest from the present, dominant father to the absent mother, a strategy comparable to the one employed by Coppélia Kahn in her essay on 'The absent mother in *King Lear*'.[11] It is, as Orgel acknowledges, a problematic strategy in so far as it deals not with the text itself but with the gaps and blanks that Shakespeare has chosen not to fill in. Indeed, he begins his study with the defensive statement 'This essay is not a reading of *The Tempest*', and worries about the possible parallels with such currently unfashionable texts as Mary Cowden Clarke's *The Girlhood of Shakespeare's Heroines*. Nevertheless, his work is highly suggestive for feminist critics in its willingness to explore a whole network of feminine allusions and absences, ranging from the obvious one of his title to more obscure issues such as the puzzling references to 'widow Dido' at II.i.70–99, Dido being a 'model at once of heroic fidelity to a murdered husband and [of] the destructive potential of erotic passion' (p. 51). He also challenges the traditional view of *The Tempest* as a happy courtship comedy, remarking that, while the play does move towards marriage, the relationships are 'ignorant at best, characteristically tense, and potentially tragic'. He sees this as typical of the author:

> relationships between men and women interest Shakespeare intensely, but not, on the whole, as husbands and wives. The wooing process tends to be what it is here: not so much a prelude to marriage and a family as a process of self-definition. (p. 56)

Current political approaches to *The Tempest* often have links with psychoanalytical approaches. Orgel exemplifies one such link as he moves from his discussion of the missing wife, by way of speculations about Shakespeare's own family experiences, to an analysis of power and authority in the play in terms of the ways these issues were conceived in Jacobean England. He points out that in setting up the contest for the island between Caliban, who claims his inheritance from his mother, and Prospero, whose authority is self-created, Shakespeare is representing positions which were available, indeed normative, at the time. Further, in his edition of *The Tempest*, Orgel goes on to consider the real-life significance of political marriages like the one in the play where Prospero goes to considerable trouble to marry his daughter to the son of his chief enemy, thereby staging a counter-usurpation of Naples by Milan.

The fact that *The Tempest* was performed at court in 1613 during the wedding festivities of King James' daughter Elizabeth and Frederick the Elector Palatine gives a further resonance to such speculations. This historical circumstance is the starting-point for Lorie Jerrell Leininger's feminist reading, 'The Miranda trap: sexism and racism in Shakespeare's *Tempest*'.[12] She imagines the 16-year-old princess as the real-life equivalent of Miranda: beautiful, loving, chaste and above all obedient to her all-powerful father. Miranda's role as the dependent female is crucial to the play's dynamics of power in so far as Caliban's enslavement is justified by his attempt to rape her: 'Prospero needs Miranda as sexual bait, and then needs to protect her from the threat which is inescapable given his hierarchical world' (p. 289). Shakespeare's play allows Miranda no way out of this situation, but Leininger invents an epilogue for a modern Miranda who refuses to participate in the play's assumptions that Prospero is infallible, that Caliban is a 'natural' slave, and that a daughter is a 'foot' in a family organism of which the father is the head.

Most political readings of *The Tempest*, however, centre on the issue of colonialism. This is the focus of Francis Barker and Peter Hulme's essay '"Nymphs and reapers heavily vanish": the discursive con-texts of *The Tempest*',[13] and of Paul Brown's essay '"This thing of darkness I acknowledge mine": *The Tempest* and the discourse of colonialism'.[14] Both employ the technique of intertextuality to relate the play to nascent seventeenth-century European colonialism, reassessing the 'sources' in the context of New World voyage materials and arguing that anxiety and ambivalence result from the struggle to create a self-justifying, colonialist discourse. We are encouraged in these readings to be deeply suspicious of Prospero and to sympathise with Caliban as the representative of an exploited Third World. Brown draws on Freudian theory to point out an analogy between the political operations of colonialism and the modes of psychic repression, and he uses the Freudian concept of 'dreamwork' to discuss the way in which Prospero's discourse subordinates that of the other inhabitants of the island, as for example when he imposes his memory of earlier events on both Caliban and Ariel in i.ii.

An explicitly feminist version of this kind of reading, and one which is moreover undertaken from a Third World viewpoint, is performed by the Indian critic Ania Loomba as the final chapter of her book, *Gender, Race, Renaissance Drama*.[15] Loomba is critical of the tendency of 'alternative' readings of *The Tempest* to seize upon Caliban as a symbol of exploitation and potential rebellion, and points out that some anti-colonialist or anti-racist readings have been unthinkingly sexist: the specific repression of Miranda has been neglected. Setting out to delineate the limits of the text's supposed 'radical ambivalence', she discusses the myth of the black rapist, the significance of Sycorax as 'Prospero's other', and the contradictory position of Miranda as typical of that of all white women in the colonial adventure: the nature of her participation confirms her subordination to white men.

Both psychoanalytical and political theoretical approaches nevertheless deny some of the pleasures experienced by earlier generations of audiences and readers who were apparently able to identify more readily with the viewpoint of Prospero as white male patriarch and coloniser. Today, white male critics in Britain and the United States understandably feel uncomfortable and guilty about participating in these attitudes. Reading the play as a woman and as a feminist, it is possible to feel good about delineating and rejecting its idealisation of patriarchy, and one can go beyond the play to consider the conscious and unconscious sexism of its critical and stage history. Reading as a white British person, my conscience is less clear: women as well as men benefited (and still benefit) from the kind of colonialism idealised in *The Tempest*.

The current situation as I have sketched it above seems to leave two major questions unanswered (and unanswerable within the scope of this essay): first, is it possible for a staging of *The Tempest* to convey anything approaching a feminist reading of the text (without rewriting it or adding something like Leininger's epilogue), and secondly, what kind of pleasure can a woman and a feminist take in this text beyond the rather grim one of mapping its various patterns of exploitation? Must a feminist reading necessarily be a negative one?

NOTES

1. Maximilian E. Novak and George Robert Guffey (eds), *The Works of John Dryden* (vol. X, Berkeley, Cal. and London: University of California Press, 1970). I would like to thank Andrew Gurr for drawing my attention to the line which forms my title.
2. References and quotations from *The Tempest* are from the Oxford Shakespeare text, ed. Stephen Orgel (Oxford and New York: Oxford University Press, 1987).
3. See *By Avon River* (New York: Macmillan, 1949). For a discussion of H. D.'s transformation of *The Tempest* in this experimental work, see Susan Stanford Friedman, 'Remembering Shakespeare differently: H.D.'s By Avon River', in Marianne Novy (ed.), *Women's Re-Visions of Shakespeare* (Urbana and Chicago: University of Illinois Press, 1990), pp. 143–64.
4. *Shakespeare's Heroines*, 1897 reprint (London: George Bell and Sons), pp. 134, 149.
5. *Shakspeare's Garden of Girls*, published anonymously (London: Remington and Co., 1885), p. 265.
6. 'The patriarchal bard: feminist criticism and Shakespeare: *King Lear* and *Measure for Measure*', in Jonathan Dollimore and Alan Sinfield (eds), *Political Shakespeare* (Manchester: Manchester University Press, 1985), pp. 88–108.
7. The First Folio's spelling, 'loose', was the normal spelling of 'lose', but most modern editors, with the exception of Stephen Orgel, print 'loose', presumably because it carries an undertone of greater sensuality.
8. In Murray M. Schwartz and Coppélia Kahn (eds), *Representing Shakespeare: New psychoanalytic essays* (Baltimore and London: Johns Hopkins University Press, 1980), pp. 33–53.
9. In Schwartz and Kahn, *Representing Shakespeare*, pp. 217–43. Passages cited are on p. 238 and p. 240.
10. 'Prospero's wife', in Margaret W. Ferguson, Maureen Quilligan and Nancy J. Vickers (eds),

Rewriting the Renaissance: The discourses of sexual difference in early modern Europe (Chicago and London: University of Chicago Press, 1986), pp. 50–64. This essay was first published in *Representations* 8 (1984), 1–13.

11. In Ferguson, Quilligan and Vickers, *Rewriting the Renaissance*, pp. 33–49.
12. In Carolyn Ruth Swift Lenz, Gayle Greene and Carol Thomas Neely (eds), *The Woman's Part* (Urbana and Chicago: University of Illinois Press, 1980), pp. 285–94.
13. In John Drakakis (ed.), *Alternative Shakespeares* (London and New York: Methuen, 1985), pp. 191–205.
14. In Dollimore and Sinfield, *Political Shakespeare*, pp. 48–71.
15. Manchester: Manchester University Press, 1989, pp. 142–58.

Rebecca O'Rourke

Fingers in the Fruit Basket: A Feminist Reading of Jeanette Winterson's *Oranges Are Not the Only Fruit*

CHOOSING THE BOOK

I chose *Oranges Are Not the Only Fruit* for the purposes of illustrating a feminist reading because I wanted to discuss a lesbian book which I could be fairly confident would be read by lesbian and non-lesbian readers alike. This decision was very easy to make and entirely partisan. Lesbian issues and lesbian writing, to say nothing of lesbian lives, are marginal within the culture I live in. I do not hear enough about them and nor do most lesbians. So, a lesbian book I thought, and asked around: What would you like to read about? 'The Well of Loneliness, people will have heard of Radclyffe Hall.' 'Crime, everyone's reading feminist crime and lesbians write the best.' I can't say I was thrilled. Radclyffe Hall, especially in *The Well of Loneliness* with its upper-class assumptions and championing of the third sex, is a terribly difficult proposition. Crime appealed, as it always does to me, but the task of choosing just one book, or just one author even was too difficult. There was also the fact that although crime as a genre, particularly feminist crime writing, has become more respectable of late, it still can be perceived as not serious or proper writing. If I was wanting to insist that lesbian writers had as much right to be considered in the mainstream as other women, then I needed a writer who was widely published and well known.

I was not exactly overwhelmed by choice. Looking through my own bookshelves and then in the library and bookshops, I was struck by how much lesbian fiction originates outside of the British Isles. Coming out and staying out has a degree of similarity whether it happens in England, Australia or the United States and where it differs, it is interesting. As someone who never has, and probably never will, travel widely I like the vicariousness of fiction, the ways in which it is possible to see what life is like in circumstances other than my own. I like the ways in which Australian fiction keeps clear, earthed connections with working-class experience, the ways in which some North American writing demonstrates a greater capacity to acknowledge and respect the differences of race between women. I am just curious about where it is and where it isn't the same. But, this lack of home-grown lesbian fiction is also a problem to me.

Partly I read for difference, but I also read for confirmation. I want to see lesbian characters inhabit a world that is imaginatively and culturally one that I recognise, intimately. And that is hard. British lesbian feminist publishing got going very late, in 1980, and is still a tiny proportion of the feminist publishing boom. Much of the lesbian publishing that there has been, has happened because of the commitment from lesbians. Onlywomen Press have been responsible for the greater part of it – their anthologies, *The Reach*, *The Pied Piper* and *In and Out of Time*, as well as the work of Anna Livia, Anna Wilson and others. Not surprisingly, they have nurtured fiction which accords with their own particular brand of lesbian politics. Sheba, another small independent publisher, has concentrated on other places in the political spectrum. Their commitment to Black writers has been extremely important and given writers such as Suniti Namjoshi, Jackie Kay and Barbara Burford a start. The Women's Press too, throughout the late 1980s, also published work by lesbians, notably Nicky Edwards, Caeia March, Frances Gapper, Barbara Wilson, Ellen Galford and the anthology *Girls Next Door*.

Although I haven't checked circulation figures, and would be delighted to be proved wrong, these publications command small circulations within the culture of lesbians and feminists. Although many bookshops now promote women's books, especially around Feminist Book Fortnight, it is rare to see Onlywomen or Sheba books on their shelves and The Women's Press titles are patchily available. In the light of this, my search for a lesbian book popular with a wide audience, the kind of book that might easily turn up on a general women's studies course, for example, or be freely available at bookshops up and down the country was narrowing down.

Of course, I'd known all along that Jeanette Winterson would fit the bill: published by Penguin and Bloomsbury, winning awards right, left and centre, fêted by Gore Vidal, amongst others, and uncompromisingly lesbian. I think I'd needed to arrive at that choice by going through the field of lesbian writing because I find it difficult to pluck books out of thin air or to accept the view that the best will rise naturally to the top and float there in singular, individual glory. That there is only one hugely successful lesbian writer to choose is a function of the market and of the culture, which both work towards the incorporation and the limiting of any potential challenges to its rules and regulations. There is only one Jeanette Winterson because there can only be one. And this is partly why I chose her, because she illustrates so clearly an insight from Tillie Olsen, whose book *Silences* is one of my touchstones of feminist criticism.

> We must not speak of women writers in our century (as we cannot speak of women in any area of recognized human achievement) without speaking also of the invisible, the as-innately-capable: the born to wrong circumstances – diminished, excluded, foundered, silenced.
>
> We who write are survivors, 'only's'. . . . Only's are used to rebuke ('to be models'); to imply the unrealistic, 'see it can be done, all you need is capacity and will'. Accepting a situation of 'only's' means: 'let inequality of circumstance continue to prevail.'
>
> (Olsen, 1980:39)

Jeanette Winterson is an 'only'. And she is a very powerful 'only', because she is a lesbian, not just a woman, and because she was born to wrong circumstances. But she's not to blame for that.

BOOKING THE CHOICE

Criticism, at least the criticism I grew up on in the early 1970s, was all about fixing judgements, agreeing lists of acceptable books and authors and deciding how to think about them. Critics told lecturers, lecturers told students and if students learnt their lessons well, then they could become lecturers too or even, if they learnt them really well, critics themselves. Originality and imagination were fine, as long as they didn't mean you strayed off the path marked 'Great Literature' into the thickets and marshes of Marxist criticism, sociology of literature or women's studies. If you did, and persisted in staying off the path, then you forfeited Literature and became a sociologist or a feminist instead.

Looking back to a course called 'Women and literature in society' that I was lucky enough to be able to take in 1975 – it was the first Women's Studies literature option offered at a British university – I'm struck by how its significance is less that we looked at the subject of women and more how we did this. Not that the subject of women should be glossed over, it was – and remains – tremendously important in a world that still treats women as trespassers. What I remember, though, is that this course allowed us to look at different sorts of books and to ask different questions about them. I think it is this that sets feminist criticism apart for me, and it is the element that has stayed constant throughout the enormous changes that feminist criticism has undergone.

In the beginning, feminist criticism was simple and polemical. Books like *Sexual Politics* by Kate Millett and *Thinking About Women* by Mary Ellmann were the inspiration behind thinking critically about the bread-and-butter patriarchal assumptions of literary criticism. A little later, Elaine Showalter, Louise Bernikow and Ellen Moers provided the drive towards the lost traditions of women's writing through their books *A Literature Of Their Own*, *The World Split Open* and *Literary Women*. Feminist criticism was a concern of women academics, but not to the exclusion of other sites of struggle. There was a great emphasis on gender issues within the school curriculum and women made a huge impact on Adult Education, especially through the Workers' Educational Association, where many branches were revitalised by effectively becoming women's branches. This grassroots Women's Studies had a very definite bias towards writing. Within the Women's Liberation Movement itself, women's writing was popular and accessible to a majority of women. It was discussed in *Spare Rib* and many smaller newsletters and newspapers, formed the basis of much women's publishing and at conferences was always a popular topic for workshops. Then it began to get rather more complicated.

Women's writing, especially contemporary work drawing on the insights and experiences of feminism, remained very popular but feminist criticism became a much more exclusive activity, almost entirely restricted to higher education. In the late 1970s and early 1980s, criticism generally was in some chaos. The old liberal humanist traditions were under attack from structuralist and poststructuralist critics who drew on the work of continental thinkers such as Louis Althusser, Roland Barthes, Jacques Derrida and Michel Foucault. Psychoanalysis, linguistics and semiology provided the tools for critical work concerned with the text and its system of meaning. Feminism, with its new way of viewing the world, was more allied to these directions in critical thought. A gap opened between women's writing, which was seen as a kind of naïve enjoyment of books and reading available to any woman, and feminist criticism, which was only possible with the assistance – and prioritising – of complex theoretical strategies and only really acknowledged if taking place within higher education; a privileged discourse indeed.

Women's Studies in higher education, especially in literature, has gained ground. I am sure it is still far from easy to be a woman working in these institutions, but something has shifted. Most advertisements for lecturers in

English Studies now ask for a specialism in feminist critical theory. Feminist criticism has arrived, but on the way I think it has shed one of its earliest strengths, which was to talk about books, their writers and their readers, rather than theories of criticism. One of the most important things I learnt about criticism from feminism, and which remains a benchmark of feminist criticism for me is this: it is only possible to reach provisional decisions and judgements about books and authors; and that there are conflicts over meanings and the books which contain them. Truth is often no more than the ability to particularise the reader, the reading and the text in such a way as to create the illusion of generality. All we do as critics is see what we see, and say what we see following the long look. It's not that I object to general statements – I make them all the time – but I try to make it clear why I think the way I do: to situate my reading, which involves questions of theory as I analyse, contextualise, compare and debate the words on the page.

I don't think I'm anti-theory, although I am concerned at what sometimes seems to be the exclusively theoretical direction feminist critical practice has taken. What I really object to is a hierarchy of reading, the critical triangle, in which general readers form the base, with their supposedly unreconstructed, a-theoretical approaches and balanced precariously on the point, is the latest darling: Mary Jacobus, Hélène Cixous, Julia Kristeva, Toril Moi, Cora Kaplan, Catherine Stimpson. The Next One and The One After. No, the criticism/theory issues have to be a circle for me, not a pyramid, and I must be able to move across it as I need and as I want. There will be history, biography, symbolism, reader-response, accumulated critical accounts, social context, textual structures, themes and language; there will be blanks for new ways of thinking about books that I do not yet know. I may spend more time in some segments than others, and have no rigid pattern for travelling this circle, but I like to see a book in a social as well as a literary context and I also like to see books within a specific literary history.

When I read a book, I do so in different ways depending upon what sort of book it is and why I am reading it: what I am expected to do next with it. *Oranges Are Not the Only Fruit* is the story of Jeanette, adopted by an evangelical family in the early 1960s and 1970s. It is set in a Northern mill town and we follow Jeanette from the age of 7 through until she is 21 and has left home. The book is a mixture of sad and funny events. We see everything through Jeanette's eyes and there is a knowingness to what she tells us and how she tells it. Jeanette is caught up in the evangelicism, too; she is a preacher and is responsible for converting a lot of people. Her and her mother's religious views set them apart from the rest of the town. During her teens Jeanette falls in love with another girl and this eventually leads to her leaving home, rejecting the church and making her own way in the world. When she returns one Christmas to visit her mother, Jeanette discovers that the evangelical movement has fallen apart under the pressure of various scandals but her mother is irrepressible: she has set up a CB radio church, call name Kindly Light. As well as telling this story, the novel has fairy tales interspersed throughout and some chapters are just short reflections on topics such as history. When I re-read *Oranges Are Not the Only Fruit* in order to write about it, I read it very differently from when I first read it, which was for my own pleasure and understanding, and from my second reading, which was to teach it on a course 'Lesbian lives and writing'.

Oranges Are Not the Only Fruit took a while to filter through to me. It was Jeanette Winterson's first novel, and the decision whether to read anybody's first novel is highly susceptible to reviews, recommendations and how appeal-ing the cover is. It didn't help that she had been published by Pandora, an imprint of mainstream publishers Routledge and Kegan Paul who had started up some time after Virago and The Women's Press. This had two effects. On the one hand, Virago and The Women's Press had established a kind of product identity for feminist writing, but Pandora also had another problem, namely a women's movement which constantly divided women and organisations into the pure and damned. Some women felt Pandora were just cashing in on the popularity of women's writing generated by the feminist presses. Not true, of course, but one legacy of the 1970s self-help political groups was a suspicion of anything that seemed too glossy and professional. Although Virago and The Women's Press quickly became very upmarket indeed, there was a residual lack of enthusiasm for Pandora books in some quarters. Mistrusting success was only one direction feminism took, for many younger women, especially those whose political experience wasn't formed in socialist or co-operative traditions, feminism was precisely about succeeding in the mainstream.

Two women, neither of them lesbians, recommended the book to me, one said it was scurrilously irreverent about religion, the other that it was painfully funny about family life. I borrowed somebody's copy and read it quickly, on holiday, and enjoyed it immensely. It was a book about growing up, told by a very clever, adult voice in the first person. I enjoyed reading a novel that wasn't set in London and featured a family that wasn't solidly middle class, and I enjoyed being able to laugh at them. But I was also uneasy about that. It is too easy to see Northerners as just good for a laugh, to make people into a freak show for your friends in the South. There was no sense in which Jeanette Winterson was writing for the people she'd left behind, and that both worried and dazzled me. It worried me because it seemed to devalue people, to lack respect for them, and it dazzled me because it took daring to be so callous, and so exuberantly defiant.

Discussions with lesbian friends about the book covered similar ground, but also took in the book's central lesbian relationships. We found it exhilarating to read a book with a lesbian heroine which had a strong plot rooted in something other than the discovery or coming to terms with lesbianism. It is impossible to separate Jeanette from her lesbianism, but at the same time much of the action of the book is rooted in quite different dynamics, such as religion, the nature of mothering, or the nature of ambition. Although we liked this, it bothered us that most of our straight friends discussed the book with barely a passing reference to lesbianism. We talked, too, about the uneasy feelings that lesbianism was once again being identified with oddness and that the book might suggest that Jeanette's lesbianism was caused by her peculiar upbringing. 'But,' countered someone, 'Jeanette is the sanest character in the book and she never blames anyone for her lesbianism.' True. The book actually makes a very strong case for that first principle of lesbian existence: lesbianism isn't the problem, people's attitudes towards it can be. There was talk, too, about how lesbian books seem to divide into the tragic or the comic, how impossible it is to have a middle-of-the-road, simply 'there' book about lesbians or lesbian issues.

Oranges Are Not the Only Fruit won the Whitbread prize for the best first novel and it was interesting to see how Jeanette Winterson's success affected both her writing and her reputation. Her reputation started to rise not just within a feminist readership but amongst the literary scene more generally, where she became a name to watch out for. Her writing, however, suffered. She brought out another novel, *Boating for Beginners* and a keep-fit book for women. Neither of them matched the promise of *Oranges Are Not the Only Fruit: Boating for Beginners* was silly and her keep-fit book fatuous. Like many writers who produce one exceptional book, she was hurried into print with subsequent titles that seriously threatened to diminish her original talent. I felt this strongly at the time, and was quite scathing about Jeanette Winterson. I wasn't the only one. 'She's bloody good, and successful, that's what feminism can't come to terms with', a friend said. And I think she was probably right. It was interesting, in the wake of *The Passion*, her next novel, to read Jeanette Winterson on the decision she'd made to move from Pandora. It was not about money – upfront anyway – at all. She'd been writing the wrong sorts of books, caught in a groove that was sapping her creativity and she'd taken the risk in order to rescue her integrity as a writer. That I admired.

But at the time, a lot of readers felt disappointed by what Jeanette

Winterson did after *Oranges Are Not the Only Fruit*, and that disappointment fed into a suspicion of success and stars fostered by the women's movement's emphasis on collectivity. There is something uneasy about feminism's desire to push women in general out into the world, to see them succeed, and how it manages the fact that such success is harder to quantify – and achieve – *en masse* than individually. By being such a public figure, Jeanette Winterson came in for a good deal of privately expressed criticism. Ruthless, self-seeking, ambitious: these were the opinions circulating about her as she struggled out of the ghastly mess she'd got herself into after *Oranges Are Not the Only Fruit* with the Penguin-published novel *The Passion*, one of the most enthralling and pleasurable books I'd read in a long time.

The Passion established Jeanette Winterson as a risen, as opposed to rising, star in the literary firmament and was followed by *Sexing the Cherry*, published by Bloomsbury, and an adaptation of *Oranges Are Not the Only Fruit* for BBC TV. Comparing my rather hostile ambivalence with the adulation around me, I had to re-think. Shortly after the TV serialisation, the Return to Learning course I tutor spent the balance of our budget on books. They returned with a varied collection, including *Sexing the Cherry* and the TV tie-in of *Oranges Are Not the Only Fruit*. These books had been chosen by a student who had watched and enjoyed the serial. I realised that I was expecting her to have trouble with them – and finding in that something else to dislike about Jeanette Winterson. What I hadn't anticipated was how much pleasure my student, Gill, found in the books, especially in *Sexing the Cherry*: how the difficulty she had in understanding was part of the pleasure, the tussle to stay with it, understand it; how she enjoyed being caught up in the semi-real, semi-fantasy world; how the play of ideas entranced her. Challenged by such enjoyment, I felt extremely churlish. Enthusiastically, she suggested I teach *Oranges Are Not the Only Fruit* next year. Perhaps I will. Finding ways to teach is an important part of feminist criticism for me, as important as any insights and accounts I might hold of the book for myself or for sharing through reviews and writing.

Oranges Are Not the Only Fruit was one of four books read and discussed on the course called 'Lesbian lives and writing'. The aim of the course was to introduce a small selection of works by twentieth-century writers and to discuss their work through the theme of autobiography. The course was run as an evening class through Hackney Workers' Educational Association for lesbians only and attracted about a dozen students, of whom half were teachers either in secondary schools or in adult basic education. The other books we read were: *Hard Words and Why Lesbians Have to Say Them* by Caroline Halliday, Sheila Shulman and Caroline Griffin, *Mirror Writing* by

Elizabeth Wilson and *Zami* by Audre Lorde. We asked these questions: Does autobiography define lesbian writing? Is this a positive characteristic; can it ever be a limitation? Is lesbianism ever just a personal issue, and if not, how are its social and political aspects present in our lives? How does the writing of other lesbians strengthen our lives and writing? The questions formed the basis of a general discussion at the first meeting and were referred to throughout the course. Each book was allocated two weeks for discussion and the expectation was that they would be read in advance.

We began the sessions on *Oranges Are Not the Only Fruit* by reflecting on and pooling answers to the following questions:

1. When did you read the novel?
2. What did you think of it?
3. Have you ever re-read it, and if so, have your views changed?
4. Would you say it was a comic book?

Only one woman's response was unchanged: each reading had provoked uncontrollable laughter. She had particularly enjoyed reading the novel out loud to her mother and relished the treatment of religion. She was also quite clear that it wasn't a lesbian book. What she meant by this was that lesbian issues were not at its heart and it was not addressed to a primarily lesbian readership. There was a lot of disagreement with her about this from people arguing that a lesbian book is defined by who writes it and not who it is written for. There was also a more complicated discussion about how central lesbianism and lesbian issues were to the novel. Most people were glad that lesbian fiction was moving on from the need to define and defend itself and was able to let being a lesbian be just one part of a more complex whole, as it is for most of us.

The majority of the women had read the novel twice and their views had changed. Coming back to it eighteen months or two years later was, as one woman said, like picking up a completely different book. The main change was that they didn't find it as funny as they had remembered it. We discussed this at length. I put forward the view that perhaps on a first reading they had been drawn into the world of the novel so effectively, so captivated by the dry, throw-away wit of the narrator that they'd read the book exactly as the author wanted it read. On a second reading, perhaps, they were finding more room for their own views, and were able to be more critical of the moral standpoint of the narrator. There was agreement that a second reading revealed more than the first: everyone was more aware of the range of characters, the various themes and issues of the book than they had been on a first reading. It was clearer, too, that humour was a way of dealing with potentially painful issues. On a first reading the shock of extreme situations being offered up in such a ribald and ironic fashion hurried the reader on past the actual content, the base of suffering the humour rested on. There was something much more sombre a second time around. It was interesting that the TV drama adopted an elegiac approach which muted the comic element.

There was a quality to the novel that disturbed most women and we tried to locate it. One suggestion was that it lay in the way everyone in the novel but Jeanette is one-dimensional. This weights her viewpoint and enables the reader to see everything as Jeanette sees it, but is a problem if you want to test Jeanette's view of the world. Going behind the main character and into the world of the novel is to find yourself in a distortedly huge landscape in which all the figures are nothing but painted cloth. 'But why,' said someone else, 'do you want to test what she says? It's only a novel, after all, it is her point of view. If fiction was fair, it would be terribly boring.'

'It's not just that her viewpoint's imposed on the novel,' said another. 'It's the way she has no self-doubt at all, not a scrap. She is right: about everything, always, and knows better than anyone else.' We discussed whether this was a deliberate aspect of the characterization, a consequence of evangelism. Those women who had experienced similar sorts of charismatic and evangelical conversion in their teens spoke about how real to them had been Jeanette's superior distance from the rest of the world. They hadn't liked it, one admitting that it reminded her too much of her own past attitudes, but they had found it accurate. This led into an interesting discussion about the ways in which the church provided a means for women to be valued and active outside the home. It was unusual for a woman to have the amount of power Jeanette had before her disgrace, and we discussed how Pastor Finch readily saw in that both symptom and cause of her fall.

In the subsequent session, we discussed *Oranges Are Not the Only Fruit* as autobiography. Our intention was not the futile task of deciding how much and in what proportions the novel was autobiographical, but rather to discuss the impact of such a novel being autobiographical. We agreed that it must have taken a certain degree of ruthlessness both to write and publish a novel which follows the broad outlines of Jeanette Winterson's life so accurately. The craft of fiction is determined by a cruel, unforgiving eye that gives very little quarter to anybody else's version of what happened and why. Members of the group who wrote themselves had the most to say about this. Some were clearly envious of Jeanette Winterson's capacity to rid herself of censors, to let creativity determine what takes shape and to give it absolute priority. 'To create was a fundament. . . . Once created, the creature was separate from the creator, and needed no seconding to fully exist' (Winterson, 1985: 46). This is 8-year-old Jeanette complaining about how little acknowledgement she received at school for the sampler she stitched for Elsie, but the statement is a useful indication of Jeanette Winterson's views on writing itself. Others, though, were wary of this, believing that the writer has a responsibility to those she writes about as well as to herself. Both views are accommodated within a feminist account of writing: the one banishes the censors and speaks the truth as seen by a woman, valorising a women's point of view; the other supports an ethic based on how others are perceived and treated, careful of feelings, careful not to blame, especially not mothers for the ills their daughters endure.

When *Oranges Are Not the Only Fruit* appeared on television it was accompanied by much advance publicity, including interviews with Jeanette Winterson. Reviewers and interviewers had two main concerns: lesbian sex scenes on TV and was it true? The lesbian sex caused far less controversy than might have been expected, a testimony to the production, which followed the writing in making it integral and unsensational. On the other question, Jeanette Winterson was most interesting. There seemed to be a conciliatory attitude towards her family, as she spoke about how they had read the novel – which she thought would never find its way to Accrington – and been hurt by it, although this was not her intention. The adaptation was a much gentler affair altogether, and the characterisation of the mother by Geraldine McEwen gave her a dignified strength that was quite different from the maniacal zeal of the novel. And as to whether it was true or not, Jeanette Winterson, interviewed in *The Guardian*, was charmingly disarming. She'd made some of it up, she said, and some of it was true, but what was what, she just couldn't remember any more.

If I were to teach this novel within an Adult Education Return to Learning context, the first difference would be that I couldn't expect students to read it at home in preparation for discussions in class. The work of reading and understanding would have to be more carefully nurtured with students who usually lack confidence about their reading and writing and who rarely have a habit of reading. I would probably aim to whet the students' appetites sufficiently so that they wanted to continue reading the novel in their own time and try to give them the skills necessary to do so. To start this, I would introduce the novel to them in a short talk, perhaps show some of the TV drama if I had access to a video copy and follow it up with selected extracts designed to illuminate the characters and some of the themes I wanted to pursue.

As I gave this summary, I would illustrate it by reading a series of very short extracts from the novel and lead the students into a general discussion about what they had heard through questions such as: Was there anything you didn't understand? Do you now want to read the whole book? Why? Why not? From what you've heard, do you like the character Jeanette, do you sympathise with her? Does the book remind you of anything that has ever happened to you or anyone you've ever met?

In subsequent weeks I would pick out a range of 2–3-page extracts for close reading and comprehension: some would be designed to get the students thinking about the characters of Jeanette and her family, others to raise more general issues to do with the family, growing up and religion. My aim would be to give students the confidence to approach unfamiliar writing and be able to look closely at it, to begin to understand it in detail. I would also be encouraging students to think around the writing, to look for what it sparked off for them, what connections it made with other writing or other experiences. The power of the church in many Afro-Caribbean women's lives, for example, could generate interesting comparisons and questions. I would encourage students to respond personally to the work in the first instance: what does this make *you* feel; what does this remind *you* of; what do *you* find interesting about this? This approach, handled skilfully, is not as naïve and anecdotal as it may appear. The differences between women, and the impact of this on how we understand and respond to fiction, can emerge through such discussion and can then be extended and developed.

Teaching like this usually involves a balancing act between reading works of fiction in order to understand what they are saying and why, and using them as jumping-off points for personal accounts and reminiscences, where the original work can quickly get left behind. With students who have not had the opportunity of wide reading and a literary training, it is important to keep the relevance of what they read at the forefront. This doesn't mean that the book must mirror their own experiences, in fact they mostly want to read about lives that are not their own – they know those all too well. But what students do want is an explanation of why they are reading something, especially if it is difficult, and they also need encouragement, or permission, simply to enjoy a work of fiction. This is as much the province of feminist criticism as the elaborated close readings of texts within more academic frameworks. Sometimes students – at whatever level – keep their heads down too low, and are so aware of the difficulty of what they are doing, the work of it, that they leave their ordinary reading selves outside the door. What this can mean is that they then don't enjoy the writing and don't connect emotionally or imaginatively with it. A book as funny as

Oranges Are Not the Only Fruit would be an excellent way of making this point. The method of taking out extracts for analysis would also work better with this novel than many others, as Jeanette Winterson has already broken the flow of the narrative, not just with the asides and fairy tales, but by adopting an episodic structure.

The novel's theme of change, of the need to break away and the consequences of doing so, would connect in exciting ways with women on a Return to Learning course. In different ways, women on these courses are beginning a process which puts them and their families under enormous pressure. Fiction is a powerful way to begin talking about these transformations, to weigh other people's choices and motives against our own. And the book would be, incidentally and fundamentally, a book about lesbianism.

REFERENCES

Olsen, T., *Silences* (London: Virago, 1980).
Winterson, J., *Oranges Are Not the Only Fruit* (London: Pandora, 1985).

ACKNOWLEDGEMENTS

My thanks to the students of Hackney WEA's Lesbian Studies classes, especially Marion Virgo for organising the video party, and to Gill.

Janet Todd

Jane Austen, Politics and Sensibility

As the mother of the patriarchal line of F.R. Leavis's Great Tradition and first gentleman of Lionel Trilling's family of liberal modern personalities, Jane Austen has been an awkward subject for feminist criticism to cope with.[1] Early in her posthumous history she was caught by Charlotte Brontë and Virginia Woolf colluding with the male desire of George Henry Lewes and the Bloomsbury men for a lady who knew her place and theirs. Charlotte Brontë found an unwomanly avoidance of the heart, while Virginia Woolf was disinclined to be left in a room alone with her.[2] After an initial reluctance, modern feminist criticism has attempted to woo Austen into the sisterhood through either downplaying or recreating her historical context. The result has been a more feminist figure than was once imagined, but its creation has demanded a determined reading against the grain or a careful selecting from literary history.

In Sandra Gilbert and Susan Gubar's *The Madwoman in the Attic* (1979), which ranged Austen with major women who came after her, the tart Austen narrator was discovered manipulating events in stereotypically feminine fashion from behind the scenes and beneath the blotter. Her texts revealed the ubiquitous madwoman, the rebellious author's double who imaged her own desire and rage in subtle patterns on the seemingly calm surface, a woman-self who strained against the female renunciation of self encouraged by society. This Austen was uncomfortable with and alienated from her cultural inheritance and her novels became the literary version of the guns in Kipling's story of the 'Janeites' who named their First World War weapons after her characters.[3] The reading was a largely ahistorical and ungeneric one, removing Austen from her contemporary context and from the other women writers who preceded and surrounded her. It made sisterhood across time but not within it.[4]

The subversive writer of Gilbert and Gubar, who is 'just plain not saying what she means' and who through her silence rather than her formal utterances indicts a patriarchy it would otherwise be impossible to indict, has been immensely helpful for feminist criticism.[5] But it is now time to accept that not all intelligent women of the past aspired to a modern feminist

71

view and that to assume that they did so is to silence them as thoroughly as patriarchy silenced enlightenment feminism. Then desire to see covert messages may partly be a disinclination to hear the overt ones – already a feature of traditional Austen scholarship. Take the remarks about fat grief in *Persuasion*, the 'large fat sighings over the destiny of a son, whom alive nobody had cared for':

> Personal size and mental sorrow have certainly no necessary proportions. A large bulky figure has as good a right to be in deep affliction as the most graceful set of limbs in the world. But, fair or not fair, there are unbecoming conjunctions, which reason will patronize in vain, – which taste cannot tolerate, – which ridicule will seize.[6]

And the historical account:

> The real circumstances of this pathetic piece of family history were, that the Musgroves had had the ill fortune of a very troublesome, hopeless son; and the good fortune to lose him before he reached his twentieth year; that he had been sent to sea, because he was stupid and unmanageable on shore; that he had been very little cared for at any time by his family, though quite as much as he deserved; seldom heard of, and scarcely at all regretted, when the intelligence of his death abroad had worked its way to Uppercross, two years before.[7]

Some critics used to say that this harshness was clearly an error and would have been removed had *Persuasion* been thoroughly revised. But why should Austen not stand by these observations, which are common-sensical though not compassionate?

In the context of earlier women's techniques, the manoeuvre here can be viewed as a rather common female strategy under patriarchy, in many ways the reverse of the coding and concealing demanded by some feminist criticism. The aside is, for example, a sad technique in the Restoration Countess of Warwick whose harsh marital life greatly tested her Puritan faith. She worked out a system of mouthing her bitterness, under her breath, and, while she repeatedly repented this activity, she simply could not give it up. So she went on moving her lips but not allowing the air to reach the open ears of her irascible spouse, although the anger was clearly expressed in her diary.[8] This is often the way of the author-narrator of Austen's novels, who comes out with statements that would be repressed in a social situation and would be impossible for the characters themselves to make. In company we all speak distress at a death, especially at the death of a child, and have been too sentimentally indoctrinated to feel at all comfortable with Austen's suggestion that some people are worthless and would be better dead. Maternal crying in such circumstances, even of the portly, is socially correct but it remains aesthetically grotesque.

Despite many influential books following Gilbert and Gubar's lead, feminist criticism of Austen in recent years has moved decisively towards the historical in its recuperation. Again the desire has been for a protofeminist but one who for historical reasons was associated less with Charlotte Brontë and Virginia Woolf than with Mary Wollstonecraft. Here the problem was the conservative Jane Austen delivered by Marilyn Butler's pre-feminist work, *Jane Austen and the War of Ideas* (1975), which argued that Austen should be included in the conservative reaction of the late 1790s. Butler noted that the novels were less permissive, individualistic and expressive than many others by women of the time; on the evidence of her work Austen herself was, in Terry Eagleton's phrase, 'just a straight Tory'. In a later Preface to this study Butler argued that Gilbert and Gubar were simply wrong in making Austen a covert radical in a man's imprisoning world because they based their views less on women writers before Austen than on a few privileged ones who came after.[9]

Using the historical method pioneered by Butler's book, several other women critics have challenged her conclusion. Margaret Kirkham in two essays in *Jane Austen: New perspectives* (1983) argued that Austen ought to be ranged with, not against the overt feminists of the 1790s such as Mary Wollstonecraft, since both desired to demystify the female character and destroy the reverential and degrading obfuscation of the real economic and social status of women. She saw Austen writing on feminist issues and considered that the authority of her fictional techniques was an aspect of her criticism of patriarchal prejudice. Fanny Price, the largest lump in the feminist throat, was relieved of her famous priggishness to become a commentary on contemporary female images. In her weakness and sexually arousing religiosity she resembled the heroines of the sort of conduct-books Mr Collins failed to read to the bored Bennet sisters in *Pride and Prejudice*. At the same time, Fanny was also intractable and rational, close to the radical woman. In the first case, Kirkham argued, irony was turned on the character; in the second, on the reader who might approve the wrong aspects. *Mansfield Park* became a great comic novel regulated by the sane laughter of a rational feminist.[10]

The problem with such an attractive reading was the exclusion of many contemporary conservative novelists from the debate, in whose pages most of the approved but ambivalent notions of the early feminist rationalist Mary Wollstonecraft could be found, such as the need for moral autonomy and serious female education. This exclusion was to some extent rectified in Claudia Johnson's tightly argued *Jane Austen: Women, politics and the novel* (1987), Mary Evans's *Jane Austen and the State* (1987) and Alison Sulloway's

Jane Austen and the Province of Womanhood (1989) which wanted to broaden the Austen context to help answer that old damning question: where are the French Revolution in *Pride and Prejudice* and the Napoleonic Wars in *Mansfield Park?* All three wished to rescue Austen from being the gentlemen critics' provincial lady and part of Marilyn Butler's Tory faithful. Johnson set the young author in the 1790s and the adult in the Regency and showed how the change was reflected not only in what she wrote but in what she could no longer write. After Godwin had published his biography of Mary Wollstonecraft, *Memoirs of the Author of A Vindication of the Rights of Woman*, in 1798, making of his wife a public and principled whore, there was no question of any modest novelist associating with her or writing a new *Rights of Woman*. The old assumption that Austen must be conservative if she came from a conservative class was agitated by the uncertain status she actually had: the fact that Walter Scott called her middle class and Madame de Staël labelled her works *vulgaire.* Claiming that most of the political novels by women were more complicated than modern commentators made them – Fanny Burney and Jane West, arch conservatives and assumed to be guardians of home and hearth, did not portray marriage idealistically – Johnson argued that under the pressure of intense reaction women including Austen developed stylistic techniques which enabled them to use politically charged material in an exploratory and interrogative rather than hortatory manner.[11] To some extent the image delivered here, although far more historically based, was not unlike the 'coding, concealing' Austen of Gilbert and Gubar.

Another version of this image was provided by Alison Sulloway who insisted on the grief and anger lying beneath the surface of the Austen satire; in *Jane Austen and the Province of Womanhood* (1989) she found these subtle forms of revenge against misogynist male writing which flourished throughout the eighteenth century. Sulloway's Austen is no 'mere conduit for the *status quo*' but instead mediates between traditional forces hostile to women and the opposing radical disruption. She becomes, like Kirkham's Austen, a radical woman speaking from the margins, attacking male privilege and female disenfranchisement, with a voice closer to the shocking Mary Wollstonecraft than to the conservative Hannah More.[12]

Mary Evans, a British writer, keener than the American Johnson or Sulloway to use the language of Marxism and the context of modern politics, pointed out that Austen endorsed values incompatible with the practices and policies of modern Toryism; she should be dissociated from conservatism since she elucidated a morality independent of the material values of the capitalist marketplace, claiming an equality of men and women and the

rights of women to moral independence and autonomy.[13] Part of this
argument is certainly true and Evans's view of Austen is an appealing one,
but some of her points depend on obliterating the specific conservatism of
the late eighteenth century, Austen's 'dear Dr. Johnson' with his dislike of
plebeian power and capitalist accumulation – of which Austen was heir but
Mrs Thatcher not. As for women, moral independence is undoubtedly
advocated and this fits with the serious concern of both radical and
conservative women of the 1790s. But women's rights, as Wollstonecraft
came to believe, included the right to express desire and sensibility as well
as independence, and this possible right was, I believe, a more openly
discussed problem than Evans and indeed Johnson or Sulloway allows.

While accepting the value of the feminist and the feminist historical
figures of Austen described above, I would like to argue for another who is
less comfortable because less conforming to present notions, closer to that
maverick among women writers that Charlotte Brontë so famously deplored.
Such a figure can be revealed through feminist literary history using empirical
generic expectations and practice. This Austen uses the codes and conventions of her contemporary novel specifically to intervene in the debates
about political, social and psychological issues, in the way that all the
historical feminist critics have emphasised. But I want to stress two aspects
of her position that they appear to have understated.

First, it is difficult to label Austen politically because it is difficult to place
single political labels on women in general and even more difficult to
distinguish a radical from conservative line on several important issues like
female education. Women called conservative or liberal such as Hannah
More, Fanny Burney and Elizabeth Hamilton, and later Jane West and Mary
Brunton, all following the conservative Edmund Burke in coalescing
national and familial interests, and women labelled radical or liberal such as
Mary Wollstonecraft, Mary Hays, Elizabeth Inchbald, and later Maria
Edgeworth, Sidney Owenson, Lady Morgan and Madame de Staël, all shared
a desire to promote the intellectual and moral woman at the expense of the
trivial lady of ornamental accomplishments which the culture appeared to
endorse.

Second, political persuasion is not immediately revealed by generic literary
habit in women. The promotion of the moral female occurred in novels
that, while varying to some extent according to political persuasion, varied
to a greater extent according to the degree of sensibility allowed into the
women characters' composition and into the composition of the novels
themselves. There is as much contrast between the sentimental and the
unsentimental treatments as there is between the conservative and the

radical, and authors can be separated from each other according to how sentimental the characters and the books were allowed to be just as much as they can be separated by politics. An attitude to sensibility *could* imply a party political line but overwhelmingly it implied a personal political one, and here it seems to me that Austen is much easier to place than she is in the party political context.

I want to suggest that the main motivator of Austen, beyond any party political purpose, is her opposition to sensibility in all its forms, whether it be romantic fantasy in young girls, spontaneous feminine understanding or intuition, political aspirations or plot expectations. If this is true, Austen will inevitably sometimes sound more like the rationalist radical Wollstone-craft in *A Vindication of the Rights of Woman* (1792) which is virulently anti-sentimental than like the conservative Burney, writer of the final emotional pages of *Camilla* (1796). But she will sound far less like the sentimental radical Wollstonecraft, author of *The Wrongs of Woman* (1798), than like the no-nonsense Jane West of *The Advantages of Education* (1793).

The eighteenth-century cult of sensibility, associating the feminine and the sentimental, brought women into the centre of culture.[14] Women's consciousness was investigated and their voice, though inevitably mediated and culturally constructed, was heard; it also brought into prominence those qualities of benevolence, tenderness, susceptibility and domesticity, thought to be quintessentially feminine. The late novel of sensibility, current when the young Jane Austen was penning her parodies, sticks to the old stock plot and characters of sentiment, suffering virtue, good daughters and bad fathers, that had done much ethical service in the past. But it was also greatly influenced by the first part of Rousseau's *La Nouvelle Héloïse* (1761) which had as its centre the story of feminine sexual and emotional desire. As a result, the later sentimental novel was more concerned with the emotive and emoting subject, with desire or self-indulgence – depending on stand-point – than with general morality. Feminine sensibility could then be purveyed in a seemingly radical novel, often in first person or letter form which could muddle the distinction of public and private. While it might suggest the importance of feminine morality, tenderness and benevolence, as all sentimental novels do, it could also preach feminine expressiveness and self-gratification – although the search for these in an anti-sentimental world would usually be disastrous. The self-expressiveness could be radically transgressive of familial pieties in its promotion of individualistic desire, as it was, for example, in Wollstonecraft's *The Wrongs of Woman* which pleaded the right of a woman to love first and beyond marriage. On the other side, sentimental conventions could be employed solely to enhance the nuclear family and domesticity, which usually appeared the direct opposite of individual expressiveness and bolstered the status quo. Edmund Burke famously employed sentimental writing against the presumptions of impious reason in his *Reflections on the Revolution in France* (1790) and Jane West would use it again in her Burkean *A Tale of the Times* (1799). Some novels such as Mary Hays's notorious *Memoirs of Emma Courtney* (1796) managed to ask for both family and transgressive self-gratification together.

To summarise the plot from the woman-authored novel of the 1780s and early 1790s: the immaculately beautiful, pure and intelligent sentimental heroine is usually orphaned at puberty. She struggles with the desire of her father or of a male substitute, a wicked uncle perhaps who has seized her property and, in a way, her person. The story of stylised victimisation becomes the fight for ownership of herself, for external marriage or friendship, creating a new nuclear family of choice. In a late radical novel the wicked male might be a husband and the freedom might become adultery as in Wollstonecraft's *The Wrongs of Woman*; in the more conservative, the wicked uncle might be a desiring rake with Godwinian or Wollstonecraftian principles and the freedom might become chosen marriage to an ethically more reliable and certainly less mastering man. If the tale were unhappy, the heroine fell and died; if happy, she gained every good through passive suffering: property, female patronage and bliss.

The sentimental heroine was usually aristocratic, but her rank delivered not power but delicious powerlessness. Consequently the heroine had all the advantages of gentility together with a victimised status while the hero, similarly aristocratic, was usually feminised out of patriarchal power, much of his heroic function being usurped by a female friend. As for techniques, one of the most obvious, used by conservatives and radicals alike, was the tableau, a static and ecstatic familial moment in which the response of the reader was described and demanded in the text, on the assumption that emotion through involuntary looking or hearing was spontaneous and immediately beneficial. The language delivering such scenes rather resembled the semiotic, pre-rational irruptions beloved of psychoanalytical feminists in the 1970s.[15] It was unbalanced, hyperbolic, eccentric and fragmented, suggesting suppressed thought by extraverbal devices like the exclamation mark and dash. A short excerpt from Mary Hays's *Emma Courtney* will exemplify:

> 'My friend sat beside me, holding my hands in her's which she bathed with her tears. "Thank God!" she exclaimed, in a rapturous accent, (as with a deep sigh I raised my languid eyes, and turned them mournfully towards her—"she lives!

– My Emma! – child of my affections!" – Sobs suppressed her utterance). I drew the hand, which held mine towards me – I pressed it to my bosom——"My *mother!*"———I would have said; but the tender appellation died away upon my lips, in inarticulate murmurs.'[16]

In this extract there are seven dashes of differing lengths, five exclamation marks, and an italicisation; these devices break up the prose to display the pre-logical character of sensibility and to convey a sense of female feeling and desire that has no easy articulation in literature.

Because of her implacable opposition to sensibility Jane Austen, although using the traditional feminine romantic and sentimental plot, simply does not seize the possibilities for political or psychological expression, articulation of desire and protest that such a plot had opened for women writers and readers. Despite valiant efforts of commentators she was, I believe, always on the side of sense against 'feminine' sensibility and so inevitably avoiding or opposing what that sensibility articulated. When in *Jane Austen* (1986) Tony Tanner, described by Hermione Lee as 'a thoughtful feminist reader', praised Austen for dramatising the abuse of language and, on occasion, properly preferring silence to sentimental expression, he colluded with her in silencing a specific kind of excessive female voice.[17]

Politically Austen revealed a kind of disenchantment; in Q. D. Leavis's words her values were 'not emotional but moral, critical, and rational', and she showed a scepticism about the possibility of human nature's changing or of political and social improvement through agitation and endeavour.[18] She mocked sentimental ideas and techniques in whatever party political context they appeared. In *Sense and Sensibility* the greedy shallow John Dashwoods employ the emotive language of familial sensibility to bolster their greed. They sentimentally refer to their small son as their 'poor little Harry' and through him set the selfish nuclear family, so much admired in conservative fiction, above the proper claims of the half-sisters and a promise to a dying man. Earlier the Dashwood patriarchal succession had been enforced by a spurt of the sentimental and misguided affection felt by an old man for a small, charming, but undifferentiated child. Throughout the book the conservatively supported nuclear family is the locus of boredom and nastiness. Mr Palmer, tired of politics, here simply the art of making everybody like him, runs from the impossible task into an irremediable and absurd marriage. The dependent male suffers from ennui, whether dependent on a morally admirable woman like Willoughby's aunt, Mrs Smith, or a reprehensible mother like Mrs Ferrars, and both men enter the close and cramped female Dashwood family in deep hypocrisy and guile.[19] Motherhood, so powerful a stimulus both to Burke's conservative polemics and to the effusions of assertive radical women like Hays and Wollstonecraft, becomes fond selfishness in Lady Middleton who reveals the mother to be 'the most rapacious of human beings', rather less preferable in her maternal habits than her predatory husband.

The oppositional use is even more insistently scorned, whether sentiment is underwriting a political, psychological or generic literary notion. Austen does not allow sentimental abilities to eradicate social distinctions, as Rousseau was famous for doing when he gave equality in love to a tutor and an aristocrat in *La Nouvelle Héloïse*, and Mr Darcy has a right to be proud and overtop the charming, intimate Wickham. Lucy Steele, from inferior society, is irredeemably vulgar in spite of her frequent displays of good nature and her natural cleverness.

Despite seeming to inhabit a sentimental plot, few Austen heroines achieve the loss of both inadequate parents, so their chances of gaining bliss and their own money in tandem, as sentimental heroines frequently do, are limited. The only mysterious orphan, Harriet, fails to live up to Emma's sentimental fantasy and proves lamentably lower middle class and unendowed. Elizabeth Bennet's misery is that she is not orphaned and that her ghastly mother and father continue to embarrass her into adulthood. Women are not amazing autodidacts as in most sentimental fiction. Fanny Price achieves no learning beyond Edmund's giving, Elizabeth Bennet does not practise the piano enough and Catherine Morland rolls down the green slope in childhood and reads romances when she grows up. She might learn the dangers of patriarchy from Ann Radcliffe's *The Mysteries of Udolpho* (1794), but her marriage indicates that she does not, and it is not she but ingenious modern readers inspired by feminist sociology and psychoanalysis who modify her conclusion that such books are not great guides to life in the Midland counties of England.

Money, so embarrassingly bourgeois when fixed in amount, is much to the fore. And, unlike in liberal sentimental novels, it remains in male hands. At the end of *Mansfield Park*, where the heroine is seemingly most unremittingly patriarchal, Fanny ends up with no female patronage but is insistent instead on patronage from her uncle: 'Fanny was indeed the daughter that he wanted.' When death completes the picture of good, Fanny and Edmund remove to the parsonage of Mansfield which grows in the last line 'as thoroughly perfect in her eyes, as every thing else, within the view and patronage of Mansfield Park'.[20] Patriarchal rule is re-established and community rests on male financial control and mutual familial selfishness, not the blissful feminine affections of sensibility.

Extra-familial friendship also gets short shrift and the possible female friend is banished to the evils of London, a sister being ensconced in her place.[21] It might be argued that patriarchy is modified in Sir Thomas's realisation that he has mismanaged his daughters and followed false values, but he *is* in place and there is nothing equivalent to the humbling of the patriarch so much a feature of sentimental fiction from Rousseau's *La Nouvelle Héloïse* to Elizabeth Inchbald's *A Simple Story* (1791). Even Sir Walter Elliot, found deeply wanting, still continues to own Kellynch Hall in *Persuasion*. The female mentors of Hays or even the more conservative Edgeworth and Burney are hardly even shadowed in Mrs Gardiner, Mrs Croft or the mistaken Lady Russell, and the affective inheritance of the estate by both partners is never a feature of Austen. It is unlikely that Elizabeth Bennet will concern herself with the rents from the Pemberley farms or Emma with the accounts of Donwell Abbey. The freakish feminists, with their excessive, expressive rhetoric such as Bridgetina Botherim of Elizabeth Hamilton's *Memoirs of Modern Philosophers* (1800), Amelia Opie's eponymous heroine of *Adeline Mowbray* (1804), Harriott Freke in Maria Edgeworth's *Belinda* (1801) and Elinor Jodrell in Fanny Burney's *The Wanderer* (1814), do not appear in Austen to be mocked, but neither is their protesting rhetoric allowed room for expression.

The expressiveness of the lady as potent victim, the staple of sentimental fiction, is likewise almost entirely absent from the mature novels. When a woman falls she does so trivially like Lydia or stupidly like Maria or even down the hill like Marianne. Although the powerful fallen woman does put in an appearance as many recent critics have noticed, pushing with odd insistence against the text of *Sense and Sensibility*, she is thoroughly silenced in the end. Despite much sentimental garrulity in the beginning about 'dear, dear Norland!' and 'ye well-known trees!', Marianne is famous now for saying nothing at certain notable points. She does so when Lucy Steele exclaims at the sweetness of the boring, selfish Lady Middleton, so that on Elinor falls the task of 'telling lies' when politeness required it. She is also silent when she receives Willoughby's cruel letter rejecting her. Only when she agrees to marry the man twice her age in a flannel waistcoat after her earlier declaration against second love does she begin again to speak – and only when she has learnt 'to talk . . . as I ought to do'.[22] Marianne is not entirely damned – she is not completely self-deluded, since Willoughby did love her at one point – she is not made into a sentimental butt like Bridgetina Botherim, a mockery of Mary Hays and her Emma Courtney who, like Marianne, pleads her right to express her feelings openly, and she is given Cowper to read like Anne Elliot, not the Wollstonecraft and Hays served up to satirised heroines in many conservative novels. But the argument that she represents, that feminine feeling must be allowed expression because authentic, is harshly mocked in the portrait of a sensibility which is discourteous, silly, feckless and impotent. Authenticity must be compromised by discretion it seems. With all her attractions, Marianne shares her name with an early French sentimental and narcissistic heroine in Marivaux's *La Vie de Marianne* (1731–41) who also rather seductively twists her ankle at the beginning of her romance but typically gets her man, as Austen's Marianne conspicuously does not.[23]

Austen refrains from the extreme attack on permanent marriage as prostitution embedded in Wollstonecraft's *The Wrongs of Woman* and the demand for female initiative in desire of *Emma Courtney*. She also avoids the interrogation of patriarchal power involved in the conservative investigation of marriage in writers such as Fanny Burney, as well as expressions of anguish at female impotence. She does this by eschewing sentimental presentation which allows protest through extreme depictions of misery and injustice and by limiting women's first-person expression through letters or other narrations. The letter in particular was *the* sentimental form, associated disparagingly and slightly anxiously with women and expressing desire that was assertive and might well be transgressive. It revealed the clash between public and private stances so central to the predicament of the woman of sensibility. In Austen these moments of expressiveness through letters are, ironically for the student of women's writing, given to men not women. When women like Isabella Thorpe or Mary Crawford write letters, it is usually to fool or deceive someone; other women like Elizabeth Bennet and Emma Woodhouse are heard a good deal directly without needing the device of the letter, although neither is given the sentimental heroine's latitude to express desire openly. It is men like Darcy, Colonel Brandon and the chastened Captain Wentworth who are silent or misunderstood in speech and it is they who can only express their inner selves and their desire in letters.[24] So a central technique of the earlier radical and liberal writers like Hays, Wollstonecraft and Edgeworth is taken from women and given to men who already, as Anne Elliot pointed out in *Persuasion*, had the pen quite firmly in their hands.

If, as Anne Elliot claims, books are not to be trusted since they largely record men's opinions, what has happened to the novels of the sister authors Austen had so proudly proclaimed in *Northanger Abbey*?

> 'Only a novel. . . . It is only *Cecilia* or *Camilla*, or *Belinda*'; or, in short, only some work in which the greatest powers of the mind are displayed, in which the most thorough knowledge of human nature, the happiest delineation of its varieties, the liveliest effusions of wit and humour, are conveyed to the world in the best chosen language.[25]

A hint of her later attitude to the writer most approved here for psychological accuracy and wit – Fanny Burney, author of *Cecilia* and *Camilla* – is given in Austen's final fragment, *Sanditon*, where Charlotte Heywood rather tartly concludes after picking up a volume of *Camilla* in the local bookshop and thinking of the expense, 'She had not *Camilla*'s Youth, & had no intention of having her Distress.'[26] It was Camilla's distressing debt that was most sentimentally treated in an otherwise largely unsentimental work and such a remark suggests that, whatever may be argued for her politics, Austen's attitude to sensibility had hardened. In the end, as at the beginning, it is generic sentimental techniques that she found most irritating.

Austen had mocked the absurd literary manifestations of sensibility when still a child in pattens, insistently placing the sentimental response in a world of other people and physical results. Long before Marianne ended up with a cold from wandering mournfully where the grass was the longest and the wettest, so becoming a liability to others, the sensitive Sophia in *Love & Friendship*, who has emoted and swooned throughout the novel, finally dies from a 'cold caught by her continual fainting fits in the open air'. Before she dies she laments that her once powerful passivity has been her downfall:

> My beloved Laura (said she to me a few hours before she died) take warning from my unhappy End & avoid the imprudent conduct which has occasioned it . . . beware of fainting fits. . . . Though at the time they may be refreshing & Agreable yet believe me they will in the end, if too often repeated & at improper seasons, prove destructive to your Constitution. . . . Beware of swoons Dear Laura. . . . A frenzy fit is not one quarter so pernicious. . . . Run mad as often as you chuse; but do not faint.[27]

Laura takes the advice and lives, but she proceeds onwards in the sensitive life, making her residence in a romantic village in the Highlands in the Celtic fringe of female emotionality. There without interruption she can enjoy her own effusions of grief and indulge in her unceasing lamentations, 'in a melancholy solitude'. The characters' knowledge of the potency of fiction, the broken language and typographical eccentricity all indicate the butt of this high-spiritedness.

Jane Austen defuses the powerful plot of feminine sensibility which takes a transgressive heroine to a nasty death, sadly or properly according to political temperament. Instead of accepting it on its own terms, she tells the reader to curb her expectations and the heroines to give up their nonsense. No doubt the first readers of *Sense and Sensibility* were as surprised as Marianne, a seemingly archetypal sentimental heroine who could have existed in conservative or radical novels, to find herself not dead after many signs that she ought to be. A large number of people in the novel assume that she is dying and need her approaching death to bring out the best in themselves. Mrs Jennings and Sir John Middleton know what to expect and act properly, but none is improved beyond the moment.[28] Most incorrigible is Willoughby, who has a fine time imagining her dying, fantasising scenarios in which she thinks of him in her last moments – though in her illness she actually raves of her mother – and finding comfort in knowing exactly what she will look like in death since his unkind action has already caused a rehearsal of the scene.

'Marianne Dashwood was born to an extraordinary fate. She was born to discover the falsehood of her own opinions, and to counteract, by her conduct, her most favourite maxims,' declares the narrator smugly.[29] She was also born to break through the sentimental plot. As semi-corpse Marianne forms the second attachment into which both sentimental characters enter in contradiction to all the rules of sentiment. Only sensible Elinor gets her sentimental first love.

The most indulged character in the plot is Colonel Brandon, physically a very prosaic lover but sentimentally the most poetic. Both Elinor and the Colonel, the standards of sense, feel the soft seduction of the feminine sentimental plot and Elinor even feels pity at the self-centred sentimental scenario of feminine death Willoughby outlines for himself. It is Colonel Brandon who brings in the seduction story of the two Elizas, both seduced and abandoned – the second by Willoughby – and it is he who insists on the sentimental connection. Whatever Marianne has learnt in the novel is not replicated by Colonel Brandon, who appears to have learnt very little indeed. He shows supreme enthusiasm for Marianne in the deathly physical predicament of Eliza the first, and his emotion burgeons when he receives her pale hand, sees the hollow eye, the sickly skin and the posture of reclining weakness. Elinor, that supposed exemplar of sense, immediately assumes the shadow, the 'probable recurrence' of the first Eliza. It might be churlish to remember the Colonel's attitude at that time: that it would have been better if the girl had died quickly.[30]

In *Sense and Sensibility* there is neither radical nor conservative security. The seemingly sensible characters are implicated in a sentimental plot that has much to do with feminine suffering, and the winners, more clearly than in the other books, are the worldly: the Dashwoods, the Middletons and Lucy Steele. The good are shadowed by the bad. Willoughby is elaborately idle, but in quieter fashion so is Edward. Both trifle with women, while other women have prior claims. It would be interesting to have the story from the point of view of Lucy Steele, who allows the actual happy ending only because she refuses to wilt under a difficult engagement and knows how to manipulate men. Or even from the viewpoint of the silent Eliza the second; it might have formed a radical novel.

Despite Colonel Brandon's example, women are far more prone than men to be caught in sentimental fantasy. On the whole, Austen's men know more what they are about. In the early 'Lesley Castle' the melancholy young man recovers speedily from the loss of love and 'thinks it very good fun to be single again', while in *Love & Freindship*, as the heroines sentimentally decline or die, the elegant and sentimental young men do not follow suit but become actors, and they are last seen on the final page of the novel exhibiting their persons at Covent Garden. The gloomy Benson in *Persuasion* throws off his gloom for one lady to pay court to another, while Willoughby speaks in the rapturous language of sentiment and means not a word of it.

Women are more persistent in sentimental blunders. Fanny Price and Anne Elliot are rewarded for sentimental waiting, but the author is pretty wry about the process in both cases. In the Kotzebue play translated by Elizabeth Inchbald as *Lovers' Vows*, rehearsed to such great effect in Mansfield Park, the heroine believes in the fantasy of romantic love, sure that a peasant can have a baron in the end if she loves enough. Maria too believes that a man's physical attraction in response to female desire can bring about marriage, but the book suggests that it well may not. Even the seemingly approved Fanny Price is mocked when, exclaiming at nature and the enraptured heart as she looks out into the Mansfield night, she believes from this rapture that wickedness and sorrow have gone from the world. But the value Fanny puts on the elevation of the moment is much diminished when she turns to find that Edmund is looking at her rival and her famous harp, himself enraptured by a sentimental scene that could have come straight out of Madame de Staël's *Corinne* (1807) or Sidney Owenson's *Wild Irish Girl* (1806).

Austen comments adversely on all the writers using sentimental, romantic motifs, be they conservative, liberal or radical. She felt herself 'Stout' against anything written by Jane West (28 September 1814), the most extreme female conservative novelist of the early nineteenth century. But she was just as stout against the later expressive writers, female equivalents of the Romantic poets about whose lofty aspirations and postures she was extremely sceptical. She dismissed Byron: 'read the corsair and mended my petticoat', while she wrote to her sister of Sidney Owenson's new novel in January 1809: 'We have only read the Preface yet; but her Irish Girl does not make me expect much. – If the warmth of her Language could affect the Body it might be worth reading in this weather.'[31]

The main accoutrement of Sidney Owenson's unappreciated wild Irish girl was the harp, that romantic symbol of sentimental femininity. In this high romance the hero is drawn to scale vertical castle walls by its sounds, exclaiming after his ascent at 'the "white rising of her hands upon the harp"; the half-drawn veil, that imperfectly discovered the countenance of a seraph; the moonlight that played round her fine form, and partially touched her drapery with its silver beam – her attitude! her air!'[32] Mary Crawford might have been trying for some such electrifying effect in the parsonage of Mansfield five years later, but had little chance with such a spoilsport creator.

For by then the harp was a veritable trade mark of sentimental romance, occurring most famously of all in Madame de Staël's *Corinne* which shares many characteristics with Sidney Owenson's book. Staël's novel tells of an exotic, unconventional, witty and harp-playing young woman, who like Hays's Emma Courtney announces her love first. She is not entirely English, and proves so unconventional that her lover pays court to her conventional sister whom he then marries. He is unhappy and after a final reunion with Corinne she dies. Shortly after *Corinne* appeared, Burney published *The Wanderer* (1814), giving her heroine Juliet some of Corinne's characteristic abilities at music. But the feminine Juliet learns that her harp-playing, though exquisite, is of no value in a world of work and duty and it will not with propriety gain her a decent living. The more radical part of *Corinne*, the plea for women's right to autonomous desire and significance, is sheered off into the masculine and eccentrically outspoken Elinor who proposes to the hero, tries romantic suicide not as abject surrender but as a female right and is in the end routed but by no means tamed. Throughout the book her fiery rhetoric, though denounced, is given much space, and a modern reader, used now to reading against the grain, might well find *The Wanderer* in two ideological minds. These two last novels are in plot something like *Mansfield Park* if the author had decided to applaud the harp-playing Mary Crawford and had intended setting her perfections off against the narrow rigidity of the country house. It seems to me possible to see Austen's work as partly an answer to this romantic permutation of sensibility, yet another swipe at unreasonable expectations and the notion that relationships can be so romantic and valuable that they may be regarded as transcendental.

As the historical feminist studies with which I began suggest, Austen is a more specifically political figure than earlier ahistorical feminist criticism had admitted. But these historical studies have not sufficiently allowed Austen to dissent from certain views and efforts of her times with which modern feminism has broadly been in sympathy. Austen turned her harshness on all party and personal political positions when they were tinged with simplicity, and her opposition to sensibility and sentimental techniques made her an uneasy ally of the sort of Regency conservatism she seemed most of the time to profess, inevitably forcing her to avoid too fixed an agenda. At the same time this opposition separated her from the company of women writers wanting to express for women both political and personal desire. The honesty that opposed the hope of sensibility – that people are good underneath some unfortunate social patina and therefore universally educable – and the specifically feminine fantasy that desire can and should be openly avowed, was a useful refiner of that sensibility, however personally and politically effective its crude employment might be. If Austen would not on the one hand assent to the naïvety required for revolutionary change or any decided amelioration of personal and social conditions, she would not on the other settle comfortably into the pieties of home and hearth. She remained always the poker of the sceptical fire, suggesting that change might make things worse but that things might already be deplorable, that children were not always loved or deserving of love, and that oppressed women might be as bitter or bad as dominating men and might do well for themselves and society by keeping their honest feelings under control.

NOTES

1. F. R. Leavis, *The Great Tradition* (London: Chatto and Windus, 1948) and Lionel Trilling 'Mansfield Park', in *The Opposing Self* (New York: Viking, 1959).
2. See G. H. Lewes, 'The novels of Jane Austen', reprinted in B. C. Southam (ed.), *Jane Austen: The critical heritage* (London: Routledge, 1968), p. 160 and 'Personalities', in *Collected Essays of Virginia Woolf* (London: Hogarth Press), II, 276. For a discussion of Woolf's complex attitude to Jane Austen see my chapter, 'Who's afraid of Jane Austen?', in *Jane Austen: New perspectives*, ed. Janet Todd (New York: Holmes & Meier, 1983).
3. Sandra Gilbert and Susan Gubar, *The Madwoman in the Attic: The woman writer and the nineteenth-century literary imagination* (New Haven: Yale University Press, 1979), p. 112.
4. In this context, see also Tony Tanner's *Jane Austen* (London: Macmillan, 1986) which argued that what mattered in Austen was not 'content' but her 'moral relation to language'. He made no reference to the major women political writers of her time and asserted that 'Jane Austen's fiction just does not include or examine a hero or heroine whose "individual fate" becomes "bound up" with matters and movements of wide public and historical significance' (p. 6).
5. See, for example, Mary Poovey's *The Proper Lady and the Woman Writer: Ideology and style in the works of Mary Wollstonecraft, Mary Shelley, and Jane Austen* (Chicago: University of Chicago Press, 1984).
6. *Persuasion* (London: Oxford University Press, 1965), p. 68.
7. *Persuasion*, pp. 50–1.
8. *Memoir of Lady Warwick: Also her diary from AD 1666 to 1667* (London: The Religious Tracts Society, 1847).
9. Marilyn Butler, *Jane Austen and the War of Ideas* (Oxford: Oxford University Press, 1975).

This book was the first to insist on the systematic discussion of the *female* literary and political context of Austen.

10. Margaret Kirkham, 'The Austen portraits and the received biography', and 'Feminist irony and the priceless heroine of *Mansfield Park*', in *Jane Austen: New perspectives*.

11. *Jane Austen: Women, politics and the novel* (Chicago: University of Chicago Press, 1987), p. xxi.

12. Alison Sulloway, *Jane Austen and the Province of Womanhood* (Philadelphia: University of Pennsylvania Press, 1989), p. xix.

13. Mary Evans, *Jane Austen and the State* (London: Tavistock, 1987), pp. ix–x.

14. I have argued this case more fully in *Sensibility* (London: Methuen, 1986) and *The Sign of Angellica: Women, writing and fiction* (London: Virago, 1989).

15. See, for example, Hélène Cixous in 'The laugh of the Medusa,' *Signs* I (summer, 1976), 875–93 and Luce Irigaray in *Le Speculum de l'autre femme* (Paris: Minuit, 1974).

16. Mary Hays, *Memoirs of Emma Courtney* (New York: Garland, 1974), II, p. 123.

17. Tanner, *Jane Austen*, p. 6.

18. Q. D. Leavis, 'Jane Austen and a changing society', *Collected Essays*, p. 59.

19. For a full discussion of the stern depiction of the family in *Sense and Sensibility*, see Johnson's *Jane Austen: Women, politics and the novel*, pp. 50–5.

20. *Mansfield Park* (London: Oxford University Press, 1966), pp. 472 and 473.

21. I have argued this case more fully in *Women's Friendship in Literature* (New York: Columbia University Press, 1980).

22. *Sense and Sensibility* (Oxford: Oxford University Press, 1987), pp. 27 and 344. See Angela Leighton, 'Sense and silences: reading Jane Austen again', in *Jane Austen: New perspectives*, pp. 128–41.

23. An interesting discussion of the relationship of Austen's novels to Marivaux's work occurs in Evelyn Farr's M.Phil. Thesis on Jane Austen, London University, 1989.

24. Marilyn Butler made this point more fully in a lecture on women writers given at Cambridge University in Michaelmas Term, 1989.

25. *Northanger Abbey* (London: Oxford University Press, 1965), p. 38.

26. *Minor Works* (Oxford: Oxford University Press, 1982), p. 390.

27. *Minor Works*, p. 102.

28. See Johnson, *Jane Austen: Women, politics and the novel*, pp. 64–5.

29. *Sense and Sensibility*, p. 378.

30. Alison Sulloway argues that Colonel Brandon's rhetoric differs from that of Austen's other secular males in being close to the unctuous tones of the disapproved sentimental conduct-book writer, James Fordyce, *Jane Austen and the Province of Womanhood*, p. 44.

31. *Jane Austen's Letters to her Sister Cassandra and Others* (London: Oxford University Press, 1969), 28 September 1814; January 1809.

32. *The Wild Irish Girl* (London: Pandora, 1986), p. 43.

Paulina Palmer

Antonia White's *Frost in May*: A Lesbian Feminist Reading*

INTRODUCTION: *FROST IN MAY*

Antonia White's *Frost in May* (1933) is one of several novels published in the inter-war years which treat the topic of female friendship in the context of school or college life. These 'novels of the gynaeceum',[1] as critics conventionally call them, share a common focus on the erc.ic aspects of attachments between women.

Whether *Frost in May* may justly be described as 'a lesbian novel' is a controversial question. In fact, one of the reasons I have chosen it as a text for discussion is that it illustrates the kind of difficulties which face the critic in deciding whether or not a work of fiction merits the identification *lesbian*. A number of factors suggest that *Frost in May* does not. Neither White nor the characters whom she creates identify as lesbian. On the contrary, as Gill Frith observes in her forthcoming book on female friendship,[2] White represents the passionate friendships which the protagonist Nanda forms with her classmates as a stage in the development of their sexual identity – an identity which, accepting the convention of her age, she envisages as heterosexual. Secondly, in keeping with this viewpoint, the word *lesbian* does not appear in the novel, and the facts of sexual relations between women are never explicitly articulated. Nanda and her friends, intense though their personal involvements are, have their perspectives restricted by the heterosexist ideology of the family and the Roman Catholic Church – with the result that the thought of a primary attachment between women does not enter their heads. When they speak, as they sometimes do, of the future, they envisage it in terms of stark alternatives – either getting married or entering a convent.

However, while these features of the novel may be cited to refute the identification *lesbian*, other features strongly support it. Love between

* For friends and colleagues at the University of Warwick

women, and the efforts made by the heterosexual, patriarchal establishment to suppress it and thwart its expression, constitute a key theme in the text. Lesbian desire and fantasy are also important motifs. Moreover, White's description of Nanda's erotic involvements with her schoolmates frequently transcends the plane of the emotional and the spiritual. It is, as we shall see, emphatically *sexual*. It is these features which give *Frost in May* its distinctive character and style. They prompt me, while acknowledging the debatable nature of my decision, to classify it as 'a lesbian novel'.

The events around which White organises her representation of female relationships in *Frost in May* are relatively straightforward. The protagonist Nanda is sent by her father, a middle-class convert to Roman Catholicism, to the Convent of the Five Wounds at Lippington, a boarding-school attended by the daughters of the Catholic aristocracy. Nanda is 9 when she enters Lippington, and 13 when she leaves. As well as feeling socially inferior to her aristocratic schoolmates, she finds the strict regime of the school and the authoritarian behaviour of the nuns irksome and oppressive. The nuns spy on the pupils' activities and censor their letters home. Seeking to restrict their access to sexual knowledge, they try to prevent them from forming 'particular friendships' with one another and confiscate any reading material which they regard, from their narrow viewpoint, as excessively worldly. However, life at Lippington, as Nanda discovers, is not all gloom and repression. After an initial period of unease, she starts to enjoy the company of her fellow pupils. Eluding the vigilance of the nuns, she forms passionate attachments with the androgynously attractive Léonie, on whom she projects the image of 'a young prince',[3] and the sensuously beautiful Clare. Her friendship with Léonie has a strong intellectual aspect. Léonie gives her a copy of the poems of Francis Thompson and, by scribbling poems and plays herself, encourages Nanda to write. Nanda's eventual expulsion from Lippington arises, in fact, from her expressing her literary aspirations in too unguarded a manner. The nuns confiscate the manuscript of a novel which she is in the process of writing and, on finding that its contents conflict with their own standard of propriety, inform her father of his daughter's transgression and demand that he remove her from the school. Like other novels of the gynaeceum, *Frost in May* ends abruptly, with the heroine's relationship with her schoolmates forcibly disrupted.

My choice of *Frost in May* as a text for discussion is also motivated by the fact that it responds very fruitfully to a reading in the light of present-day lesbian theory. Such a reading, as I shall show, illuminates both thematic and stylistic features of the text. White's description of the repressed nature of female desire and of the obstacles which women encounter in relating to one another in a phallocentric culture are significant here. So too is the emphasis she places on an alternative female sexual economy. They look forward to the interests of lesbian theorists such as Adrienne Rich and Luce Irigaray who are writing at the present time. White also concentrates attention on the subversive aspects of women's writing and reading. And, in describing the erotic involvements between Nanda and her friends, she employs strategies of indirection and displacement. These aspects of the novel are relevant to lesbian literary studies and to debates about 'lesbian aesthetics'. Both topics are important to critics working in the area of lesbian writing.

Before discussing these features of *Frost in May*, however, I need to clarify the context of this essay. The practice of 'lesbian reading' and the current situation of the lesbian reader are themes which seldom receive attention in schools and colleges in the United Kingdom. They require a word of explanation.

LESBIAN READING, SECTION 28, AND SEXUAL POLITICS

A lesbian reading of a text can take one of several forms. It can be purely personal in nature, existing on an imaginative plane and created solely for the satisfaction of the reader – as is the kind that Alison Hennegan describes in her fascinating essay 'On becoming a lesbian reader'.[4] As Hennegan observes, in the period of the 1950s and 1960s, before the advent of the feminist publishing houses made lesbian fiction easily available, the only course open to those of us who identified as lesbian or bisexual was 'to create our own "popular fiction", develop our own much cherished canon' (p. 169). Hennegan describes how, as a teenager starved of lesbian fiction, she constructed characters and situations with which she could identify by appropriating and imaginatively reworking materials from the heterosexual literary canon, such as the novels of Jane Austen.

Another kind of lesbian reading, besides the personal type which Hennegan describes, is, of course, possible. The reading can be more formal, composed to be read by other people, and employing lesbian theory as its base. The one I shall construct will be of this kind. However, despite their differences, both kinds of reading share a common aim. They seek to counter the marginalisation of lesbian experience and literary representation, and to challenge heterosexist perspectives. Heterosexism has been defined by theorists as 'the set of values and structures that assumes heterosexuality to be the only natural form of sexual and emotional expression – "*the* perceptual screen provided by our patriarchal cultural conditioning"'.[5] 'The perceptual screen' of heterosexism, as it is aptly termed, is depressingly evident in the United Kingdom today. The setting up of feminist publishing houses and bookshops has made lesbian texts available, in urban areas at least, but in many spheres of life the lesbian reader continues to suffer discrimination and to be treated as an outsider. One such sphere is institutionalised education. In the majority of colleges and universities in the United Kingdom facilities for lesbian and gay studies are either non-existent or, at the best, sparse.

There are signs that in the present period of the 1980s and 1990s such facilities as exist for lesbian and gay studies, either at the basic level of sex education in schools or at the more advanced level of the study of lesbian literature and history in colleges and universities, are not improving but are in decline. The political gains achieved by the lesbian and gay liberation movements in the 1970s, reflected in more tolerant social attitudes and in the setting up of gay centres and lesbian lines,[6] are now under attack from a homophobic backlash. Section 28 of the Local Government Act, which prohibits the so-called 'promotion of homosexuality' and discriminates against lesbian mothers by describing their families as 'pretended', both epitomises and exacerbates this trend.[7] Job shortages and threats to tenure in the field of education also discourage work in the area of lesbian and gay studies. Teachers in all branches of education are understandably nervous of discussing lesbian topics and texts in the classroom or lecture theatre. In this hostile social climate, in which lesbian perspectives are increasingly marginalised or erased, lesbian readings of texts are important from the point of view of sexual politics and civil liberties. As well as clarifying lesbian critical approaches, they make visible aspects of experience and literary representation which a reading based on the dominant heterosexual culture is likely to ignore. My reading of *Frost in May* will illustrate this.

THEORIES OF 'LESBIAN CONTINUUM' AND 'AN ALTERNATIVE ECONOMY OF FEMALE DESIRE'

The strategies of indirection and displacement, which, as I mentioned in the Introductory Section, are characteristic features of the text of *Frost in May*, are particularly apparent in White's representation of female erotic relationships. A passage describing an encounter between Nanda, portrayed as innocent of sexual matters, and Clare, her senior who is depicted as more knowing, illustrates these strategies at work.

White has already established the fact that Nanda is attracted to Clare and regards her as a 'romantic' figure. Clare's aura of romanticism stems, we are told, partly from her good looks, and partly from the fact that she occupies in the mythology of the school the intriguingly mysterious role of 'poor inquiring heathen' (p. 110). Unlike Nanda and the other pupils, Clare is Protestant by religion. Her parents only send her to the Roman Catholic bastion of Lippington because they find her unruly behaviour impossible to control at home. In the passage describing the encounter between the two girls, Clare flirtatiously exploits the fact of her alien religious identity. Having provocatively asked Nanda to explain certain thorny points of Roman Catholic doctrine relating to sex, namely 'the fornication and all wilful pleasure in the irregular motions of the flesh' mentioned in the Ten Commandments, she playfully touches on the topic of 'conversion':

> 'Besides, you may be converting me,' [Clare said.] 'Who knows?'
>
> 'I shouldn't dream of trying, Clare,' asserted Nanda. 'Catholics don't try and convert people like that. They just answer your questions and . . . and . . . pray for you.'
>
> Clare leaned over and touched Nanda's arm with a hot quivering hand that burned through her holland sleeve. 'Do you pray for me, baby?'
>
> 'Of course,' said Nanda in a very matter-of-fact voice, but she blushed all the same. Clare's touch embarrassed and delighted her; it gave her the queerest shivering sensation in the roof of her mouth. Why was it that when everyone else seemed just face and hands, Clare always reminded one that there was a warm body under her uniform? (p. 113)

The erotic impact of this passage is remarkable. A number of different factors contribute to its effect. As well as describing Nanda's response to Clare's caress with exceptional vividness, White humorously and provocatively juxtaposes references to sacred and profane love. Clare asks with mock piety, '"Do you pray for me, baby?"' – while simultaneously 'touching Nanda's arm with a hot quivering hand that burned through her holland sleeve'! White also creates a dialectic between the desiring female subject and the repression of female desire. This is a key theme in the novel. It is represented here by Nanda's sudden intense perception, which constitutes the climax of the passage, of 'the warm body' concealed 'under Clare's uniform'.

The sexually provocative humour of the passage is increased by certain other features White introduces. There is, for example, the play on the word 'convert', which the two girls flirtatiously bandy about. Though referring ostensibly to religious conversion, the word acquires in the erotic context of the passage connotations of lesbian seduction and 'proselytising'. There is also the ironic incongruity of the name Clare. Associated in Roman Catholic culture with the religious Order of Poor Clares, the name conjures up an image of extreme purity and unworldliness – attributes which are obviously foreign to Nanda's friend.

White's oblique description of female erotic relations in the passage quoted above is illuminated by reference to the ideas of the radical feminist theorist Adrienne Rich and the French psychoanalyst Luce Irigaray. Despite differences in their approaches to lesbianism, both Rich and Irigaray have contributed to the lesbian feminist attempt to redefine female desire as a separate sexual economy. They argue that, since female desire differs radically from its male counterpart, it cannot be defined within masculine parameters. The current re-evaluation of female desire, and the challenge this poses to the unitary subject positions produced by a phallocentric culture, are, in my opinion, one of the most exciting aspects of lesbian feminist discourse.

Rich's theory of the 'lesbian continuum' is pertinent here. Rich complains that the word 'lesbian', on account of the clinical associations it has acquired, has the effect of separating female friendship and camaraderie from the erotic, and thus 'limiting the erotic itself'.[8] She introduces the concept of the lesbian continuum to describe a shifting spectrum of female relationships:

> I mean the term *lesbian continuum* to include a range – through each woman's life and throughout history – of woman-identified experience: not simply the fact that a woman has had or consciously desired genital sexual experience with another woman. . . . As we deepen and broaden the range of what we define as lesbian existence, as we delineate a lesbian continuum, we begin to discover the erotic in female terms: as that which is unconfined to any single part of the body or solely to the body itself. (pp. 20,22)

Rich's concept of the lesbian continuum is relevant to Nanda's erotic involvement with her schoolmates. These flourish in the context of school-girl camaraderie. They are expressed in forms which are fluid and diffuse, 'unconfined to any single part of the body or solely to the body itself'.

Rich's theory of the lesbian continuum, as its critics complain, tends to underplay the sexual aspect of lesbian relationships by representing them in terms of woman-bonding. Thus, while highlighting the diffuse nature of Nanda's relationships with her friends and their element of camaraderie, the theory fails to illuminate their specifically sexual aspect. Here the psychoanalytic analysis of female sexuality formulated by Irigaray is useful. Observing that 'Woman's desire most likely does not speak the same language as man's desire', she claims that 'her sexuality, always at least double, is in fact *plural*.'[9] Irigaray associates the diffuse, multiple nature of female sexuality with the imaginary realm of the pre-oedipal mother/daughter dyad. Describing female desire as repressed and concealed by the structures of phallocentric culture, she points out that 'it is recuperated only secretly and in hiding.'

Irigaray's analysis of the repressed 'Minoan realm'[10] of woman's sexuality sheds light on White's description of the multiple nature of female erotic response, as well as on her representation of the dialectic of desire/repression. It also illuminates the complex pattern of references to mother/daughter relationships which inform the novel. On entering the Convent, Nanda is handed over from the care of her biological mother Mrs Grey to a set of surrogate mothers – Mother Frances, Mother Poitier and the other nuns who supervise the regime of Lippington. These nuns, with their petty rules and tyrannical behaviour, fulfil, in general, the roles of Dorothy Dinnerstein's figure of 'the malevolent mother, the source of ultimate distress',[11] and of the cruel stepmother portrayed in fairy tales. However, Nanda is fortunately able to find comfort and nurture in yet a third source of maternal care which White depicts – the affection of her friends Clare and Léonie. Terms of endearment such as 'baby' and 'my child', by which they playfully address her, foreground the relation between female erotic attachments and the realm of maternal nurture.

MARGINALISATION, REPRESSION, INVISIBILITY

The emphasis which Irigaray and other theorists place on the repressed nature of female desire is relevant not only to White's description of the encounter between Nanda and Clare, discussed above, but also to other features of *Frost in May*. The repression and invisibility of female relationships and desire are, in fact, key themes in the novel. They are apparent at the level of content in the nuns' attempts to prohibit 'particular friendships' amongst the girls and to confiscate any questionable reading material. They are also reflected, it is interesting to note, in White's methods of characterisation and her representation of female subjectivity. White portrays the characters she creates – both the pupils and the nuns who teach them – in terms not of unitary identity but of contradiction and fracture. By concentrating on the split subject and the girls' irrational behaviour, she foregrounds the importance of the unconscious as the repository of repressed desire, and highlights its power to undermine and subvert the 'common-sense' realm of rational thought.

Nanda and Léonie behave irrationally and inconsistently – in a manner they themselves do not understand and cannot explain. Nanda finds the regimented nature of life at Lippington unbearably oppressive. However, when her father unexpectedly gives her the opportunity to leave, she finds herself 'overwhelmed with a passionate affection for the place', and ends by rejecting his offer (p. 176). White highlights the conflict between conscious and unconscious levels of thought which Nanda experiences on this occasion:

> Her own nature saw the sense of her father's suggestion, even wanted to fall in with it. Yet here was some force she had never reckoned with, bursting up in her mind, taking possession of her, driving her to protest with a violence she did not consciously feel. (p. 177)

Léonie too is portrayed in terms of contradiction. She is openly sceptical about Roman Catholic doctrine, and shocks Nanda by questioning the existence of God. However, she paradoxically insists that, far from intending to leave the Church, she plans to remain a Catholic – and may even eventually become a nun.

As for the nuns themselves, though Nanda initially regards them as unitary, unchanging figures, they are presented, in fact, as comprising a disconcerting combination of attitudes, both sacred and secular. Nanda is surprised to discover that the tyrannical Mother Frances, who makes her life a misery by confiscating her precious copy of *Dream Days* and spying on her friendships, has led a romantic and pleasure-loving youth. She was exceptionally beautiful, enjoyed riding to hounds, and spent the night before she entered the Convent not in prayer but dancing at a fashionable ball (pp. 94–5). The culture of the Roman Catholic Church, and the school building that houses and represents it, display a similarly confusing mingling of the sacred and the secular. The parlour was previously a ballroom (p. 57), and the picture of the Virgin Mary which adorns the adjacent chapel is unexpectedly worldly in style. (p. 58).

As well as foregrounding the splits and fractures in female subjectivity and in Roman Catholic culture, White highlights the disruptive potential of the unconscious. Nanda and her friends appear hypersensitive to stimuli, and are described as experiencing sudden, involuntary fits of emotion – either laughter or tears. Nanda suffers from irrational periods of 'pleasurable melancholy' (p. 120), while her efforts to concentrate on the religious dimension of life are frequently disrupted by a sudden, overpowering awareness of the sensuous and the erotic. At her first Communion she is distracted from thoughts of God 'by the smell of Joan Appleyard's newly-washed hair above the lilies and the incense' and the expression of ambiguous ecstasy (religious or erotic?) on her friend Theresa's face: 'Theresa Leighton's head was thrown back; she had closed her prayer-book and was gazing at the altar with a rapt, avid look, her mouth a little open' (p. 84). White's choice of the name Theresa is, of course, ironically appropriate. It recalls the mystic St Teresa of Avilard and Bernini's famous representation of her in ecstasy. Jacques Lacan relates St Teresa's mystical experiences to the nature of female eroticism, arguing that it exemplifies woman's ability to enjoy 'a *jouissance* beyond the phallus'.[12]

White's emphasis on the emotional sensitivity of the girls and their sudden shifts of mood is a strategy to illustrate the sudden, unexpected eruption of desire. It also lends conviction to her representation of their passionate involvements. She describes these very vividly. Nanda, Léonie, Clare and Rosario (the four chief characters) are portrayed teasing and writing verses to one another, quarrelling and making up, in the emotionally turbulent manner associated with lovers.

White's introduction of gaps and absences in the text also alerts the reader to the importance of the unconscious and the realm of repressed desire. These gaps and absences relate to a variety of different dimensions – material, psychological and cultural. There are the missing pieces of the jigsaw puzzle which Nanda tries to solve when, on account of an attack of flu, she is in the school infirmary; and the inked-out paragraphs of *St Winifred's or the World of School*, a novel she reads, the flyleaf of which bears the repressive message: 'Certain pages of this book have been cut out, as the matter they contain is both vulgar and distasteful to the mind of a modest reader' (pp. 101–2). There are also the answers to certain questions which puzzle Nanda. If God expects her to renounce the world, then why has He made it so attractive? What is the meaning of the word 'Purity' (pp. 68–9)? What is the impure word, the utterance of which caused St Aloysius Gonzaga to faint? The innocent Nanda conjectures that it must be 'belly', since this is 'a word so dreadful that she only whispered it in her very worst, most defiant moments' (p. 69). However, the reader, positioned by White into a more worldly point of view, surmises that it has to do with sex.

There are also certain phenomena and events which, though the nuns' interference prevents them from fully materialising or achieving fruition, none the less play a significant role both in Nanda's imagination and the novel's narrative design. These include numerous 'particular friendships' between the girls which the nuns, in the name of morality, insist on breaking up; and the dramatised version of Dante's *Il Paradiso* rehearsed by Léonie and Rosario. The nuns decide at the last moment to substitute an alternative cast who speak the lines with less passion, and the full performance of the play never takes place. There are also several abortive literary works, such as Léonie's play about Socrates and Nanda's unfinished novel, which are either destroyed or remain incomplete.

All these gaps and absences bear witness to a vast realm of repressed knowledge and experience, much of which relates to sex, to which the girls are denied access. They also illustrate White's interest in exploring the themes of frustrated desire and the compensatory function which fantasy performs in the life of the female subject.

Patriarchal relations

One of the most convincingly depicted features of *Frost in May* is the world of Lippington itself – not only the Convent buildings but also the compelling atmosphere and distinctive organisation of the place. Like the characters and the Roman Catholic culture, Lippington is described by White in terms of contraries. On the one hand, it is identified with an ethos of extreme repression and a system of surveillance which rivals that of a police state. On the other hand, the heady aura of the religious and the erotic which the Convent exudes causes Nanda to comment appreciatively on its 'rare, intense element' (p. 176). On certain exceptional occasions, such as the fête set up to celebrate the canonisation of the foundress, it becomes transformed into a place of almost orgiastic revelry, with the girls 'dancing like *bacchantes*' in the flickering light of the festive bonfire (pp. 124–5).

While many different interpretations of Lippington are possible, I intend to concentrate on one particular reading: the symbolic relation which the school bears to the structures and organisation of patriarchy. For, despite the fact that Lippington is peopled almost entirely by women, its organisation and codes of conduct reproduce and perpetuate patriarchal values.

One of the best-known commentators on patriarchal institutions and organisations is the American radical feminist Mary Daly. In *Gyn/Ecology: The metaethics of radical feminism* Daly discusses what she calls 'the sado/ritual atrocities'[13] which patriarchal institutions inflict on women, citing as an example the witch-burnings carried out in Europe by the Christian Church. Many of the points she makes are relevant to White's account of the repressive aspects of Lippington. Patriarchal institutions, Daly argues, maintain and perpetuate their authority by perpetrating 'sado/ritual atrocities' against women. These atrocities, carried out under the pretext of purifying society, are generally performed with an obsessive attention to orderliness, ceremony and detail. The emphasis on ritual deflects attention from the women's suffering and, in addition, has the effect of rendering 'the unacceptable acceptable and even normative' (p. 132). Men seldom carry out 'the ritualized atrocities' themselves but, instead, employ women as 'scapegoats and token torturers'. This tactic masks the male origin of the crimes and buttresses male power. It also has a divisive effect on the female population, preventing women from achieving resistance and solidarity.

Daly's description of the workings of patriarchal power sheds light on the social structures of Lippington. The fact that the Convent of the Five Wounds is an all-female domain, as well as the emphasis placed by the nuns on the cult of the Virgin Mary and the female saints, has the effect of masking the male-dominated character of both the Convent itself and the religion which it promotes. Only on a few rare occasions, such as the appearance at the Convent of Nanda's father (who is responsible for paying her fees) and the ceremonial visit of the Cardinal (who represents the higher echelons of the Church) are we allowed to glimpse the patriarchal origins of Lippington's economic and intellectual power-bases. The nuns, divided from the pupils they teach by a conflict of interests, unknowingly perform the role of 'scapegoats and token torturers'. Rules of conduct are enforced by means of a fiendishly intricate system of exemptions, permissions, penalties, different coloured cards and even the coding of gloves according to transgression (pp. 39–40, 63). This compulsive concern with order and detail (euphemistically described by Nanda's father as a respect for 'formality and tradition'!) deflects attention from the suffering of the pupils and, as Daly suggests, renders 'the unacceptable acceptable and even normative'. Numerous episodes in the novel illustrate the sadism and perversity informing the nuns' treatment of the girls. A striking example is the anecdote, recounted by Reverend Mother not as a cautionary tale but an exemplary one, of little Molly who, on having her ear accidentally pierced by a large safety-pin when being dressed in her Communion veil, refused to draw attention to her plight but chose to suffer in silence. This bizarre example of sado/masochism ironically suits the location in which it occurs – the Convent of the Five Wounds. Another perversely cruel incident is the expulsion of Léonie and Rosario from the dramatised version of Dante. The two girls are dismissed from the cast of the play not because they act badly but because they perform the roles with too much passion (p. 169).

Whereas Daly sees patriarchal structures as having a consistently destructive effect on female relationships, the psychoanalytic critic Maria Ramas regards them in a much more ambiguous light. She argues that they perform a contradictory function, one which is alternately mediatory and disruptive. In her commentary on Freud's case-study *Dora* Ramas discusses the erotic relationship which the young Dora formed with Frau K, an older woman with whom Dora's father was sexually involved. Ramas convincingly demonstrates that patriarchal relations, heterosexual fantasy and the actions of individual men were, in fact, necessary to the establishing of the relationship between the two women.[14] They facilitated the attachment in its initial stages and, by masking its lesbian component, enabled it to flourish – for a limited period at any rate. In the long run, however, as Dora's feelings of betrayal both by her father and by Frau K herself indicate, they had a disruptive, destructive effect.

Nanda's situation, in relation both to individual men and to patriarchal structures in general, displays interesting similarities to Dora's. Whereas Dora occupies the role of object of sexual exchange, handed over by her father to Herr K in exchange for his wife's favours, Nanda occupies the role in a 'religious' sense.[15] Her father hands her over to the Convent of the Five Wounds in exchange for acquiring spiritual peace of mind. By placing Nanda in the Convent, he unintentionally facilitates her passionate relationships with Léonie and Clare, and by treating her in an apparently adult manner, wins her trust. However, in the final episode of the work, where he sides with the nuns in their bigoted condemnation of the novel she is writing, he betrays her. At this point he reveals himself, despite his previous pretensions to liberalism, as the stereotypical paterfamilias, the representative and harsh enforcer of patriarchal law. By doing the nuns' bidding and removing Nanda from the Convent, he is, of course, instrumental in destroying her friendships with Léonie and Clare.

The patriarchal social structures of Lippington and the male-supremacist Roman Catholic culture associated with it play a similarly ambiguous role in the erotic relationships which Nanda forms with her friends. Although, from an ideological point of view, these structures and culture are inimical to the girls' relationships, they none the less frequently perform a mediatory function, helping to promote and cement them. The Convent, though dominated by the nuns and their repressive attitudes, contains numerous chinks and crannies (both literal and figurative) where the girls can meet and pursue their involvements. The religious, heterosexist culture of Roman Catholicism is transformed by the inventive readings which Nanda and her friends construct, with the result that it takes on a subversively sexual and homoerotic slant. 'Elita's lazy, veiled contralto', White comments, 'would make the O *Salutaris* sound like a love-song' (p. 107); while the reference to the sensual touch of 'a girl's soft arms' in a poem Nanda reads acts as a prelude not to a heterosexual love scene but to her erotic response to Clare's caress (p. 105). White's most explicit reference to the subversive effect of the creative female reading of a text occurs in relation to Nanda's exuberant interpretation of a poem by Francis Thompson. White tells us that, though Nanda cannot understand the rational meaning of the verse, she:

> read on, enraptured. . . . She followed the poem vaguely as she followed the Latin in her missal, guessing, inventing meanings for herself, intoxicated by the mere rush of words. And yet she felt she did understand, not with her eyes or her brain, but with some faculty she did not even know she possessed. (p. 103)

The reading which Nanda produces in this elated state, White further observes, 'had nothing to do with God' but, on the contrary, is sensuous and erotic (p. 104). On this occasion in White's text, as in Hennegan's teenage readings of the novels of Jane Austen discussed above (page 91), the materials of the dominant culture are appropriated and imaginatively reworked by a member of an oppressed, subordinate group. In this way, their ideological content is effectively subverted and undermined.

LESBIAN AESTHETICS AND 'THE LESBIAN TEXT'

In her Introduction to the Virago edition of *Frost in May* Elizabeth Bowen remarks on the 'cool exactness' of White's descriptive technique and praises her style of writing for being 'precise, clear and unweighty' (p. vii). Bowen's choice of words, though obviously intended as a compliment, is, in actual fact, inappropriate. The text of *Frost in May*, as my analysis has indicated, far from displaying attributes of 'exactness' and 'clarity', is intriguingly devious and indirect. The strategies of obliquity and displacement which White employs, though most strongly in evidence in her description of female relationships, also characterise the novel as a whole.

White's indirect style of narration and description serves to relate *Frost in May* to yet another branch of lesbian studies – that of 'lesbian literary aesthetics' and 'the lesbian text'. As Bonnie Zimmerman illustrates, these topics are controversial.[16] Critics argue about precisely what constitutes a lesbian text. They debate the questions: to what degree can lesbian writing be seen as a stable, 'essential' entity, or to what degree is it a cultural construct which differs from writer to writer and from age to age? In an attempt to define the 'essential', 'universal' features of lesbian writing, critics have pin-pointed certain themes and images, such as unrequited longing, strong female characters, a rhetoric of non-violence and the use of natural imagery, which they claim constitute standard components.[17] Their practice is clearly faulty. These themes and images, while undoubtedly playing a part in some lesbian texts, are certainly not reliable indicators of lesbian writing *per se*. On the contrary, they appear in a number of heterosexual texts while being absent from many lesbian ones. As Zimmerman observes, 'Violence, role-playing, disaffection, unhappiness, suicide and self-hatred, to name a few "taboo" subjects, all exist within lesbian culture, and a useful criticism will have to effectively analyse these as *lesbian* themes and metaphors, regardless of the dictates of ideological purity' (p. 197). She believes that a constructionist approach, which focuses attention on historical and cultural differences in the representation of lesbianism, is preferable to an essentialist one. She argues that 'Lesbian criticism and cultural theory in general must continue to grow by developing a greater specificity, historically and culturally' (p. 198).

Elaine Marks likewise concentrates attention on historical and ideological differences in images of lesbianism. She points out that, with the advent of the lesbian feminist movement in the 1970s, 'The lesbian in literature has undergone a radical transformation from impertinent young woman, fragile couple, solitary writer, ecstatic schoolgirl, to aggressive lover and namer'.[18]

The debate about essentialist and constructionist approaches to lesbian writing relates, of course, to the debate about whether lesbian sexuality itself is 'innate' or 'socially constructed'. An intelligent discussion of the distinction between essentialist and constructionist approaches, as well as of the links between the two, is provided by Sarah Franklin and Jackie Stacey in a recently published essay.[19] They point out that in the past fifteen years the feminist representation of gender and sexuality as socially constructed has led to the constructionist approach dominating the discussion of sexual identity. However, this approach, though effective in challenging the view of patriarchal institutions such as male supremacy, compulsory heterosexuality and the family as 'natural' and universal, none the less reveals certain weaknesses. These failings are defined by Carole Vance, who cogently remarks that:

> In its emphasis on deconstruction and discontinuity, social constructionism threatens to make sexuality disappear altogether and to dismantle the very sexual identities which we seek to affirm and preserve. And in its emphasis on the denaturalization of sexuality, it tends to exclude the body from its considerations, thus denying the materiality of its subject of study.[20]

As Franklin and Stacey illustrate, the relationship between essentialist and constructionist approaches to lesbianism is not, as people generally assume, one of irreducible opposition. There are many different versions of essentialism which themselves are socially constructed, emerging at different historical periods in response to specific circumstances and events.[21]

The comments voiced by Franklin, Stacey and Vance are highly relevant to lesbian writing and criticism. The constructionist approach to lesbian writing, which dominates feminist and academic discussion at the present time, is useful in challenging the view of lesbian writing as an unchanging, universal entity. However, if taken to extremes, it reveals disadvantages. In concentrating on difference, discontinuity and deconstruction, it ignores the continuities in theme and style which link writers of different periods. It also runs the risk of making 'the lesbian text' and 'lesbian studies' disappear as topics of study.

The strategies of deviousness and indirection employed in *Frost in May* link the novel to the fictional treatment of lesbianism and themes of woman-identification in the first half of this century, the period prior to the advent of the lesbian feminist movement of the 1970s. In *Frost in May*, as in the fiction of Willa Cather and Virginia Woolf,[22] devices of metonomy and displacement play an important part in the text. Instead of treating female erotic relations explicitly, White creates a metonomic discourse focusing on 'hands', 'arm' and 'mouth'. In the passage describing Nanda's erotic encounter with her friend Clare, which I quoted above (page 93), the facts of sexual arousal and response are not represented directly by reference to intimate parts of the body such as the breast or genitals, the mention of which was socially unacceptable at the time. They are represented indirectly by reference to other, less intimate parts, the mention of which is permissible. White tells us that 'Clare leaned over and touched Nanda's arm with a hot quivering hand that burned through her holland sleeve' (p. 113). The caress 'embarrassed and delighted Nanda; it gave her the queerest shivering sensation in the roof of her mouth' (p. 113).

On other occasions in the novel White displaces the theme of female sexuality onto images of nature. For example, the enclosed garden where Nanda and Léonie meet is described as 'small and secluded, spicy with the smell of azaleas' (p. 80). White's use of the oblique devices of metonomy and displacement can be explained by reference to the stigmatised and taboo nature of lesbian relations in the inter-war years, as well as by the lack of an accepted language to represent female sexuality. As Lucy Bland comments, 'We face a past and a present in which there has never been a language allowing us to think about and define women's sexuality.'[23]

A motif which Zimmerman describes as occurring frequently in fiction treating lesbian relations and themes of woman-identification is 'the dialectic between freedom and imprisonment'.[24] This motif plays a central part in *Frost in May*, and assumes a variety of different forms. The spacious grounds of the Convent with their secluded gardens, where the girls can meet unobserved, contrast with the confined interior of the building, with its maze-like corridors and interconnecting rooms, where they are subject to the nuns' scrutiny. The gardens in the grounds are associated with emotional and sexual liberation. On going to keep her tryst with Léonie, Nanda experiences a sudden delightful impulse of *jouissance*: 'The warmth [of the sun] playing on her skin made her feel quite dizzy with happiness; she wanted to tear off her thick serge and shake her hair loose from its plait' (pp. 80–1). Needless to say, she performs neither action. Because of the oppressive patriarchal codes operating at Lippington, the image of the liberated female body and its desires function in the text chiefly on the level of fantasy, and seldom achieve material substance.

The major arena in which the dialectic of freedom/imprisonment is played out is *the female body itself*. One of the rules of conduct which puzzles and irritates Nanda when she first enters Lippington is the nuns' expectation that, when in bed, she will sleep on her back with her arms folded, instead of curled up in her usual 'comfortable ball' (p. 35). She also has to confine her hands in gloves and wear her hair bound in a tight plait. The motif of hair is of particular interest. The different styles in which the female characters wear their hair – whether tightly plaited, cropped or flowing free – take on the significance of a sexual code, indicating different degrees of repression or liberation. Nanda, White tells us, submitted patiently while an officious schoolmate 'pulled her hair back and twisted it into an agonisingly tight rope. The efficient bony fingers tied it tighter still until Nanda's eyes felt as if they would start from her head' (p. 34). The element of linguistic excess in White's description of the plaiting of Nanda's hair alerts the reader to the symbolic function of the motif.

In view of the link which theorists make between 'the economy of female desire' and the pre-oedipal mother/daughter bond,[25] it is appropriate that it should be Mrs Grey, Nanda's mother, who voices a complaint about the brutal treatment of her daughter's hair. '"But darling," she wails, on visiting her daughter at the Convent, "what have they done to your lovely hair?"' (p. 38). She also complains about Nanda's hands being encased in gloves, and about the numerous rules and regulations which the nuns impose (pp. 38–9).

The cropped hair of the nuns functions in the text as an image of de-sexualisation. Nanda is deeply worried by the fact that the beautiful Moira

Palliser, a young postulant whose appearance fascinates and attracts her, is about to become a nun. Her anxieties focus predictably on the traumatic moment of the cutting of Moira's hair (p. 55).

Whereas the motif of bound or cropped hair functions in the text as an image of sexual repression, hair which flows free is an image of liberation. One of the most overtly erotic episodes in the novel is the occasion when Nanda and her friends spend the evening together in the school infirmary. Rosario and Clare loosen their tresses and compare their respective lengths, while Nanda and Léonie watch them with evident pleasure.

Another feature which links *Frost in May* to other fictional representations of lesbianism and woman-identification produced in the first half of this century is its circuitous narrative structure.[26]. The novel's circuitous and maze-like structure stems partly from White's frequent introduction of gaps and absences in the text, a feature I have discussed above, and more particularly from the pronounced emphasis which she places on the motif of story-telling. The nuns and the pupils they teach, though generally portrayed in a state of conflict, do share one common interest. Both groups of women are enthusiastic raconteurs. The nuns tell the pupils improving, though fanciful, stories of the lives of saints, along with Gothic tales about ghosts and skeleton-infested mansions, while the pupils entertain one another with anecdotes about their holidays and exaggerated accounts of their parents' possessions and wealth. A few of the more intellectual pupils, like Nanda and Léonie, surreptitiously experiment with creative writing. The stories recounted by the nuns and pupils interweave, giving the text the appearance of a tissue of interlinking narratives. This intricate exercise in intertextuality is further complicated by the variety of different genres and kinds of writing which White introduces. The primary narrative line is frequently fractured by excerpts from letters, poems, diary entries and notes on religious retreats – as well as by literary quotations and allusions. These are remarkably eclectic – and create a wittily provocative interplay of the sacred and the secular, the serious and the frivolous. Quotations from the Magnificat and from the French Romantic poets mingle with allusions to *The Arabian Nights*, Hans Andersen's *Fairy Tales* and Lewis Carroll's Alice novels.

This profusion of stories, different kinds of writing and literary allusions has some interesting intellectual consequences. It foregrounds the fact that culture and subjectivity are constructed in a variety of different, conflicting discourses. It also has the effect of breaking down the division between fact and fiction, life and art. Nanda and the reader discover that, contrary to the doctrine of the Roman Catholic Church which dominates Lippington, there is no such thing as absolute, unmediated truth. There are, on the contrary, only numerous, conflicting *versions* of reality. Léonie is assigned the role of spokeswoman for this heretical point of view. Defending her irrational allegiance to Roman Catholicism, she announces to the shocked Nanda: 'I like the Catholic way of looking at things. Any way of looking at life is a fairy story, and I prefer mine with lots of improbable embellishments. I think angels and devils are much more amusing than microbes and Mr Wells's noble scientists' (pp. 148–9).

It is appropriate that White should assign to Léonie the subversive role of destabilising Nanda's views about Roman Catholicism and the absolutist concept of truth which it promotes. Léonie functions as a refreshingly subversive presence throughout the novel. In the manner of the old-style image of the lesbian, popular in the first half of this century, she destabilises conventional ideas of sexual difference by her disconcerting combination of masculine and feminine attributes and dress-codes.[27]

The interplay of literary allusions and of different kinds of narrative which characterise the text of *Frost in May* also alerts the reader to the fact that cultural and literary practice is itself a contested area. In the struggle which the nuns and pupils wage over the issue of repression/liberation both parties appropriate works of literature and art as weapons. The pupils manifest their defiance by reading prohibited novels, while the nuns retaliate by confiscating the books or by deleting the passages they regard as impure. As we have seen, the pupils also make their own spirited personal contribution to cultural practice. They write poems and love letters to one another, romantically comparing the rays in the beloved's eyes to 'chips of emerald' (p. 142). The rebellious Monica exploits her talent at drawing dogs to create caricatured portraits of the nuns, while Nanda and Léonie write novels and plays on unacceptable worldly themes.

For Antonia White, as for us who live in the 1990s in the age of Section 28, literary and cultural practice constitutes a key arena of sexual-political struggle.

NOTES

1. See Elaine Marks, 'Lesbian intertextuality', in Elaine Marks and George Stambolian (eds), *Homosexualities and French Literature: Cultural contexts/critical texts* (Ithaca, NY: Cornell University Press, 1979), pp. 353–77; and Gill Frith, *The Intimacy which is Knowledge: Female friendship in the novels of women writers* (Ph.D. dissertation, University of Warwick, 1989), pp. 304–35. Frith's dissertation will shortly be published.
2. Frith, *The Intimacy which is Knowledge*, p. 318.

3. *Frost in May* (1933; London: Virago, 1978), p. 79. Subsequent references are to the Virago edition and are in the text.
4. In Susannah Radstone (ed.), *Sweet Dreams: Sexuality, gender and popular fiction* (London: Lawrence and Wishart, 1988), pp. 165–90. Subsequent references are in the text.
5. Bonnie Zimmerman and Julia Penelope Stanley, in Zimmerman, 'What has never been: an overview of lesbian feminist criticism', in Gayle Greene and Coppélia Khan (eds), *Making a Difference: Feminist literary criticism* (London: Methuen, 1985), p. 179.
6. Lines in the United Kingdom include London Lesbian Line, 071-251 6911, Monday and Friday 2–10 p.m., Tuesday, Wednesday, Thursday 7–10 p.m.; and Cambridge Lesbian Line, 0223-311753, Fridays 7–10 p.m.
7. Section 28 (previously Clause 28) of the Local Government Act was sponsored by a group of Tory backbenchers and, despite considerable opposition, came into force in the United Kingdom on 24 May 1988. It prohibits local authorities from (a) promoting homosexuality or publishing material that promotes homosexuality, (b) promoting the teaching in maintained schools of homosexuality as a pretended family relationship or (c) giving financial assistance to any person for either of these purposes. Though intended primarily as an intimidatory piece of legislation and not a prescriptive one, Section 28, as Duncan Fallowell points out, has given 'official approval to homophobia in the country at large' (*The Guardian*, 1 December 1989, p. 36). For discussion of Section 28 and its significance see *Spare Rib*, 192 (June 1988), p. 42; and Madeleine Colvin with Jane Hawksley, *Section 28: A practical guide to the law and its implications* (London: National Council for Civil Liberties, 1989).
8. *Compulsory Heterosexuality and Lesbian Existence* (1980; London: Onlywomen Press, 1981), p. 22. Subsequent references are to the Onlywomen Press edition and are in the text.
9. 'When the goods get together', in Elaine Marks and Isabelle de Courtivron (eds), *New French Feminisms* (Hemel Hempstead: Harvester Wheatsheaf, 1981), pp. 101–2.
10. Marks, 'Lesbian intertextuality', p. 362.
11. *The Rocking of the Cradle, and the Ruling of the World* (1976; London: Souvenir Press, 1978), p. 95.
12. Juliet Mitchell and Jacqueline Rose (eds), *Feminine Sexuality: Jacques Lacan and the école freudienne* (London: Macmillan, 1982), pp. 145–7.
13. *Gyn/Ecology* (1978; London: Women's Press, 1979), pp. 130–3. Subsequent references are to The Women's Press edition and are in the text.
14. 'Freud's Dora, Dora's hysteria', in Charles Bernheimer and Claire Kahane (eds), *In Dora's Case: Freud – hysteria – feminism* (London: Virago, 1985), pp. 162–5.
15. Irigaray's analysis of woman's role as object of exchange in a phallocentric culture is also relevant ('When the goods get together', in Marks and de Courtivron, *New French Feminisms*, pp. 107–10).
16. Zimmerman, 'What has never been', pp. 177–9, 183–5.
17. *ibid.*, pp. 185, 197, 202. Subsequent references to Zimmerman are in the text.
18. Marks, 'Lesbian intertextuality', p. 371.
19. 'Dyke-tactics for difficult times', in Christian McEwen and Sue O'Sullivan (eds), *Out the Other Side: Contemporary lesbian writing* (London: Virago, 1988), pp. 220–32.
20. *ibid.*, p. 225.
21. *ibid.*, p. 223–5.
22. See Sharon O'Brien, '"The thing not named": Willa Cather as a lesbian writer', in Estelle B. Freedman, Barbara C. Gelpi, Susan L. Johnson and Kathleen M. Weston (eds), *The Lesbian Issue: Essays from Signs* (Chicago: University of Chicago Press, 1982), p. 67–90; and Catherine R. Stimpson, 'Zero degree deviancy: the lesbian novel in English', in Elizabeth Abel (ed.), *Writing and Sexual Difference* (Hemel Hempstead: Harvester Wheatsheaf, 1982), pp. 246–7.
23. 'Purity, motherhood, pleasure or threat? Definitions of female sexuality 1900–1970s', in Sue Cartledge and Joanna Ryan (eds), *Sex and Love: New thoughts on old contradictions* (London: The Women's Press, 1983), p. 9.
24. *ibid.*, p. 202.

25. See Irigaray, 'When the goods get together', pp. 107–10; Margaret Whitford, 'Re-reading Irigaray', in Teresa Brennan (ed.), *Between Feminism and Psychoanalysis* (London: Routledge, 1989), pp. 106–26; Stimpson, 'Zero degree deviancy', pp. 256–7; and Joanna Ryan, 'Psychoanalysis and women loving women', in Cartledge and Ryan, *Sex and Love*, pp. 196–209.
26. Marks comments on the meandering narrative structure of the novels of Colette and Renée Vivien. She suggests that this structure mirrors the characters' bisexuality and their uncertainty about their sexual orientation ('Lesbian intertextuality', p. 366).
27. See Elizabeth Wilson, 'Forbidden love', Wilson, *Hidden Agendas: Theory, politics, and experience in the women's movement* (London: Tavistock, 1986), p. 181.

Rebecca Ferguson

History, Memory and Language in Toni Morrison's *Beloved*

In an interview with *City Limits* magazine in March 1988, a few months after *Beloved* was published, Toni Morrison restated with special urgency a point which has often been made about America and its history:

> We live in a land where the past is always erased and America is the innocent future in which immigrants can come and start over, where the slate is clean. The past is absent or it's romanticised. This culture doesn't encourage dwelling on, let alone coming to terms with, the truth about the past. That memory is much more in danger now than it was 30 years ago.[1]

These observations point to a crucial concern of many Afro-American novelists; to an unusual degree, they place memory at the forefront of their writing, in full awareness that their own history has been (to take a phrase from the closing passages of *Beloved*) 'disremembered and unaccounted for'.[2] Similarly, the act of writing – writing from and about that past – has special significance for authors who are conscious of belonging to a race once legally proscribed from attaining literacy or having access to education. So on both fronts, black writers find themselves in a complex position; theirs is a history of oppression, but one that must be remembered and accounted for, and while the language of the dominant culture and the written word itself have all too often been potent instruments in that oppression, not to have mastery of them is to be rendered impotent in ways that matter greatly. An awareness of both points is evident in much recent writing by black women:[3] in Alice Walker's *The Color Purple* with its emphasis on the liberating act of letter-writing, in certain of her short stories, and in the merging of both documented and mythic history in Walker's *Meridian* or Morrison's *Song of Solomon*, which moves backwards historically and southwards geographically to rediscover a heritage where oppression and liberation are paradoxically drawn together.

It is understandable too that the response of these writers to such contemporary concerns as the tenuous nature of our conceptions of history and identity and the instability of the language system itself is especially problematic. Michael Cooke has remarked that, notwithstanding the ludic experimentation of a text like Ishmael Reed's *Mumbo Jumbo* (1972) and the formal boldness of Ellison's *Invisible Man* (1952), 'the fabulator's sense of life as unreal and mad, though this might seem highly germane to black experience, has not really taken hold in black writing.'[4] Yet it is the term 'fabulation' as used by Robert Scholes to denote 'a return to a more verbal kind of fiction . . . a less realistic and more artistic kind of narrative' which Bernard Bell finds particularly appropriate to describe the work of black American postmodernists. Bell points to a crucial difference in what they are doing, however: 'unlike their white contemporaries, [these writers] are not merely rejecting the arrogance and anachronism of Western forms and conventions, but also rediscovering and reaffirming the power and wisdom of their own folk tradition: Afro-American ways of seeing, knowing, and expressing reality.' Thus, to leave behind the constraints of realism and naturalism does not mean abandoning 'such traditional narrative modes as myth and legend', nor does it have to entail the neglect of history.[5]

In this context, Toni Morrison's own comments on the question of modernism and postmodernism in the arts are especially interesting, since she too is concerned with essential distinctions between what this has meant for white culture and what it has meant within black culture and experience. She locates the inception of modernism, as she locates so many of her novels, in a time of radical *transition*, observing that it began in the West with writers and painters who registered the impact of industrialisation and 'the great transformation from the old world to the new', while at the same time Africa was being put through a parallel and extreme experience of severe dislocation:

> Modern life begins with slavery. . . . in terms of confronting the problems of where the world is now, black women had to deal with 'post-modern' problems in the nineteenth century and earlier. These things had to be addressed by black people a long time ago. Certain kinds of dissolution, the loss of and the need to reconstruct certain kinds of stability. Certain kinds of madness, deliberately going mad in order, as one of the characters says in the book, 'not to lose your mind'.[6]

Slavery, she contends, must be called more than an ideology or an economy; it was also a *pathology*, the effects of which are with us still. Whites 'have had to reconstruct everything in order to make that system appear true', and this in itself is a form of madness.

Though I would be wary of dwelling too much on the precise import of words which were after all delivered orally, 'reconstruct' none the less seems an important term in the way it is applied by Morrison to two subjects; to blacks, who were forced to reconstruct *themselves* as an act of survival, and to whites who (then as now) found themselves reconstructing the very order of things to sustain their supremacy. Reconstruction is also that time of attempted, though inadequate, transition between the Civil War and the new order of America which followed it, when – nominally at least – the institutions of slavery were ended. It is the era in which a significant proportion of *Beloved* is set; although it is most obvious to regard it as a novel 'about slavery', and although the use of narrative tenses and the interactions of past with present are so fluid, it is still apparent that Reconstruction constitutes the predominating 'present tense' of the novel, the point where it begins and ends, and the point to which we are constantly being returned.

Of the remarks quoted above, one of the most interesting – concerning pathology – is made again and expanded in a recent article by Morrison.[7] Discussing the suggestion that the white whale in Melville's *Moby Dick* represents the ideology of race,[8] she writes that, if it is understood in these terms,

> what Ahab has lost to it is personal dismemberment and family and society and his own place as a human in the world. The trauma of racism is, for the racist and the victim, the severe fragmentation of the self, and has always seemed to me a cause (not a symptom) of psychosis.

It is significant that she focuses on the idea of that fragmentation being bodied forth as a literal dismemberment, especially as this emerges as such an important figure in *Beloved*.

My concern in this essay is to examine how these perceptions on madness, dissolution and pathology are expressed by Morrison in *Beloved*, a work which is formally very demanding – in ways that can sometimes evoke the 'postmodernist'[9] – but which is at the same time very exact in its reference to recorded history, a history which Morrison had carefully researched.[10] In handling this material, she is aware of dealing with what can best be described as a repression; but, as she has remarked, for blacks themselves 'the struggle to forget which was important in order to survive is fruitless', and this is a novel about living *with* the memory and surviving it. It is not only concerned with the claims the past may make upon the present, but with how far those claims may conceivably be met and on what terms. Behind the writing of the novel lay Morrison's conviction that (despite the published slave narratives) the records on that subject are still only an outline, and that the experience of slavery had never been adequately described on the imaginative level. Perhaps the most notable gap in the history is the beginning, and the absence of any but the barest records of the 'middle passage' on the slave ships – the most traumatic of the horrors a first-generation slave would have undergone.[11]

Along with this central concern with history and memory, there is also a compelling emphasis in the novel upon the survival of women within and beyond the structures of slavery – on their struggle to establish continuity through the protection of their children, their men and the community – and upon the possibilities for the shaping of the self within these changing structures.[12] It is striking that the dynamics and rivalries of the family should have such force within this novel where the orthodox conception of the 'nuclear family' is so tenuously formed and so conspicuously (sometimes comically) crowded out.[13] By the very nature of Sethe's drastic choice – to kill her baby daughter rather than let her be returned into slavery – the bonds of mother and daughter and the responsibilities they entail are probed with particular depth. In this sphere, as well as in the sphere of a 'disremembered' history, Morrison is attempting to express the inexpressible, to speak the 'unspeakable' partly by exploring domestic space and the space and language of the pre-Oedipal. The house, 124, is occupied by three women (daughter, mother and grandmother), plus the spirit of a fourth, after the two male children have departed and before Paul D appears; when he does, he is run off by Beloved and the household of women is re-established before it finally disintegrates. This is not to say that the place of the male is marginal within the novel, however; on the contrary, Paul D's story and his interactions with Sethe and her household are crucial to its development.[14] Morrison does not privilege mother–child over adult bonds, female over male, or 'the things behind things' over the future that is 'becoming', but she does demand that we give due weight to all of these as a part of survival.[15]

Beloved is dense with 'unspeakable thoughts, unspoken' (*Beloved*, p. 199). While those parts of the narrative that deal with the Reconstruction era set up a linear, progressive chronology, the text is fragmented – shattered, one might say – by what is termed 'rememory': the continual entry and re-entry of past into present.[16] From the beginning, with the abrupt entry into the house, the reader is confronted with a network of allusions from which full meaning is withheld, with constant intimations that sinister, even traumatic referents lie beyond them. 'Rememory' is ambivalently merged with individual acts of remembering, sometimes triggered by Proustian catalysts (notably when Sethe smells hair burning in the fire, and is suddenly rocked with repressed memories concerning her mother's death). But through individual memory – as well as in a host of other ways – there is the growing, insistent sense that a larger memory is pressing itself upon our attention. This deeper memory is expressed above all in a constant emphasis on the recurrent and on synchrony; the text dwells on images, sensory impressions, phrases and metaphors which connect and repeat themselves so often that it has the force of an obsession, a highly poetic haunting. As in Morrison's other novels, 'the psychological, like the sensual and sexual, is also historical'.[17] History is never over and done with; it exists always in the realms of the mind and senses as well as in specified places, and as I will show, in Morrison's writing it is constantly being called up by metaphor and analogy. In all these respects, *Beloved* is a deeply imagined historical novel, in which what is commonly called the supernatural is also the manifestation of history. When Paul D first touches the scars left on Sethe's back from her beating, the house explodes with the baby ghost's disturbance, and we witness the force of Beloved's jealousy, her will to obstruct any living person from appropriating Sethe's past, her guilt or her 'responsibility'.

Like Freud's 'uncanny', Beloved's disturbance manifests itself precisely within what is most intimately known and domestic (not only in her presence as poltergeist but later as occupant of 124). She is, in Freud's words, 'something repressed which *recurs*', something supposedly 'dead' returning painfully to life, through the supernatural at work in the 'world of common reality', yet 'in reality nothing new or alien, but . . . familiar and old-established in the mind'.[18] 124 is thus a space which is both empty and full, intimate and strange. Denoted by a 'mere number', one which opens each section of the book, like all haunted houses it becomes 'personalised by its own activity'.[19] Through it, our attention is also fixed on the *differences* that have marked out the choices made by Sethe and Paul D, who share a large measure of the same past on the plantation Sweet Home; the focus is displaced from the potential questing male hero, the 'long gone ramblin' man' of black myth and fiction, to Sethe's choice of staying put and living with the worst of her own history, of piecing together – within very definite, cautious limits – an existence in the same place where she killed her child.[20] In this respect their stories become very different; it is not until much later that Paul D is able to 'put his story next to hers', and then this is only possible in so far as he has stayed long enough to hear and understand it.

Through Beloved's presence, which guards the very threshold, 124 is invested with an immense, disremembered suffering peopled by all the ghosts of those who died through slavery. Like many of Sethe's own memories, this is latent though potent until Paul D arrives; then Beloved makes herself known, insists upon her claim and interposes herself in the world of the living, demanding to be seen, heard and understood. And as Amy Denver says as she rubs Sethe's numbed feet back into feeling, '"anything dead coming back to life hurts"'. Parts of the narrative treat Beloved's physical rebirth and the unsettling evidence of her identity through the conventions of the ghost story (her specific uncanny knowledge of her mother's song, her earrings and so on), yet despite this clear evidence of past links it is especially significant that the second daughter Denver – who should, after all, know least about it – is the first to establish a close and sympathetic bond with her. Her mother represses the knowledge for as long as possible – even though it is registered at once in her body – until she is ready to handle it; but Denver instantly recognises, in her isolation and loneliness, that Beloved is her sister, and she knows too that she is 'more than that'. Paul D acknowledges in a confused way that '"she reminds me of something; something, look like, I'm supposed to remember"',[21] while the grandmother Baby Suggs sees more wisely that there is nothing so exceptional about her as a ghost, that there can be no house in the district that is not 'packed to its rafters with some dead Negro's grief'. Since Beloved brings the whole traumatic experience of slavery with her, she not only knows more than she could otherwise have known in her previous short life, but she also contains the *effects* that slavery had, its profound fragmentation of the self and of the connections the self might have with others.[22] The dependency she shows towards Sethe is in the face of this fragility, and her confusion is profound; she is dislocated in herself as well as dislocated in time, full of grief and need, love and resentment. For Sethe, Beloved *is* above all a connection, the reconnection with and restoring of all that was lost when she was driven to kill her; even so, what appears to be an end, a closure in a healing restoration, is really only the beginning. Beloved yearns to make connections, but those she does make grow without restraint to become destructive, to break down rather than 'reconstruct'. While she strives to re-enter and lay hold on the world to which her lived history connects her, she is also strenuously holding herself together, defending herself from being engulfed or exploding in the space between the two worlds where she simultaneously exists.

This last point is vividly illustrated when Beloved comes close to a ghostly disappearing, 'eaten alive by the dark', in the shed where she was originally killed and where Denver was almost killed too. Returning, she tells Denver, '"I don't want that place. This the place I am"' (p. 123), willing herself into a single place and a present tense, but she is also able to point to herself as she exists in the other place, crouching and rocking in a foetal position. The physical posture suggests a regression, and what is especially striking is that Beloved's double presence, for all its potency, suggests equally powerfully a kind of absence. Being in both realms, she seems to exist fully in neither.

Likewise, although being swallowed and exploding appear perhaps as opposite figures, both express the same physical instability, the potential for fragmentation and dissolution that the text so often invokes. Denver is herself overwhelmed by it as she faces the ultimate loss defined by her sister-companion's vanishing:

> If she stumbles, she is not aware of it because she does not know where her body stops, which part of it is an arm, a foot or a knee. She feels like an ice cake torn away from the solid surface of the stream, floating on darkness, thick and crashing against the edges of things around it. Breakable, meltable and cold. . . . Now she is crying because she has no self. Death is a skipped meal compared to this. She can feel her thickness thinning, dissolving into nothing. She grabs the hair at her temples to get enough to uproot it and halt the melting for a while. (p. 123)

The melting away of both body and self is experienced by Denver as the accumulation of all the losses she has sustained, death and leaving understood in terms of one another. Even within the microcosm of 124, where she and Sethe are given a wide berth by the local community, the only interactive relationships she has known (with her brothers, her grandmother, her mother) are seen as leading inexorably to this loss. On the very threshold of adulthood, Denver both chooses and is pushed back into a lost childhood, which is part of what Beloved represents for her. Her own dependency on her mother is very evident, and she jealously guards that relationship against the male interloper – she is waiting instead for an idealised father, an 'angel man' who is definitely not, for this time, Paul D – but what may come as more of a shock to the reader is the later revelation of her aggression and of her self-protective fears concerning Sethe. Through her suppressed knowledge of Beloved's fate she has been taught that, quite literally, 'mother love is a killer', and having only a limited sense of why this became so in the specific context of slavery, she has no way of knowing whether 'the thing that happened that made it all right for my mother to kill my sister could happen again' (p. 205).[23] The fantasy she has about being decapitated by Sethe ambivalently merges both responses, as it is both a murderous and a loving act, carried out 'carefully' with the same necessary pain as combing tangled hair. Hence, her own disappearance is one of the deaths that Denver anticipates, while Beloved's return from the other side seems to affirm that this fear could be exorcised. To possess Beloved is partly to protect her from Sethe, and partly to repossess a part of herself that has not been realised. It could be viewed as both regression *and* growth, and her first response to Beloved is jealously to mother her.

The episode within the shed is one of a number where the sense of both connection and disconnection is very strong; as I will show in discussing two more of these episodes, they also incorporate certain passages which demand to be read in a specific *historical* context which functions as both an analogy and an integral part of their meaning. Those I will refer to are, first, the set of passages late in the novel which deal with the 'unspeakable thoughts, unspoken' of the three women alone in the house, and, secondly, the earlier passage which tells of Beloved's first physical appearance on the tree stump outside 124.

Morrison's placing of the passages on the women's thoughts is arresting in its narrative context, which strongly marks the distinction between the exterior and the interior through the boundaries of 124. Stamp Paid, coming as he hopes to make his peace with Sethe, is unable to get any further than the door of the house, since all around it are the 'roaring' voices of the dead and dispossessed. Within, the scene is correspondingly peaceful and excluding; all he sees, as he peers through the window, is the backs of Denver and Beloved, preoccupied only with each other.[24] Morrison's rendering of the women's interior 'voices' (in which speech and thought are indistinguishable) powerfully conveys that absorption. Indeed, the phrase with which they are introduced – 'unspeakable thoughts, unspoken' – is resonant with complexity. All that is here presented is implicitly not speakable, nor writable, yet it articulates the deepest level of self expression and dialogue between Sethe, Beloved and Denver. What they say is for themselves alone, interactive yet intensely private, inexpressible yet 'overheard' by narrator and reader. Throughout, the narrator's intimacy has helped to direct us towards this, but now that mediation is withdrawn. Sethe's outpouring of memories (pp. 200–4) is addressed both to Beloved and to herself, as if the two were one. All the incidentals and details of memory – as urgently meaningful as they are – come down to the central affirmation that Beloved is her daughter, as Sethe would have been a daughter to her own destroyed mother, who 'left' her. This restoration is thus not only the return of her own child, but the restoration of herself *as* a child; she projects Beloved in a maternal and filial fantasy as a perfectly dutiful daughter who 'came right on back like a good girl' (p. 203) and 'understands everything already', effectively denying Beloved the expression of *her* anger at the savage separation.[25] Here, memory is above all a path to explanation, and explanation a plea for forgiveness; ironically, all of it is framed by the declaration that 'I don't have to explain a thing', capturing the ambivalent innocence and guilt in Sethe's moving, involved narrative.[26]

Beloved's first stream of ideas, impressions, recollections is still more complex in its shifting of pronouns, identities, and bodily parts; hers is an open, seeking, concentrated language of elision, approaching most nearly Julia Kristeva's concept of the pre-Oedipal 'semiotic'.[27] In the spaces between words, as much as in the words themselves, the traces of desire – and loss – are strongly felt. Within its poetry (a poetry of recurrent themes, images and statements), Beloved refers above all to the place where she 'crouched' in the dark among others who were dying, and how Sethe went into the sea and left her. For her, it is an eternal present, 'All of it is now', and a large part of the experience being described is recognisably that of the slave ships, where the men 'without skin' – white men – bring less than is necessary to keep their cargo alive:

> I am always crouching the man on my face is dead his face is not mine his mouth smells sweet but his eyes are locked some who eat nasty themselves I do not eat the men without skin bring us their morning water to drink we have none . . . someone is thrashing but there is no room to do it in if we had more to drink we could make tears we cannot make sweat or morning water so the men without skin bring us theirs
> one time they bring us sweet rocks to suck we are all trying to leave our bodies behind (p. 210)

Throughout the passage there persist ambiguous impressions of separation and connection, but Beloved is clear that the face of the man dying on top of her is not her own face, while the woman who has her face, and whose face she wants, is Sethe. Again, the self exists both subjectively and objectively, but never integrally, since the sea is the place where all connections are lost. In this narrative of suffocation, starvation and death merging with the struggle to join and survive, Morrison has placed Beloved directly within a historical experience which (as the baby daughter of a second-generation slave) she could not actually have undergone; the displacement here is backwards in time, appropriately to the time when the fragmentation began, and Sethe is a part of it too with the iron collar about her neck which Beloved wishes to bite off. The slave ship represents the very worst time of transition, and the dispossession of which Beloved speaks is having '"no one to want me to say me my name"'. The closing of this section is in a willed union with 'the face that left me' so that 'now we can join' (p. 213).

A major aspect of this semiotic discourse, intimately bound in with the impressions of the slave ships and Beloved's earliest memories of her mother picking leaves, is the struggle to represent the infant's still fluid sense of 'identity', 'self' and 'body'. It is a process in which apperception and mirroring are active, so that there is no settled distinction between nor unification of images, and images cannot be pressed into language. Beloved's very existence is merged in the face and responding smile of her mother, corresponding closely to what Winnicott has described as 'the mother's role of giving back to the baby the baby's own self':[28]

> I AM BELOVED and she is mine . . . how can I say things that are pictures I am not separate from her there is no place where I stop her face is my own and I want to be there in the place where her face is and to be looking at it too a hot thing[29]

While the overriding impression in this passage is of the depth of that pre-Oedipal bond, there is also a sad irony in that the nearest Beloved comes to seeing herself as 'separate' is when she is lost into death. Dissolution is forced on her at the very point when a fragile process of individuation might begin, in the midst of becoming, and Beloved finds that she is 'going to be in pieces'[30] just when she was striving to join: '"I see me swim away a hot thing I see the bottoms of my feet I am alone I want to be the two of us I want the join"' (p. 213). Beloved's will to return again is to *exist*, to 'find a place to be', to identify 'the face that left me' so that finally when this is achieved, 'Sethe sees me see her and I see the smile' (p. 213). Hence, the second section representing Beloved's consciousness begins as a more articulate, clarifying version of the first, establishing that recognition and union; it soon shifts into dialogue between Sethe and Beloved, sometimes returning to the ambiguous separation and merging of identities through complex use of pronouns ('will we smile at me?'), while Denver's voice begins to enter as a more wary consciousness warning against too much love. Where the previous section had been made up of statements, this becomes a series of questions, answers, pleas and reproaches – active, responsive and troubled.

While the rediscovery of possession and belonging here is deeply moving, none the less the troubled aspects lie within the very framework of the language, and arguably they are a prelude to a process which becomes progressively more destructive than constructive in the reuniting of Beloved with Sethe. That destructiveness resides partly in Sethe's desire to lose herself in her daughter – a feeling which she first equates with sleeping and dying (p. 204) – and even more in what Beloved herself cannot rationalise, articulate or understand. Even her rebirth is into a repetition of babyhood and early childhood, in her long exhausted sleeps, her incontinence, her craving for sweet things, her demands and tantrums as well as in her devotion. There is always that aspect of the child and of the dislocated being in Beloved which cannot be mediated, even though it so powerfully communicates with Sethe and Denver.

The same sense of disconnectedness is once more conveyed through historical reference when Beloved first appears at 124. As mystifying as she is, Paul D relates her bewildered state of mind and the slow and painful spelling of her name to his recollections of the crowds of stunned, exhausted Negroes wandering the roads after the Civil War had ended. Seeking their relatives against all the odds, they are only capable of spelling out their names or bearing them on scraps of paper for others to decipher (p. 52). As we are told, 'the War had been over four or five years then, but nobody white or black seemed to know it'; the wandering groups, 'dazed but insistent', are chiefly made up of women and children, while the adult men have either been killed or driven off, living by stealth on the run. The code they adopt for survival is also a mute, cautious one; partly as a defensive necessity (too much information only spells danger), partly because the stories of their fugitive lives are too charged with trauma:

> chased by debts and filthy 'talking sheets', they followed secondary routes, scanned the horizon for signs and counted heavily on each other. Silent, except for social courtesies, when they met one another they neither described nor asked about the sorrow that drove them from one place to another. The whites didn't bear speaking on. Everybody knew. (p. 53)

Again, Morrison has linked Beloved with a critical *transitional* point in black history, with the exhaustion (like her physical exhaustion) of the passage over from one era to another, the notional freedom from slavery still dissipated by the lack of any established framework within which freedom could be realised. What is stressed once more is the experience of dislocation, inarticulacy (whether through the pointlessness or the sheer danger of speech), and the near-impossibility of risking or achieving connections. What Paul D first supposes about Beloved, then, is by no means wide of the mark. She grasps, yet can barely understand, the connection she is trying to make, and where she came from, all is confused, she knows no names. In the time and place that Paul D is thinking of, little is happening that could really be described as Reconstruction;[31] it is only now that he is trying to make a tentative homecoming, a settling down, just as Beloved is. This is one of the reasons why, as far as she is concerned, he is in the way; each of them is jealously convinced that there is only room for *one* to come home, while for both of them, Sethe is the centre.

As to this homecoming, despite the vital differences which Morrison has pointed to as distinguishing 124 from the plantation Sweet Home,[32] there are also certain analogies. Both are places overcharged with meaning which is intimately related to personal experience (meaning in which some are included while others appear to be excluded), and both can and do become places of enclosure. Denver's heartfelt dislike of stories about Sweet Home is understandable, because it marks out the difference between her own and Sethe's relationships to the past. Sethe was born into slavery, Denver was born (at another significant transitional point) in the waters of the Ohio River which formed the boundary between slavery and a vulnerable freedom. She has been protected from the worst of that experience, but still – for all her resentment of Sethe's anecdotes – she knows that she is being kept from something. Sethe is both unconsciously and consciously guarding the territory of her memory, not only because it is a responsibility and a site of bottomless terror for her, but because everything in it exists as 'rememory' and will never cease to be a threat to her children:

> 'Someday you be walking down the road and you hear something or see something going on. . . . It's when you bump into a rememory that belongs to somebody else. Where I was before I came here, that place is real. It's never going away. Even if the whole farm – every tree and grass blade of it dies. The picture is still there and what's more, if you go there – you who never was there – if you go there and stand in the place where it was, it will happen again; it will be there for you, waiting for you. So, Denver, you can't never go there. Never.' (p. 36)

Because Denver knows what it is to be excluded from the past which is such a deep link between Sethe and Paul D, and because she knows what it is to be closed away from others in 124, she has an intuitive recognition of what the baby ghost feels: 'lonely and rebuked'. Just as Beloved feels rage at her exclusion from the living, so Denver feels dispossessed of her father's memory when her mother and her lover speak of him so that even 'her own father's absence was not hers' (p. 13). Even as a ghost, Beloved's presence fills that gap for her, supplying 'the downright pleasure of enchantment, of not suspecting but *knowing* the things behind things' (p. 37). When her mother does tell stories about the past, Denver prefers to hear only the one that relates to her, the story of her own birth; and when this is recounted in the text (pp. 28–35), Morrison introduces two significantly different narrative patterns. The first begins with Denver, playing in her secret boxwood bower, then looking in at 124 from the outside and seeing her mother praying with the mysterious white dress holding her waist. In her mind, she connects the approach to the story of her birth (which begins 'way back') with the approach to 124, whose single front door can only be reached by a circuitous route from the back. It is as if all her history was invested in the house, yet this does not prevent her from feeling in some respects isolated from it. By contrast, the other narrative pattern takes the story well beyond Denver's exclusive concerns and conceptions of things. It moves us instead much further back, from the white dress which reminds Denver of the white girl (Amy) who helped at her birth, to the detailed account of the circumstances of Sethe's escape, to Sethe's childhood memories of trying to identify her own mother among the slave workers. Unobtrusively, Morrison has allowed the reader to connect the line of mothers, a genealogical link which serves to make us aware of what Denver does *not* know (and what Sethe barely recalls), because the links between families were ruptured by slavery.[33] For her own part, Denver can only draw her history from Sethe in fragments, which may be cut short at any moment of the telling.

The intensity that characterises the relationship between Denver and Beloved, then, lies in a shared need and a *mutual* feeding – in Denver's desire to know about the place Beloved came from, and of course to have a companion, and in Beloved's desire to find out from Denver about the shape of things in the world and the history of the living. It is important to recognise that the people living have their own present 'history' – that is, one which is understood in terms of shared experience and kin relationships – and in so far as Denver knows something about these, she has something valuable to offer Beloved. Even so, Beloved's deepest needs are always for Sethe; in her she is seeking the strongest of her connections. She says as much to her sister, brutally: '"She is the one I need. You can go but she is the one I have to have"' (p. 76).

The double isolation of Denver, her existence in a limbo somewhere between a lost past and a lonely present, is of great importance to the closing sections of the novel. The process begins with Sethe and Paul D cautiously opening the Pandora's box of their shared memories, and continues with Beloved herself as the chest of hidden treasure which her mother cannot bear to lose again. Once Paul D has left, the pattern becomes one of dangerous obsession, with Sethe feeding only on her guilt, and Beloved, like an over-demanding child or a succubus, growing fat on it. If at first we are enfolded in the self-sufficient warmth and depth of one of Morrison's 'three-woman utopian households',[34] we later see that (like the parallel household of *Song of Solomon*) it cannot sustain itself indefinitely.[35] Eventually, Denver's and Sethe's physical and spiritual starvation develops to a crisis. The paradox we have to face is that Beloved's claim on them (on Sethe especially) is both just *and* excessive, a literally wasting claim to which there would be 'no end'. The starvation is both the outcome and opposite to an abiding theme within the novel: the linking of memory with food and the preparation of food.[36] The point at which Denver decides that she must break the boundary of the house and seek help in contact with others also has to be understood in its connection (through analogy and through textual metaphors) with the only other time she experienced a brief period of community. This was when she tentatively crept over to peer in from a side window on the classes where Lady Jones was teaching other illiterate black children to write. At that time Denver is forthrightly invited in, and for the first time becomes part of a group, engaged in a shared, constructive exercise. It is a personal unfolding, a liberation in the 'magic' of the chalk: 'the little i, the sentences rolling out like pie dough'[37] (here it is *language* that is linked to food). What throws her back into immediate and literal deafness is the question put by her classmate Nelson Lord about her mother's past; she cannot bear to hear her mother's answer because she has latent memories of her own (prison and rats) that tell her the story is true.

The significance of this network is that Denver's enclosure in the prison, her self-enclosure in silence and deafness, and the now closed world of 124 begin to share common ground, even though Denver herself associates her fear of the prison and the trauma that closed her in silence with the *outside* world (p. 243). The reader may also be reminded of those passages in which Sweet Home is revealed as a delusory cradle where, despite Garner's comparative liberality, his slaves remain illiterate and powerless. Ironically, in so far as they have any choices, they choose (all but Halle) to remain in that state; as Paul D later reflects, they imagined themselves free and whole men because they were permitted: 'to buy a mother, choose a horse or a wife, handle guns, even learn reading if they wanted to – but they didn't want to since nothing important to them could be put down on paper' (p. 125). Garner, like any other slave master, appropriates them in giving them names, and the system of slavery itself dictates their real impotence: 'One step off that ground and they were trespassers among the human race. Watchdogs without teeth; steer bulls without horns; gelded workhorses whose neigh and whinny could not be translated into a language responsible humans spoke.'[38]

Within the context of slavery, language and all its written definitions may well appear no more than the instrument of the oppressor – Schoolteacher with his books and his coachbox full of paper arriving to break Garner's slaves, measure Sethe's head and inscribe her (with the ink she herself has made) as 'animal'. Or the newspaper cutting which reports Sethe's crime, in black marks which neither she nor Paul D can decipher and which Sethe knows will say all about the what and nothing of the reasons why. From the slave's and the ex-slave's point of view, nothing could seem more hostile and less relevant than this controlling word.[39] Yet historically, the first movements towards a degree of constitutional freedom and the first concerted attempts to teach literacy to blacks were taking place in the Reconstruction years.[40] For Denver, living in that time, the outside world still **appears** fearful, but communication is even so the keyword in her course of action at the novel's end. She rightly recognises that in order to survive she is going to have to reconnect, and that nothing the past can offer will make up for the loss of a future. Initially, she is passing on to a second 'mother' in her second encounter with Lady Jones, who reads her face with complete familiarity as if it were her child's and addresses her with maternal sympathy; yet Morrison also describes her inauguration into the world 'as a woman' in terms of a place which she reaches following 'a trail . . . made up of paper scraps containing the handwritten names of others' (p. 248). Gifts of food from others appear on the very tree stump where Beloved had formerly materialised, and Denver's personal connection with the donors begins through her deciphering the names they leave, or alternatively through identifying their plates, pie dishes and so on. From that halting beginning, she proceeds to risk conversations and the social encounters that conversations entail. She finally shares in the wider history that the community is able to fill in for her, but only on the condition that she in turn tells *them* everything. Thus, when Nelson Lord next speaks to her, 'she heard it as though it were what language was made for. The last time he spoke to her his words blocked up her ears. Now they opened her mind' (p. 252).

The period in which Denver opens up again to wider verbal communication and interaction is bound in with the renewal of her formal education, first through Lady Jones and later through the (white) Bodwins. Throughout this part of the narrative, we are never allowed to forget how Denver is bridging a world which is full of terror, even though she has only heard about the terror that lies beyond the confines of her house; but she finds that at this stage and in this place, it no longer need be quite so terrifying.[41] Likewise, Morrison seems concerned to show that, as history can be outlived, so language can be enabling, not only as an instrument of power but because it is one of the crucial means by which we express and communicate.[42] However compelling the claims of the past may be – and this novel never ceases to make them so – it cannot interpret itself for us; we can only develop that understanding. Beloved's final disappearance, the fading of her traces, is gradual but necessary; it happens quite simply as others progressively forget her. In part it is a willed forgetting, since 'remembering seemed unwise'; thus, 'although she has claim, she is not claimed'. Morrison's final statement, that 'it was not a story to pass on', none the less sustains a paradox in its double reference, voicing the concern with both connection and disconnection which is expressed throughout the text. Within the frame of the narrative, the black community has chosen to close the door on this particular claim, and we have been shown the reasons why. The narrator, on the other hand, *is* passing the story on, and to do so is unquestionably to acknowledge its claim, at the very time when the traces seem to be vanishing.

NOTES

1. 'Living memory', *City Limits* (31 March–7 April 1988), 10–11.
2. James Baldwin also observes that 'in the context of the Negro problem neither whites nor blacks, for excellent reasons of their own, have the faintest desire to look back', but maintains that the past will 'remain horrible' for as long as it is not honestly assessed. Furthermore, 'This horror has so welded past and present that it is virtually impossible and certainly meaningless to speak of it as occurring, as it were, in time' (*Notes of A Native Son*, 1955; London and Sydney: Pluto Press, 1985, p. 6, xii).
3. Margaret Homans examines the question of language and its adequacy in the work of contemporary women writers, white and black; see '"Her very own howl": The ambiguities of representation in recent women's fiction', *Signs* 9, 2 (1983), 186–205, and Valerie Babb, '*The Color Purple*: Writing to undo what writing has done', *Phylon* 47, 2 (June, 1986), 107–16.
4. Michael G. Cooke, *Afro-American Literature in the Twentieth Century: The achievement of intimacy* (New Haven and London: Yale University Press, 1984), p. 4; see also his general remarks on p. 14.
5. Bernard W. Bell, *The Afro-American Novel and Its Tradition* (Amherst, Mass.: Massachusetts University Press, 1987), pp. 283–4; Robert Scholes, *The Fabulators* (New York: Oxford University Press, 1967), p. 12. Bell rightly points out that while many black modernist and postmodernist writers 'are definitely influenced by the traditions of Western literature and committed to the freedom of hybrid narrative forms', none the less their experience of racial oppression and their sense of responsibility means that most 'are not inclined to neglect moral and social issues in their narratives' (p. 284). See also Robert Elliot Fox, *Conscientious Sorcerers: The black postmodernist fiction of LeRoi Jones/Amiri Baraka, Ishmael Reed, and Samuel R. Delany* (New York and London: Greenwood Press, 1987).
6. 'Living memory', p. 11.
7. 'Unspeakable things unspoken: the Afro-American presence in American literature', *Michigan Quarterly Review* 28, 1 (1989), 1–34; 15–16.
8. See Michael P. Rogin, *Subversive Genealogy: The politics and art of Herman Melville* (New York, 1979; California: University of California Press, 1985).
9. Elliott Butler-Evans in *Race, Gender and Desire: Narrative strategies in the fiction of Toni Cade Bambara, Toni Morrison and Alice Walker* (Philadelphia: Temple University Press, 1989) follows Fredric Jameson in characterising postmodern discourse as entailing among other features 'the emergence of a schizophrenic textual structure; a displacement of history by "historicism", in which the past is reread and reconstructed in the present' (p. 152), and also cites Jean-François Lyotard's definition of the postmodern as 'that which searches for new presentations . . . in order to impart a stronger sense of the unpresentable' (pp. 152–3).
10. Extracts from a range of source material are reproduced in *Black Women in White America: A documentary history*, ed. Gerda Lerner (New York: Random House, Pantheon Books, 1972), including passages concerning the case of Margaret Garner on which Sethe's story is based (pp. 60–3). Despite the notoriety of the case, such acts of infanticide by slave mothers were not in fact uncommon.
11. Henry Louis Gates has observed that for the slaves themselves, the general absence of written records to mark out their lives and their past history, together with the fact of their

illiteracy, amounted to a radical undermining of their sense of time and of self. 'Slavery's time was delineated by memory and memory alone. . . . the slave had lived at no time past the point of recollection' (*Figures in Black: Words, signs, and the 'racial' self* (Oxford: Oxford University Press, 1987), pp. 100–1).

12. These aspects of *Beloved* (New York: Plume, p.b. edition, 1988; first published New York: Alfred A. Knopf, 1987) are briefly but brilliantly explored by Marianne Hirsch in *The Mother/Daughter Plot: Narrative, psychoanalysis, feminism* (Bloomington: Indiana University Press, 1989); see especially pp. 5–8. As she observes, the novel begins with the mother and allows her a voice to express her rage at the loss of a child, while it also considers deeply 'the hierarchy of motherhood over selfhood' (p. 7). It owes as much to the 'woman-centered' myth of Demeter and Persephone, with its emphasis on the cyclical plot of loss and rebirth, as it does to the linear and fatal Oedipus plot, although Sethe is 'neither the silent Jocasta nor the powerful Demeter' (p. 6).

13. Hirsch notes that 'Familial structures in this novel are profoundly distorted by the institution of slavery', and that whenever a nuclear family group begins to frame itself, it is 'repeatedly broken up as a *fourth* term either supplements or replaces the third' (p. 6).

14. Paul D has a special place in relation to women from the first, when Morrison emphasises their sense of frank intimacy with him (p. 17); they 'told him things they only told each other'. At the novel's end, Sethe carries over this same intimacy with him to express her particular sorrow as mother and as daughter and as a self (p. 272). Similarly, he thinks of her as a woman who can leave his humanity and manhood intact in the midst of slavery's humiliations, and piece together his fragmented self (pp. 272–3).

15. Morrison acknowledges that black women 'are of compelling interest to me' (see *Black Women Writers at Work*, ed. Claudia Tate (New York, 1983, Oldcastle Books: Harpenden, 1985, p. 119), but she repeatedly stresses in interviews the necessity for interaction between men and women and for an inclusive vision encompassing both ('Living memory', p. 11, and 'Rootedness: the ancestor as foundation', in *Black Women Writers 1950–1980*, ed. Mari Evans, New York: Doubleday, Anchor Books, 1984, pp. 339–45). As she observes, in the circumstances in which Sethe is placed, she *is* her children, and also the community. However, Elliott Butler-Evans (*Race, Gender and Desire*, pp. 3–9) sees a tension between the discourses of race and gender in Morrison's work and in that of Alice Walker and Toni Cade Bambara.

16. This model of 'rememory' is akin to Freud's model of the psyche, which moved away from the notion of linearity and 'stages of development' towards 'a theory of imbrication, parallels, simultaneity, and diachronology. . . . a complex "time" of space, not a simple "time" of place' (Juliet Mitchell, *Psychoanalysis and Feminism*, Harmondsworth: Penguin, 1974, p. 22).

17. Susan Willis, *Specifying: Black women writing the American experience* (Madison: University of Wisconsin Press, 1987), p. 102.

18. Sigmund Freud, 'The "uncanny"' (1919), in *The Standard Edition of the Complete Psychological Works of Sigmund Freud*, trans., ed. and rev. James Strachey (1955; London: Hogarth Press, 1971), XVII. Reprinted in *New Literary History* 7 (1976), 619–45. See pp. 634, 641. Freud takes his hint from Schelling, that '"*Unheimlich*" is the name for everything that ought to have remained . . . secret and hidden but has come to light' (p. 623), and dwells at length on the connotations of the word 'heimlich' as 'belonging to the house', 'intimate', 'not strange', and yet also (conversely) 'concealed, kept from sight . . . withheld from others'. The apparent contradictions in the use of the word are, he proposes, an expression of an overlapping meaning, a common ground within apparent difference; this is suggestive with regard to the qualities of 124 in *Beloved*.

19. Morrison, 'Unspeakable things unspoken', p. 31.

20. Morrison comments that black women 'seem able to combine the nest and the adventure', to be 'both inn and trail' (Tate, *Black Women Writers at Work*, p. 122); this encompasses the distinction between the 'male' and 'female' plot, and helps to point up the fact that what takes place in Sethe's house makes it *both* a haven and a trail.

21. Morrison, *Beloved*, p. 35. The point at which Paul D is forced to remember is presented as Beloved's seduction of him, with the ambivalently sexual injunction to '"touch me on the

inside part and call me my name"'. To be made to *speak* her name is to enact a kind of 'performative', that is to declare and seal a bond which he has striven to suppress; it is followed by his intercourse with her, which opens up the sealed tobacco-tin of his memory and touches the 'red heart' in its place (p. 117).

22. In another sense, Beloved could be described as the symptom of what the trauma of slavery entailed, so that the story unfolds as a case history would unfold, backwards from the phenomenon which confronts us and through the intricacies of how it came to be. See Mitchell, *Psychoanalysis and Feminism*, pp. 14, 20, 27.

23. Beyond this specific context, there is a recognition here of the child's 'active wishes' towards the mother, expressed in the desire both to mother her and to kill her. 'There is a fear in both sexes of being killed by the mother and so there is a shift to activity in an aggressive death-wish against her' (Mitchell, *Psychoanalysis and Feminism*, p. 58).

24. Roberta Rubenstein, in *Boundaries of the Self: Gender, culture, fiction* (Urbana and Chicago: University of Illinois Press, 1987), refers to Gaston Bachelard's analysis of 'the values of inhabited space, of the non-I that protects the I' as an important one for women writers especially. Houses may appear 'other' yet intimate in this sense, or may themselves represent bodily boundaries (pp. 4–5). See also Frances Bartkowski, *Feminist Utopias* (Lincoln and London: University of Nebraska Press, 1989), chapter 4.

25. Beloved's repeated reproach at this primal deprivation, '"You left me"', is echoed by Sethe's sad declaration, '"She left me"', at the novel's end.

26. Innocence is much more clearly the keynote in Sethe's final recognition of Beloved's identity (p. 176), where the colour white is emphasised in the domestic scene of the pan of milk, the snow, the 'lily-white stairs' which Sethe ascends 'like a bride'. Again, Stamp Paid is outside, fingering the red ribbon of the lynched girl.

27. Kristeva writes of 'a divided subject, even a pluralised subject, that occupies, not a place of enunciation, but permutable, multiple, and mobile places' (*Desire in Language*, Oxford: Basil Blackwell, 1986, p. 111).

28. D. W. Winnicott, *Playing and Reality* (Harmondsworth: Penguin, 1971); acknowledging 'the delicacy of what is preverbal, unverbalized, and unverbalizable except perhaps in poetry', Winnicott goes on to ask:

> 'What does the baby see when he or she looks at the mother's face? . . . what the baby sees is himself or herself. In other words the mother is looking at the baby and *what she looks like is related to what she sees there*. (p. 131)

See also Mitchell, *Psychoanalysis and Feminism*, pp. 39–40. Ronnie Scharfman challenges the idea of the self-alienation or splitting of the subject entailed in the mirroring process as propounded by Jacques Lacan and Jean Paul Sartre, arguing that because of identification with the mother the process may be different for girl children ('Mirroring and mothering in Simone Schwarz-Bart's *Pluie et vent sur Télumée miracle*, Paris: Editions de Seuil, 1972; and Jean Rhys, *Wide Sargasso Sea*, *Yale French Studies* 62, 1981, 88–106).

29. See also Steven Marcus, 'The psychoanalytic self', *Southern Review* 22 (1986), 308–25.

30. The way in which the body is figured in Beloved's passage and in some other parts of the novel can be related to Lacan's representation of the *pre*-mirror stage, 'a period in which an infant experiences its body as fragmented parts and images', figured in images of 'dismemberment . . . devouring, bursting open of the body' (Ellie Ragland-Sullivan, *Jacques Lacan and the Philosophy of Psychoanalysis*, London and Canberra: Croom Helm, 1986, pp. 18–19).

31. Eric Foner takes issue with Morrison's representation of the Reconstruction years as 'a time of unrelieved sordidness and corruption', arguing that this echoes a long-standing misrepresentation of the positive accomplishments of that period ('The canon and American history', *Michigan Quarterly Review* 28.1, 1989, 44–9). However, Morrison has previously spoken of the unusual split in Ohio, between the northern part representing freedom and the southern part, 'as much Kentucky as there is, complete with cross burnings' (Tate, *Black Women Writers at Work*, p. 119).

32. 'Unspeakable things unspoken', p. 31; the difference lies in the absence of adjectives or

connotations applied to 124, while Sweet Home is marked by the postures of 'arrivistes and estate builders . . . laying claim to instant history and legend'.

33. This disruption of the family, and the need to survive that rupturing, still presents an important issue for black women and black feminists; see Angela Y. Davis, *Women, Race and Class* (New York: Random House 1981; New York: Vintage Books, 1983), pp. 14–15, Deborah A. King, 'Multiple jeopardy, multiple consciousness: the context of a black feminist ideology', *Signs* 14.1 (1988), 42–72, and Alice Walker's *In Search of Our Mothers' Gardens* (New York: Harcourt Brace Jovanovitch, 1983; London: The Women's Press, 1984).

34. Willis, *Specifying*, p. 106.

35. Morrison comments on this in *Black Women Writers*, ed. Evans, p. 344.

36. *Beloved*, pp. 16–17, 73.

37. It is significant that the letter 'i' is the one singled out here, representing Denver's fragile sense of an unfolding self, her sense of herself as a subject and of 'becoming' through the command of language symbolised by writing.

38. Denver also remembers her father's attitude to these issues as recounted by Baby Suggs; Sixo declared that it would

> make him forget things he shouldn't and memorise things he shouldn't and he didn't want his mind messed up. But my daddy said, If you can't count they can cheat you. If you can't read they can beat you. They thought that was funny. (p. 208)

39. Morrison stresses a fundamental difference between this coercive use of the word (where 'definitions belonged to the definers') and the Word which is 'given' to Baby Suggs, a suasive Call rather than a directive sermon. Compare the sermon of Mr Pike in Harriet Jacobs' *Incidents in the Life of a Slave Girl*, Section XIII (in *The Classic Slave Narratives*, ed. Henry Louis Gates, New York: New American Library, 1987, pp. 397–8).

40. See note 31 above, and *Black Women in White America*, ed. Lerner, pp. 92–113. Henry L. Gates also observes, 'In literacy was power . . . the correlation of freedom with literacy not only became a central trope of the slave narratives, but it also formed a mythical matrix out of which subsequent black narrative forms developed' (*Figures in Black*, p. 108; see pp. 104–8 generally).

41. Denver's fear is partly offset by the intervention of her grandmother's voice, telling her not that the world is safe but that she must go on anyway. The importance of the link with Baby Suggs strongly resembles that of grandmother and granddaughter in Schwarz-Bart's *Télumée* (see Scharfman, note 28 above). Scharfman argues that 'through her grandmother's eyes, Télumée comes to know the world', including its political reality. She also prepares Télumée for connection with the community in which she will again be mirrored (pp. 91–6).

42. Julia Kristeva's assertion in *About Chinese Women* that we can only gain entry to social experience and to the 'temporal scene' of political affairs at the cost of 'identifying with the values considered to be masculine (dominance, superego, *the endorsed communicative word* that institutes stable social exchange)' is castigated by Gayatri Chakravorty Spivak as a directive for 'class- and race-privileged literary women . . . identifying the political with the temporal and linguistic'. See the extract from *About Chinese Women* reprinted in *The Kristeva Reader*, ed. Toril Moi (Oxford: Basil Blackwell, 1986), pp. 138–59, and Spivak, 'French feminism in an international frame', *Yale French Studies* 62 (1981), 154–84; p. 158.

Andrea Nye ('Woman clothed with the sun: Julia Kristeva and the escape from/to language', *Signs* 12, 4, 1987, 664–86) makes a case for acknowledging 'interpersonality' in language in the face of Kristeva's 'idealism', which (following Lacan) 'reduces all to the "I" and "me"; "you's" and "they's" are seen only as projections of an otherness first discovered within the subject' (pp. 682–3). Interpersonality, argues Nye, is 'not missing from language but only from Kristeva's representation of it', and it can be presented as 'the obvious reality of linguistic communication' (p. 683).

Claire Buck

'O Careless, Unspeakable Mother': Irigaray, H.D. and Maternal Origin

The figure of the mother has long been a central locus of most theoretical accounts of femininity regardless of ideological persuasion. The maternal role defines the nature of femininity for all women, both in accounts which reduce femininity to the functions of reproduction and nurturing, and in feminist interrogations of the relationship between femininity and maternity. The vast amount of feminist work on the mother, crossing different disciplines, is principally defined by two projects. First, a systematic critique of the containment of women within the biologically reductive parameters of a culturally endorsed reproductive role. A second, and often overlapping project, has been the investigation of the role of mother in the construction of femininity as actual women live it. The feminist psychologist, Nancy Chodorow, offers a compelling account of the girl's acquisition of gender through identification with the mother. Julia Kristeva employs poststructuralist psychoanalysis to theorise the function of the maternal body in a psychic and cultural history of masculinity and femininity. In a rather different frame the other two stars of new French feminism as it has penetrated Anglo-American feminism, Luce Irigaray and Hélène Cixous, have attempted to map alternative models of femininity and female desire through the deconstruction of existing psychoanalytic models. Woman writes as a feminine subject, indeed writes her femininity, through the white ink of her mother's milk, according to Cixous.[1] For Irigaray, women have been systematically denied the use of the mother to fantasise their origin as feminine subjects. The woman's relationship according to Irigaray is to the man's mother, her mother-in-law, and not to her own mother. In this essay I want to explore Irigaray's proposition and use it to reflect on *Helen in Egypt*, the long poem sequence by the modernist American poet, H.D.[2]

The first translations of Irigaray's work in Britain and America elicited the charge of essentialism. Debates over the accuracy of this charge have since dominated Anglo-American writing about her work. It is only recently that feminists, such as Margaret Whitford, Kaja Silverman and Jan Montefiore, have moved beyond a defensive position to examine the positive critical potential of Irigaray's work.[3] I do not intend here to give a full account of the debate over Irigaray's essentialism. This has been fully discussed by Whitford, Silverman and Carolyn Burke.[4] However, Irigaray's discussion of the mother is a part of what has been seen as essentialist in her writing. And in order to understand the role Irigaray gives to the figure of the mother it is necessary to understand how her ideas fundamentally differ from essentialism. Her argument that women are denied a specific feminine relationship to a maternal origin can easily look like an argument for a natural and pre-given feminine libido originating with the mother, but repressed by a patriarchal culture.[5]

For Irigaray the subject's (whether man's or woman's) relationship to a maternal origin is a matter of fantasy. This is clear, for example, in her discussion of the substitutions and symbolisations which make up the man's relation to origin. The girl, unlike the boy, 'will never give the mother a drink of sperm from her penis, in a substitute-reversal of the lost breast and milk; she will never reproduce her (like) self inside the/her mother'.[6] Here, the significance of the sexual act, and the wishes it embodies, whether for the boy or the adult man, evidently belong with fantasy. Likewise, 'The blind spot of an old dream of symmetry', the text on which I will concentrate in this study, depends heavily on recent psychoanalytic theories of fantasy for its concept of origin. Fantasy, within this context, is not opposed to reality on the side of illusion and fiction, but is fundamental to subjectivity as a form of psychical reality. Psychical reality is one of the most important propositions of psychoanalysis, 'as immutable a force in our lives as any material circumstances'.[7] Freud's analysis of the unconscious motivations behind slips of the tongue would be one example of its effectiveness. As a key element of psychical reality, fantasy becomes the term which sidesteps natural accounts of sexuality. Desire is not simply a natural, biological force, 'an upsurge of the drives, but is articulated into the fantasy'.[8] Fantasy, as it is often put, is the theatre, or *mise-en-scène*, in which wishes are staged. It is a 'setting for desire'.[9]

Once the concept of origin is located within an account of fantasy rather than a real moment of origination or causality, it then becomes a question of an imaginary which structures the human subject and its desires. According to Laplanche and Pontalis, the child creates myths of origin to explain itself and the enigmas which necessarily confront it: where the child comes from, the child's relations to its parents and the puzzle of the child's difference from the other sex. The myths or primal fantasies which the child elaborates explain and represent the self through imagining its origins: 'the primal scene pictures the origin of the individual; fantasies of seduction, the origin and upsurge of sexuality; fantasies of castration, the origin of the difference between the sexes' (*Speculum* 19). In other words, the child uses the question of where I came from to answer the question of who I am. The form of these fantasies of origin is not simply subjective. Freud's concept of fantasy supports a theory of the relationship of individual subjectivity to the cultural imperatives which predate the individual.[10] Fantasy supports a commerce between the culturally permissible forms and routes desire can take, resistance to those forms, and the specific history of the individual.

Irigaray's concept of origin is similarly a question of a necessary structuring of the subject and its desire via fantasy. However, her analysis is a critical reading, 'between the lines', of Freud's essay 'Femininity'. She provides an implicit corrective to Laplanche and Pontalis's formulation. Central to Irigaray's account of origin is the radical imbalance between the man's and the woman's relationship to these fantasies of origin. These fantasies are irreducibly marked by a masculine libido, or perhaps more precisely, a phallic *modality*, since the possibility of alternative 'economies' of sexual difference is fundamental to Irigaray's project. Irigaray's woman is destined to support the image of the man in what she calls an economy of the Same.[11] In both the discourses of psychoanalysis and metaphysics the radical otherness of the woman is reduced to a mirror in which the man can perceive himself without breaks or lack. In Freud's concept of 'penis-envy' we can see in operation Irigaray's argument that woman functions as a support for man's narcissism. The image of the woman both lacking and desiring a penis, and 'envious' of the man's possession, ensures the value of the penis which comes to signify all that desire can be. The penis acquires the status, that is, of the phallus. Thus the woman's 'penis-envy' 'soothes the anguish man feels, Freud feels, about the coherence of his narcissistic construction and reassures him against what he calls castration anxiety' (S 51).[12] The mother's role in this phallic economy of the same is to 'facilitate the repetition of the same, in contempt for her difference' (S 54). The mother represents the place of origin for the man. His relation to that origin must then represent and repeat it in terms which ensure his narcissistic coherence. Thus the man tells his story of his relation to origin according 'to the desire for sameness and to the repetition-representation-reproduction of sameness' (S 43). Woman's position within the story is one of woman's lack.

Irigaray's account suggests a variety of fantasies about this relation to the mother, not all of which are specifically phallic. For example, the early oral relationship to the mother is structured by the child's attempt to 'reabsorb its material cause' (S 40), so that food has the function of 'repeating-representing closeness to the mother' (S 41). Thus one element of the fantasy concerns a healing of the inevitable separations which are involved in the mother–child relationship. A second element involves the substitution-reversal I referred to above. The child does to the mother what she did to it: for example, in the child's play with dolls. However, Irigaray's point is that through the threat of castration these instances are reinscribed within a phallic economy in which the possibilities of satisfaction are a matter of the subject's relation to the phallus. The substitution-reversal is then appropriated by the man who has the penis. He can in fantasy heal the break with origin, 'go back inside the mother'; 'give the mother a drink of sperm' and crucially reproduce himself inside the mother by producing his own son. It is the woman's role to take the place of the man's mother in these metaphoric substitutions. Rather than stage her own specific fantasy of a relation to origin, she 'will herself be the place where origin is repeated, re-produced and reproduced, though this does not mean that she thereby repeats "her" original topos, "her origin"' (S 21). The role is forced on her because of the loss of any means to symbolise the daughter's relationship to the mother as *her* mother.

The daughter's relation to her mother within a Freudian model is primarily one of rejection, contempt and loss.[13] She 'recognises' her own lack through the discovery of her mother's 'castration' and responds with contempt and fury because her mother cannot supply her with the desired organ. This is the classical psychoanalytic account which has so long troubled feminism. The girl turns away from her mother to her father, propelled into the positive Oedipus complex by castration. Her 'proper' femininity involves a simultaneous repudiation of her mother as object of desire and an identification with her as feminine. She identifies with what she contemns. She is the 'castrated' daughter of a 'castrated' mother. On this model her desire for origin 'will henceforth pass through the discourse – desire – law of man's desire' (S 42).

Irigaray's account of origins within what she calls a phallic economy assigns both mother and daughter as supports for the narcissistic coherence of masculinity. Thus she introduces a question already implied by Freud's pre-oedipal, phallic and castrated mother: Who is the mother? Is she the son's mother or the daughter's mother in Irigaray's formulation? Both Freud and Irigaray are asking us to think of the way the mother operates as part of our psychic reality, within a series of fantasies. This is very different from a sociological account of the mother, such as Chodorow's, which depends on an empirical account of 'real' mother–child relations.[14] In Irigaray's account these real relations are only comprehensible within the context of the fantasies surrounding the figure of the mother. The advantage of Irigaray's analysis is that like Freud she establishes that the mother has multiple meanings and functions fundamental to sexual difference and desire. The mother's femininity and its role in her daughter's femininity or son's masculinity have no pre-given significance. Unlike Freud, Irigaray attempts to rethink the mother's relation to the daughter (and hence to the son), through a critical account of the phallic story. Irigaray proposes a feminine myth of origin, the daughter's relation to *her* origin and *her* mother, as the foundation for an alternative modality of libido, a feminine one not subject to the phallic definition of lack as the property of women. [15]

I now want to turn to H.D.'s *Helen in Egypt* in the light of Irigaray's thesis about the mother–daughter relationship. The poem, written between 1952 and 1954, takes as its subject the proliferation of myths about the classical heroine, Helen of Troy. In the three sections which divide the 161 lyrics of *Helen in Egypt*, 'Pallinode', 'Leuke' and 'Eidolon', a series of voices offer Helen's story. Predominant among these are Helen's own voice and that of the poet who is represented in the prose headnotes which introduce and interrogate each lyric. The other voices belong to Helen's three lovers, Achilles, Paris and Theseus, and to Achilles' goddess mother, Thetis. These classical myths are used to stage an investigation of the terms for a feminine self. [16] Helen, as chief protagonist, explores the often contradictory stories of her as cultural emblem of female beauty: 'the face that launched a thousand ships'. The poem's quest for the true story of Helen is set against the absence of a single meta-narrative. Consequently the poem uses myth to explore the cultural inscription of femininity in some of the founding texts of Western culture, rather than to establish a true femininity beneath the defamatory fiction. Helen's investigation of her 'story' also entails the scrutiny of the masculine narrative.

Achilles' relationship with his mother, Thetis, is a major focus of the poem, filling the last three books of 'Eidolon'. Part of the poem's project is to reform maculinity in order to enable a new utopian version of sexual difference. This transformation rests on the relationship of both man and woman in the poem to the mother, Thetis. As Rachel Blau DuPlessis has said, the poem 'shows that all desire is matrisexual: that all polarities, including major oppositional conflicts (love and death, eros and conflict), can be sublated through the mother'. [17] Thetis's power, we learn in 'Eidolon', 'was measureless'. [18] However, the poem is also more enigmatic about the identity of this mother and her relationship to Helen than DuPlessis's comment suggests. The mother who dominates H.D.'s poem is not the daughter's mother, Leda, but the son's mother, Thetis. Leda, raped by Zeus in the shape of a swan, appears solely as a womb/eggshell. It is here that it is useful to draw on Irigaray's proposition that 'woman's symbolization of her beginning, of the specificity of her relationship to the origin, has always already been erased' (S 60). She offers a way of understanding why the focus of a story of matrisexual desire should be the son's mother, and specifically why Helen should tell this story in place of the story of the daughter's mother.

Helen's power over Achilles, in the face of her role in the destruction of his male-bonded guard, the Myrmidons, is attributed to her use of the mother's name:

> 'Isis,' he said, 'or Thetis,' I said,
> recalling, remembering, invoking
> his sea-mother
> (*Helen in Egypt* 14)

Helen is identified therefore with her new lover's mother in the traditional position assigned the woman in psychoanalytic theory. Freud writes that 'it is in this identification [with her mother] too that she acquires her attractiveness to a man, whose Oedipus attachment to his mother it kindles into passion'.[19] Irigaray, quoting this, notes that the identification is with 'his mother' (S 109). H.D.'s use of this formula in her poem need not be surprising given that she was analysed by Freud; she even includes a Freud figure in the poem in the character of Theseus.[20]

The identification of Helen with the man's mother is echoed too in her relationship with Paris: 'I lost the Lover, Paris, / but to find the Son' (*HE* 155). The poem narrates these relationships within a psychoanalytic discourse coded as mythical by means of explicit references to Oedipus. For example:

> O, Paris, beautiful enchanter?
> you would re-live an old story,
> Oedipus and his slain father,
>
> you would re-create Troy
> with Helen, not Hecuba for mother,
> did I ever stand on the ramparts?
> (*HE* 223–4)

The psychic terrain of the poem is thus marked to justify and enable the mobile identifications in which Helen may be alternatively lover, mother or even sister to Achilles and Paris. However, the above example evokes the oedipal structure only to dismiss it as an old story. In a headnote within the same sequence of lyrics we learn what Helen lost through her place in the Trojan war: 'she had lost her childhood or her child, her "Lord's devotion" or the devotion of the conventional majority' (*HE* 227). The word 'conventional' suggests that the costs of the loss were worth paying, but the lyric itself is a passionate evocation of the loss of the child: 'how could I remember all that?' (*HE* 228). I will return to this in detail below. Here, my point is that the placing of the lyric and headnote just after Helen's refusal of the role of mother in Paris's oedipal drama marks the implications of woman's role in a masculine drama. That is, the woman becomes the means by which the man re-enacts his relationship to a maternal origin thus securing his privilege; but this is at the cost of the daughter's relationship to her mother, '"her" original topos, "her" origin' (*S* 41).

If the stake of the oedipal drama enacted by Paris is easily revealed, the network of identifications cast around Helen and Thetis by Achilles presents a more complex interrelating of masculine and feminine investments. The identification of Helen with Thetis in the lyrics is made from Achilles' point of view. We see him remembering his obsession with Helen in a way which turns out to be at odds with the warrior cult of masculinity. On the one hand he is 'the Achilles of legend, Lord of the Myrmidons, indisputable dictator with his select body-guard' (*HE* 51). However, he turns to the sight of Helen pacing the walls of Troy as 'a new oracle' (*HE* 53). In the lyric that follows they exchange a glance:

> you say, I could not see her eyes
> across the field of battle,
> I could not see their light
>
> shimmering as light on the changeable sea?
> all things would change but never
> the glance she exchanged with me.
>
> (*HE* 54)

The exchange is presented as against reason: 'you say I could not see'. But the image H.D. uses for Helen's eyes is that of 'light on the changeable sea', linking Helen with Thetis the sea-goddess. Helen's attraction for Achilles is a consequence of this identification.

The identification Achilles makes, and his recognition of his mother in Helen, are also marks of his value and the unacknowledged power of the mother. Although he makes the conventional identification of mother and lover, that identification is also indicated as narrated from elsewhere. It is Helen who invokes his mother's name at their first meeting. The identification which should 'guarantee a certain representation of the place of origin' (*S* 42) for the man is turned against masculinity in this poem. H.D. uses the psychoanalytic sub-text to display the relationship of the mother to the man's castration fear. The child, Achilles, makes a secret carving, an eidolon or image, that 'filled the eyes of the child / with terrible fire – ' (HE 285). The eidolon stands in for her:

> but he forgot her,
> the charm, the eidolon,
> when his own mother came,
>   (HE 292)

This representation is explicitly related to the mother, but as a mark of her absence:

> so he went to the prow
> of his love, of his beloved,
>
> feeling her flanks,
> tearing loose weed from her stern,
> brushing sand from her beams,
>
> not speaking, but praying:
>   (HE 248)

In the psychoanalytic terms with which the poem deals, the 'eidolon' and the 'prow' form fetish objects which allow the man to disavow his own castration through a disavowal of the mother's. The poem marks these as representations and substitutions, albeit exerting a powerful hold on both mother and son. Typically, H.D. engages with the psychoanalytic narrative, but distances herself from it by its very explicitness. Here, the man's stake in the narrative is revealed when the mother fails to ensure his narcissistic coherence, 'she cheated at last':

> she had promised him immortality
> but she had forgotten to dip the heel
> of the infant Achilles
>
> into the bitter water,
> Styx, was it?
> O careless, unspeakable mother,
>   (HE 253)

The theme of castration is present for both mother and son in this lyric. The Achilles heel and the son's death are both linked to the failure of the mother: 'so she failed at last' (HE 254). This reflects the Freudian account, and too the threat the 'castrated' woman represents for the man, in that as much as she confirms his own possession through her mutilation, she also displays its possibility, or worse the possibility of 'a nothing to see':[21]

and worse than failure,

the mockery, after-death
to stumble across a stretch
of shell and the scattered weed,

to encounter another
whose eyes slant in the old way:
is she Greek or Egyptian?
(*HE* 254)

However, the poem locates the castration narrative within a different project, the rewriting of masculinity. Thematically, H.D. uses Achilles' unconscious desire for his mother to rewrite and reform masculinity. His unconscious desire for his mother turns out to be the Achilles heel which will carry him beyond the warrior-cult.[22]

Achilles is stripped of his masculine and militaristic armour and 'as the new Mortal, / shedding his glory', he 'limped slowly across the sand' (*HE* 10). Achilles both loses and displays his glory in the pun on 'shedding'. This new being also limps, the Achilles heel of the legend, the man's castration becoming the motif of regeneration. The man's acceptance of castration becomes the sign of a new form of masculinity predicated on the retrieval of his relationship to his mother: 'the ecstasy of desire . . . / . . . melted him quite away, / till he knew his mother' (*HE* 260–1). This new man can be united with Helen in an image of 'androgyny' or 'bisexuality'. Their child, Euphorion, becomes the bisexual offspring of this utopian rewriting of sexual difference. 'The promised *Euphorion* is not one child but two [underlined words indicate author's emphasis]. It is "the child in Chiron's cave" [Achilles] and the "frail maiden," stolen by Theseus from Sparta [Helen]' (*HE* 288).[23]

Up to this point I have concentrated on Achilles' story as if masculinity were the poem's primary concern. However, *Helen in Egypt* tells another story – that of the daughter's desire for her mother. Helen 'knows' Achilles by 'the sea-enchantment in his eyes / of Thetis, his sea-mother' (*HE* 7). Thus Achilles' desire for his mother, the 'sea-enchantment', draws Helen to him. Here we have the mother as object of desire for Helen as much as for the man, and moreover, not as a locus of identification. Confirmation of this erotic link between Helen and Thetis can be found in the way *Helen in Egypt* narrates the son's story. Significantly, Achilles' story is told by Helen. From its beginning we learn that 'we see with the eyes of Helen' (*HE* 243) and that 'Helen recalls the scene of his boyhood' (*HE* 284). This is in spite of the frequent use of the first person, as if it were Achilles speaking as he does elsewhere in the poem. 'The memory', we learn, 'is really that of

Achilles but she lives it with him' (*HE* 260). Helen and Achilles are doubled in the telling of the story – it is her story as well as his. It is Helen who speaks Achilles' unconscious desire for his mother in his place: 'O mysterious treasure, / O idol, O eidolon, / with wings folded about her' (*HE* 291). This suggests Irigaray's proposition that the woman lacks a symbolisation of the daughter's story of her own mother. The story which locates her desire is that of the man and the man's mother. I would argue, however, that Helen has to use Achilles' story, the man's story of his mother, in order to tell a story of her erotic attachment to the mother, one which is not reducible to penis envy.

Although Helen's desire is for the man's mother, by ghosting Achilles' story she tells a story of desire, of the daughter for the mother, and not a story of identification. Identification would place her in a phallic narrative in which to be 'properly' feminine she must accept her lack and identify with her mother as 'castrated'. In this narrative her wound can be healed by giving birth to a son: 'she will be recompensed for her narcissistic humiliation, she will be able to love the "bearer of the penis", "perfectly" and "without ambivalence"' (*S* 107). The identification here is not however with the mother, and thus 'not the repetition, re-presentation, representation of *her* relationship to *her* mother' (*S* 107) since she is not 'a mother *like* her mother, mother of a daughter' (*S* 107). If she is 'mother of a daughter' then she reproduces her lack. A maternal identification for the woman within a phallic economy of representation leaves her with nothing that does not reconfirm the value of what she is not. Helen's ghosting of Achilles' desire for Thetis speaks the possibility of the woman's desire, and the reconstruction of the son's story at least represents a struggle to move beyond the definition of woman as 'castrated', although arguably Thetis still represents a pre-oedipal or phallic mother.

The difficulty of representing the specificity of the daughter's desire for *her* own mother as anything other than a narrative of betrayal and loss can be seen if we turn to the treatment of daughters' mothers in *Helen in Egypt*. H.D. implies that mothers are interchangeable in fantasy; one can just as well stand for another: 'your mother, / Leda, Thetis or Cythereaea' (*HE* 165), Thesus tells Helen. However, the representation of the daughters' mothers in the poem belies this confidence and tends to support Irigaray's argument that the daughter is exiled from her own mother.

The two principal versions of the daughter's mother are Leda and Helen herself as mother of Hermione. Leda, as I have already said, is little more than an eggshell. She is imaged as a womb to which Helen is invited to return for renewal: 'return to the Shell, your mother' (*HE* 165). Her significance is as a pre-oedipal fantasy of unity. In so far as gender enters into it, Leda represents the fantasy of a bisexual origin. She gives birth to two sets of twins of either gender – Helen and Clytaemnestra, and the brothers Castor and Pollux. The twinning is offered as a coming together of opposites, a fantasy of bisexuality, mortal and spirit, male and female, in Leda's womb/ shell. Thus Helen's origin is fantasised as a bisexual origin rather than a daughter's origin, so that the divisions and imbalances of sexual difference reappear. And although there is a promise of resolution this depends on the reformation of masculinity which is the poem's work.[24]

Helen's relationship to her daughter, Hermione, represents a narrative of betrayal, loss and abandonment. I have already briefly discussed the lyric in which Helen remembers the daughter whom she lost. The moment is registered as a break by the dropped work-basket:

> my child
> prattling of a bird-nest,
>
> playing with my work-basket;
> the reels rolled to the floor
> and she did not stoop to pick up
>
> the scattered spools but stared
> with wide eyes in a white face,
> at a stranger – and stared at her mother,
>
> a stranger – that was all,
>
> (HE 228)

The mother's loss is registered also as the child's loss of her mother and Helen's loss of her own relationship to herself as child. Thus the recovery of the relationship to the mother in the Thetis narrative heralds the birth of Euphorion and the recovery of herself as a child:

> and if I remember a child that stared
> at a stranger and the child's name is Hermione,
> it is not Hermione
>
> (HE 290)

This recovery of a lost and innocent self invokes the early Helen through her own abandoned daughter. Hermione therefore stands as a point of identification for Helen, as a moment of lost innocence prior to the Trojan war: 'Familiar fragrance, / late roses, bruised apples,' (HE 227). However, memories of the lost child propel her back into a narrative of betrayal and separation even as they enable a fantasy of a mother–daughter relationship in which Helen would be the child. That fantasy is supported by the autobiographical narrative on which the poem leans.

A familiarity with both H.D.'s biography and her earlier writing indicates the extent of the poem's autobiographical reference. The classical dramatis personae is as clearly autobiographical as the *roman-à-clef*, *Bid Me to Live*, with its contemporary London setting. Theseus, for example, is easily identified with Freud, and Achilles with Hugh Dowding, the Second World War air commander wih whom H.D. became preoccupied in the 1940s. The poem is not explained by these autobiographical details, which are not anyway available to all readers. The autobiography does however open another scene of writing. This scene is outside the poem, a reference to the poet's actual life, but nonetheless another text which the poem refers to and engages. H.D.'s mother's name is Helen, and Hermione is the name H.D. uses for the daughter in an autobiographical novel of the 1920s. H.D. herself describes the uncanny experience of making a sound recording of parts of the poem in 1955:

> I was alone and felt that I had an alter-ego, this *Helen*, speaking with my own voice, but with a self-assurance that I generally lack in everyday life . . . I had found myself, I had found my alter-ego or my double – and that my mother's name was *Helen* had no doubt something to do with it.[25]

She ghosts and is ghosted by her mother. Helen's fantasy of a return to childhood and lost innocence through an identification with the deserted daughter, Hermione, displaces the fantasy of a reunion with the daughter's mother onto the autobiographical scene. The autobiographical reinscribes the story of the daughter's mother, and the desire for her. Thus the poem registers the story of the daughter's mother by memorialising the loss of the mother, and the fantasy of a return to that origin as a daughter's rather than a bisexual origin.

It is Irigaray who theorises the stake of that fantasy outside the more familiar account in which the adult seeks to escape the divisions and losses of sexual difference through a return to the pre-oedipal mother. In a discussion of the child's desire to have a child with the mother, which might be represented in the child's play with dolls, Irigaray speculates on the difference which would be made to the woman were the Freudian account of femininity to entertain the idea that this child might be a girl:

> this fantasy of the woman-daughter would mean that the little girl, and her mother also, perhaps, want to be able to represent themselves as women's bodies that are both desired and desiring – But all this would require the repetition-displacement of the maternal function as it has been cathected by man. (S 36)

However, this fantasy is not simply accomplished in *Helen in Egypt*. The poem equally investigates the difficulties which lie in the relationship of the woman to the mother who stands as guarantor of the man's claim to the phallus. 'Is it true', H.D. wondered, 'that the only way to escape a war is to be in it?'[26]

NOTES

1. See 'Laugh of the Medusa', *New French Feminisms*, ed. Elaine Marks and Isabelle de Courtivron (Hemel Hempstead: Harvester Wheatsheaf, 1981), p. 251.
2. For more information about H.D. and good discussion of *Helen in Egypt* see Rachel Blau DuPlessis, *H.D.: The career of that struggle* (Hemel Hempstead: Harvester Wheatsheaf, 1986); Susan Stanford Friedman, *Psyche Reborn* (Bloomington: Indiana University Press, 1982).
3. Jan Montefiore, *Feminism and Poetry: Language, experience, identity in women's writing* (London: Pandora, 1987); Margaret Whitford, 'Rereading Irigaray', in *Between Feminism and Psychoanalysis*, ed. Teresa Brennan (London: Routledge, 1989), pp. 106–26; Kaja Silverman, *The Acoustic Mirror: The female voice in psychoanalysis and cinema* (Bloomington: Indiana University Press, 1988), pp. 141–86.
4. Whitford, 'Rereading Irigaray'; Margaret Whitford, 'Luce Irigaray and the female imaginary: Speaking as a woman', *Radical Philosophy* 43 (summer 1986) 3–8; Silverman, *The Acoustic Mirror*, pp. 143–7; Carolyn Burke, 'Irigaray through the looking glass', *Feminist Studies* 7, 2 (1981) pp. 288–306.
5. Lynne Segal, *Is the Future Female? Troubled Thoughts on Contemporary Feminism* (London: Virago, 1987), pp. 132–3; Kate McLuskie, 'Women's language and literature: A problem in women's studies', *Feminist Review* 14 (summer 1983); Janet Sayers, *Sexual Contradictions: Psychology, psychoanalysis and feminism* (London: Tavistock, 1986).
6. *Speculum of the Other Woman*, trans. Gillian C. Gill (Ithaca, NY: Cornell University Press, 1985), p. 42. Hereafter page references will appear in the text.
7. Victor Burgin, James Donald and Cora Kaplan, *Formations of Fantasy* (London: Methuen, 1986), p. 2. See also Sigmund Freud on psychical reality in 'The interpretation of dreams', *The Standard Edition of the Complete Psychological Works of Sigmund Freud*, ed. J. Strachey, vol. IV–V (London: Hogarth Press, 1953–74), p. 620.
8. Jean Laplanche and Jean-Bernard Pontalis, 'Fantasy and the origins of sexuality', in Burgin, Donald and Kaplan, *Formations of Fantasy*, pp. 27–8.
9. Laplanche and Pontalis, 'Fantasy and the origins of sexuality', p. 27.
10. See Laplanche and Pontalis for a discussion of the function of primal fantasy and phylogenesis in Freud's work.
11. Irigaray's concept of the same is one point at which her debt to Derrida is clear. For a discussion of this see Burke, 'Irigaray through the looking glass'.
12. For other critiques of Freud's concept of penis-envy see Rachel Bowlby, 'Still crazy after all these years', in *Between Feminism and Psychoanalysis*, ed. Brennan, pp. 40–59; Jacqueline Rose, *Vision in the Field of Difference* (London: Verso, 1986).
13. In 'Femininity' Freud does distinguish between two strata of identification for the woman. One is with the pre-oedipal mother who she takes as her model; the other is with the oedipal mother whom she rejects in favour of her father. Freud is unclear, however, as to the difference in the boy's and the girl's relationship to this pre-oedipal figure. See Silverman, *The Acoustic Mirror*, pp. 119–26.
14. *The Reproduction of Mothering: Psychoanalysis and the sociology of gender* (Berkeley: University of California Press, 1978), pp. 166–7.
15. Although Irigaray has sometimes been seen as supporting the concept of separate masculine and feminine libidos, her argument is that these would be different modalities of a single

libido. This avoids the problem of a gendered, natural sexual instinct. See Whitford, 'Rereading Irigaray', pp. 118–21, for a discussion of Irigaray's interest in a female imaginary as the support for a female sociality.

16. The turning round of classical myth to expose the place of femininity represents a woman's turn to modernist uses of myth. For a full discussion of this point see Alicia Suskin Ostriker, *Stealing the Language: The emergence of women's poetry in America* (London: The Women's Press, 1987), pp. 210–38.

17. DuPlessis, *H.D.*, p. 114.

18. *Helen in Egypt* (New York: New Directions, 1961), p. 293. Page references will hereafter appear in the body of the text.

19. 'Femininity' (1933), *The Complete Introductory Lectures on Psychoanalysis*, trans. J. Strachey (New York: Norton, 1966), p. 598.

20. H.D. went to Freud for psychoanalysis in 1933, and then again in 1934. For a full account see her *Tribute to Freud* (Boston: David R. Godine, 1974).

21. Irigaray writes that 'the woman, supposedly has *nothing* you can see. She exposes, exhibits the possibility of *a nothing to see. . . .* the 'signifier', of the possibility of an *other* libidinal economy . . .' (*Speculum*, pp. 47–8).

22. It should be remembered here that H.D. lived through two world wars in London, and the nuclear bombings of Japan. *Helen in Egypt* dates from the early years of the Cold War. The metaphors of sexual difference and militarism are inalienably linked in her writing. See Sandra M. Gilbert and Susan Gubar, *No Man's Land: The place of the woman writer in the twentieth century* vol. I, *The War of the Words* (New Haven: Yale University Press, 1988).

23. The bisexual child is also a key figure in H.D.'s memoir *End to Torment* (New York: New Directions, 1979), pp. 11–33.

24. For a discussion of the problems with bisexuality as a feminist concept see Hélène Cixous 'The laugh of the Medusa', in Marks and de Courtivron, pp. 253–4; and Irigaray, *Speculum*, pp. 25–33.

25. 'Compassionate friendship' (1955), TS. H.D. Papers. Beinecke Library, Yale University, pp. 14–16.

26. 'Compassionate friendship', p. 17.

Lynne Pearce

John Clare's *Child Harold*: The Road Not Taken

At length I came to a place where the road branched off into two turnpikes one to the right about and the other straight forward . . . I then suddenly forgot which was North or South and though I narrowly examined both ways I could see no bush or tree or stone heap that I could reccolect [*sic*] I had passed so I went on mile after mile almost convinced I was going the same way.

John Clare, 'Journey out of Essex', *Autobiographical Writings*, p. 157.

I confess it was with some reluctance that I accepted the invitation to write this essay. My clearest response to John Clare today is that he took up five years of my life that could have been much better spent doing something else. This resentment is augmented, in the immediate present, by the frustration of another summer spent patiently negotiating feminist readings of other male authors; first, my book on the representation of women by Pre-Raphaelite writers and artists, and latterly, my annual stint as reviewer for the Victorian Poetry section of *The Year's Work in English Studies*.[1] Such evidence of scholarship is all very well, but at this stage of my academic career (30 years old, just embarking on my first permanent post as university lecturer) I feel an urgent need to abandon the re-reading of 'dead male authors' and to actively engage with feminist writing, especially by women of my own generation. For this reason, when Susan Sellers first invited me to contribute this essay I asked, instead, to be allowed to work up a paper I had given earlier in the year on Jeanette Winterson and the lesbian construction of Romantic Love.[2] Since Rebecca O'Rourke had already chosen to write on the same author, my appeal failed and I was abandoned, once again, to John Clare.

I have prefaced this reading with these personal details (themselves against the grain of my usual critical practice) because I do, indeed, perceive my 'involvement' with John Clare to have been pre-determined by institutional forces. Clare was made my academic destiny when I was just 20 years old and submitting my applications for postgraduate research. John Clare, my tutor suggested, was a 'safe bet': on the margins, but respectable. He told me that 'a good book on Clare' had yet to be written. Not knowing what I really wanted to do, the subject of my doctoral thesis was thus decided for me.

By the time I took up my place at Birmingham University, I already knew that John Clare was not what I was primarily interested in: that my *pleasure* was in twentieth-century women's writing. In retrospect this seems hardly surprising: what 'education' is it that trains women to exert so much energy on texts that are implicitly (or, indeed, explicitly!) addressed to a male audience, when now, in the late twentieth century, we are surrounded by an ever-increasing store of contemporary feminist writing and 'reclaimed' women authors? Texts, that is, which speak directly to (and for) us, and which deal with matters of great relevance and political urgency.

Since my academic career has been founded on it, I naturally subscribe to the continuing importance of 'feminist critique'; this said, all the sexual politics in the world cannot now prevent me from looking back on my five years exploring 'John Clare and Mikhail Bakhtin: the dialogic principle' without regret. As I say to anyone who asks me why, in these days of radicalised gender consciousness, I should want to dedicate all my energies to contemporary women writers ('when there is so much good writing by men around'!): time is short. Despite what seems to some of my friends and colleagues to be a blind partisanship, I know that my bookshelves are still dominated by male authors and that at least 90 per cent of my teaching to date has been directed to re-reading, revising, but ultimately *upholding*, the male canon. And my activities this summer will have done the same. For this reason, readers will appreciate that the reading which follows is inscribed in resentment: that its resentment is the site of its feminism.

TOWARDS A FEMINIST READING OF *CHILD HAROLD*

It is significant that although I was practising feminist criticism when I began work on Clare, it never occurred to me that my thesis should involve feminist critique. From the beginning, the questions I asked – about voices, about the function of the personal pronoun, about Clare's attitude to language and the role of the imagination – were non-gender-specific. These were broad textual/theoretical problems supposedly above and beyond gender: problems, so I believed, that were available to any reader (regardless of sex) to do what he/she liked with.

What I propose to do in this essay is go back over those readings and write in the gender. It seems especially shocking to me now that I could have

looked so closely into the function of the voice and intonation in Clare's work
– terms that are *necessarily* gender-specific – without ever directly confronting
the sex of the speaker, listener, or reader. Although I was concerned to
establish a power-dynamic amongst Clare's different speakers, the *sexual politics*
of the relationship was never addressed. How texts 'position' their readers has
become a matter of increasing concern in recent literary theory, and in my re-
reading of Clare's love-poem I shall be especially interested in the way in which
it welcomes or excludes a female audience.[3] Needless to say, my initial response
to the text – as an asexual, liberal-humanist reading subject – was unencumbered by such anxieties. Not only could I suppose Clare was speaking to me,
'the reader', but also that his voices were ones that I could read through,
'identify with'. The 'I'/'You' dynamic that Bakhtinian criticism made so
productive in theoretical terms might be 'stitched' to a material context in a
way that has made it especially attractive to Marxists, though few readers have
yet examined how that dynamic is circumscribed by gender and sexuality.[4]
This relates to the second preoccupation of my re-reading: namely, the
representation of Romantic Love in *Child Harold*, and the literary traditions to
which that representation belongs. As with the question of the voices, I see
now that any reading which ignores the specifics of the discourse – man as
lover, woman as object of love – is undermining its politics. For me, this has
been a painful reproof. Like Marion Shaw *vis-à-vis* Tennyson, I am haunted by
lines of Clare's poem which occur to me at 'times of grief', stress, and doubt.[5]
My theoretical consciousness now tells me that such 'empathy' across gender is
wholly problematic: not only are Clare's speakers heterosexual males, but they
also belong to literary traditions that constitute the female merely as object.
Although, as I have argued in my book on the Pre-Raphaelites, women *can*
appropriate such texts 'against the grain', there is usually a *context* which makes
such a procedure unacceptable.[6] That context, I shall argue here, is the obverse
of the Romantic Love discourse: Clare's writing, in prototypically Victorian
manner, generates Romantic Love against, and out of, discourses of profound
misogyny. Amid a whole spectrum of clichés, the Virgin and the Whore (or,
more particularly, Mary and Martha) are the cornerstones of Clare's love
poetry: even as *Child Harold* celebrates the idealised love of childhood
innocence, so does *Don Juan* (located in the same originating manuscript)
torrent violent, scatological abuse on all women. While I was advised to avoid
Don Juan as a graduate student, re-reading these manuscripts from a feminist
perspective means that such evasion is entirely impossible. What other critics
have read as Clare's tender, enduring love for his childhood sweetheart is
inextricable from the fear and loathing that circulate on the other side of the
discourse; on the other side of the page.[7]

CHILD HAROLD: TEXT AND CONTEXT

At this point it is necessary that I provide some basic information for readers not familiar with John Clare and his work. Usually grouped with the Romantics, although his career extends well into the Victorian era (1793–1864), Clare has traditionally been presented as a 'nature poet' whose unhappy life, from 'peasant' to 'madman', is better known than his actual work. Critical interest in the twentieth century, moreover, has divided fairly evenly between those who prefer to cast him in his former role (the 'nature poet' whose peasant origins give his verse an 'authenticity' lacking in Wordsworth *et al.*), and those who have seen, in his later works, the off-beam genius of another Blake.

The only biographical information that is of particular relevance to what follows here concerns his education and his relationships with women. With respect to the former, it should be noted that Clare's education, though assisted by good schooling, was largely that of a self-made man.[8] He learnt to write poetry through a sketchy apprenticeship of reading it, and throughout his life his debts to other writers are obvious, sometimes to the point of plagiarism.[9] As with the Brontës, it was the folly of much early Clare criticism to suppose that because he lived outside recognised cultural circles his inspiration was somehow 'non-literary': almost the exact opposite is the case. Clare's work, from beginning to end, carries more visible traces of his literary forebears and contemporaries than many other writers. His poems exist as testaments to the competing literary traditions which informed his education: not only was he Stephen Duck (an earlier peasant poet), he was also Marvell, Crabbe, Byron. The belief in a quintessential 'John Clare', the authentic voice of rural labour, is somewhat misplaced. In fact, the aspects of Clare's writing which appear to render him most 'authentic' – his use of dialect words, his use of colloquial language – themselves belong to another tradition: that of the ballad.[10]

As far as Clare's relationships with women are concerned, the Mary and Martha of his poems do have their counterparts (though not necessarily their *origins*) in actual life. The received history is that Clare met Mary Joyce when he was about 16, and she 12, and that they enjoyed a 'romantic friendship' until, at the age of 17, Mary's parents objected to her liaison with a labourer's son (Mary's parents were small farmers at Glinton). Sometime after this, Clare met, courted and impregnated Martha Turner ('Patty'), whom he subsequently married and lived with until his removal to High Beech asylum in 1844.

After Clare 'escaped' from Matthew Allen's establishment and made the extraordinary 100 mile walk back to Northamptonshire, Patty agreed to 'try him at home again', but this failed and six months later, he was admitted to Northamptonshire Lunatic Asylum where he spent the remaining twenty years of his life.[11]

It is not known whether Clare had any relationships with women beyond these two, but his journals – and certainly his asylum manuscripts – show that he had an obsessional 'eye' for them. The catalogues of names and addresses found in Northampton MS 19, for example, are as disturbing as those sometimes found amongst the documents of sex-murderers.[12] It is not clear whether or not Clare actually got to know any of these women, but their proximity seems to have caused him deep sexual excitement, as is evidenced both in his journal entries and his many (unsent!) letters:

> My Dear Eliza
> How I long to see you and to kiss that pretty Face – I mean 'Eliza Dadford' how I should like to walk with you in the snow where I helped to shake your carpets & take the oppertunity [sic] we neglected then to kiss on the green grass & Love you even better then before . . .
> I am My Dear Eliza Dadford yours forever
>
> J. Clare [1849–50][13]

The letters are one of the most visible indexes of Clare's fluctuating attitudes to women: the tenderness of his 'devotion' to Mary Joyce (his 'Angel'), contrasting with his domestic fondness for Patty, and contrasting again with these lascivious propositions to the women of his fantasy.

His divided loyalty to Mary and Martha is a recurrent motif in the asylum manuscripts, and central to *Child Harold*, in which he repeatedly admits to the crime of bigamy and evinces considerable torment over his duty to his 'two wives':

> My dear wife Mary
> I might have said my first wife & first love & first everything – but I shall never forget my second wife & second love for I loved her once as dearly as yourself – & almost do so now so I determined to keep you both for ever . . .
> your affectionate Husband
> John Clare [May? 1841][14]

What I propose we see in this muddle of emotion towards the opposite sex is not the confusion of a deranged individual, but rather the site of competition between a number of prototypical Victorian discourses on women and sexuality. In the same way that Clare's poems are the palimpsest of numerous literary traditions, so is his representation of women a revealing catalogue of their confused and contradictory status in mid-Victorian culture.

CHILD HAROLD: TEXT AND THEORY

Child Harold was never published in John Clare's own lifetime. Written
during his stay at Matthew Allen's Asylum in High Beech, Essex, it is to be
found in two main manuscripts, identified in the Northampton Public
Museum Collection as MS 6 and MS 8.[15] Of these sources, MS 8 is the
earliest, being the small pocket-book Clare kept during his time at the
asylum and then during his 'escape'. As I have shown in my thesis, MS 8 is
an extraordinary document in which poems, letters, biblical paraphrases,
quotations and accounts are bizarrely juxtaposed.[16] *Child Harold* and *Don
Juan* are the two major poems contained in the manuscript, while entries to
the Journal ('Journey out of Essex') frequently occur at the foot of the pages
containing the poems.[17] MS 6 is the larger manuscript book into which
Clare made 'fair copies' of his poems, paraphrases and journal.

One of the objectives of my doctoral thesis was to explore the relationship
between the formal presentation of texts in these manuscripts, and their
'polyphonic' nature. Although previously registered as a simple sign of his
derangement, all readers coming to Clare's later poems must recognise their
general instability in terms of lyric and/or narrative voice. Whatever
'essential' John Clare may be constructed from the early poems, there is no
single unitary ego to be found in a text like *Child Harold*. Instead, the reader
is presented with a collection of different voices or 'personae' which lack a
controlling authorial consciousness. By using Bakhtin's celebration of the
'polyphonic text' in his *Problems of Dostoevsky's Poetics* I was able to convert
this apparent 'weakness' (critics had generally dismissed *Child Harold* in terms
of its lack of 'coherence', 'development', 'resolution') into aesthetic
precociousness:

> The new artistic position of the author with regard to the hero in Dostoevsky's
> polyphonic novel is a *fully-realized and thoroughly consistent dialogic position*, one
> that affirms the independence, internal freedom, unfinalizability, and indeter-
> minancy of the hero. For the author the hero is not 'he' and not 'I' but a fully-
> valid 'thou', that is, another and autonomous 'I' ('Thou art').[18]

Despite my repeated transcription of passages like the above, with its
'innocent' perpetration of the masculine pronoun, I never pursued the
feminist implications of my masculine theoretical model any more than I did
the gender of the speakers in the poem. Both were accepted as 'givens', and
while I was actively performing feminist analyses of male-authored texts
elsewhere, my preoccupation with the technicalities of 'dialogic art' allowed
blatant patriarchal collusion.

The highlight of my research on the asylum manuscripts was the discovery that the MS 6 version of *Child Harold* has been carefully divided into groups of stanzas and songs according to a system of line divisions.[19] I subsequently used this formal organisation of the text to support my own 'polyphonic reading', arguing that it contained at least six identifiable speakers, most of whom could be linked to a specific literary tradition.[20] Needless to say, all these speakers were male and although one way I distinguished between them was according to social class (the 'aristocratic rake' and the 'peasant lover'), I persistently failed to register the implications of the power-dynamic *vis-à-vis the female subject of the text.*

Central to my system of classification was also Bakhtin's notion of 'intonation', which critics like Katerina Clark and Michael Holquist have seen as a crucial element in Bakhtin's dialogic view of language, in that it registers any utterance as a *contextual experience*, involving the speaker, the listener (the addressee in the text) and the reader.[21] By focusing on the relationship between the speaker in a text and his/her addressee, we are able to characterise him/her in terms of relative power. All speech-acts (whether in living conversation or in texts) reveal the relative status of the speaker according to the attitude he/she adopts towards his/her interlocutor. In my reading of *Child Harold* I therefore used this means of 'identifying' speakers according to the 'tone' they adopt towards their interlocutors to distinguish between the different voices which comprise the poem, aided by the fact that intonation is also a register of social (and in this case *socio-literary*) context (see Clark and Holquist above).

RE-READING *CHILD HAROLD*: SPEAKER/LISTENER/READER

It now seems to me extraordinary that I ignored the gender implicit in such a context: failed to observe that the power-dynamic existing between the different speakers is *always* gender-specific. If we take the first of the voices, that of the 'Byronic lover', we see that his authority – what I earlier described as the register of his social class – is manifested through the arrogance with which he treats his female subjects. Although in the final stanza of the sequence beginning 'My life hath been one love – no blot it out' (*Later Poems*, 1, p. 45), this speaker extends his contempt (like Byron's Manfred) to the world in general ('Cares gather round I snap their chains in two / & smile in agony & laugh in tears'), the real site of his supremacy is his droit de seigneur:

> I have had many loves – & seek no more –
> These solitudes my last delights shall be
> The leaf hid forest – & the lonely shore
> Seem to my mind like beings that are free
> Yet would I had some eye to smile on me
> Some heart where I could make a happy home in
> Sweet Susan that was wont my love to be
> & Bessey of the Glen – for I've been roaming
> With both at morn & noon & dusky gloaming
>   (*Later Poems*, 1, p. 47)[22]

While in my earlier readings I focused on Clare's rhetorical debt to Byron in stanzas such as this one, it goes without saying (or, at least, I allowed it to go without saying!) that the rhetoric was concomitant with a particular discourse of sexuality.

Where this leaves the feminist reader is not, however, immediately obvious. In theoretical terms we have supposedly moved beyond simple moral/political outrage at the perpetration of such negative images, and most recent work on the representations of women in Victorian culture has concentrated on dispassionately elucidating the discourses which give rise to them.[23] This work aside – and one of the purposes of this essay is to demonstrate the contradictory discourses in Clare's poem – I feel there is a need for the twentieth-century feminist reader to consider the way in which she is *positioned* by such texts; the way in which she is excluded, silenced, rendered invisible. For my overwhelming impression on re-reading the 'Byronic' passages of Clare's poem is that they dispense with the female reader as contemptuously as they dispense with the female subject. Clare's speaker addresses his remarks to a male auditor: women are merely items of linguistic/cultural exchange.

It is wholly significant that the Byronic persona of *Child Harold* habitually refers to Mary, as well as to women in general, in the third person. She is the object of his address, not the subject, no matter how indulgently he presents her:

> From school days of boyhood her image was cherished
> In manhood sweet Mary was fairer than flowers
> Nor yet has her name or her memory perished
> Though absence like winter oer happiness lowers
>   (*Later Poems*, 1, p. 43)

When we turn to the other speakers, however, the situation is quite opposite. In the Petrarchan sequence beginning with the stanza 'This twilight seems a veil of gauze & mist' (*Later Poems*, 1, p. 49), the speaker is suppliant to his lady in the manner of the courtly love tradition: he is obstensibly her *victim*:

> Remind me not of other years or tell
> My broken hopes of joys they are to meet
> While thy own falsehood rings the loudest knell
> To one fond heart that aches too cold to beat
> Mary how oft with fondness I repeat
> That name alone to give my troubles rest
> The very sound though bitter seemeth sweet –
> In my loves home & thy own faithless breast
> Truths bonds are broke & every nerve distrest
>
> Life is to me a dream that never wakes
> Night finds me on this lengthening road alone
> Love is to me a thought that ever aches
> A frost bound thought that freezes life to stone
> Mary in truth & nature still my own
> That warms the winter of my aching breast
> Thy name is joy nor will I life bemoan –
> Midnight when sleep takes charge of natures rest
> Finds me awake and friendless – not distrest
> ...
> For her for one whose very name is yet
> My hell or heaven – & will ever be
> Falsehood is doubt – but I can ne'er forget
> Oaths virtuous falsehood volunteered to me
> To make my soul new bonds which God made free
> Gods gift is love & do I wrong the giver
> To place affections wrong from Gods decree
> – No[w] when farewell upon my lips did quiver
> & all seemed lost – I loved her more than ever
>   (*Later Poems*, 1, pp. 49–50)

Temporarily leaving aside the sexual politics of this convention, it is important to consider the significance of this dynamic for the *female reader* of the text; to ask whether or not the power reversal positions *her* differently? Beyond Mary's representation as 'love-object' there is a case for arguing that the intimate dialogue between speaker and addressee in these stanzas does, at least, tolerate the presence of a female reader. If she is not directly included in the text, she may, nevertheless, 'eavesdrop'. More problematic, however, is whether she may legitimately transgress gender boundaries and position herself 'alongside' the speaker (i.e. identify, 'empathise', with him). In liberal-humanist terms, the confused expressions of desire, loss, helpless-ness, distress, may be seen as part of the 'universal condition', yet as soon as we begin to examine the sexual politics of the text hitherto suspended, rather than the dialogic exchange *per se*, any innocent alignment becomes untenable. Put simply, as long as we read these stanzas as a particularised exchange between one individual and another – the 'I'/'You' dynamic – the question of gender can be suspended. The lyric form allows us to substitute a female speaker or, indeed, to insert ourselves in her place. As soon as we begin to *contextualise* the lines, however – to identify the conventions they use and the literary traditions to which they belong – we (as female readers) are once more denied the possibility of vicarious identification. Although Marxists and feminists have perceived the political potential of the 'social context' implicit in the dialogic model, there is still a tendency to observe its constraints only selectively. Hence my ability to consider the differential class-locations on Clare's speakers, without observing the conjunction of gender.

The problematic relationship of speaker, listener and reader present in the Petrarchan section of *Child Harold* is repeated in many of its songs and ballads. These include some of the poem's most 'powerless' voices; speakers who are not only humble before the beloved, but who are also helpless. In the song 'I think of thee at early day', for example, the simplicity of the verse-form (regular abab quatrains) combines with the impotence of the statement (he is able to do no more than 'think of her') to create a speaker whose experience and expectations are severely limited:

> I think of thee at early day
> & wonder where my love can be
> & when the evening shadows grey
> O how I think of thee
> (*Later Poems*, 1, p. 72)[24]

I would suggest, however, that, as with the Petrarchan sequence, the conventions of the tradition – the fixing of the speaker as male and the addressee as female – will ultimately militate against full involvement. As feminist film theorists have suggested *vis-à-vis* Hollywood cinema, the woman viewer can only enter such texts by becoming a surrogate male, or by a process of what Teresa de Lauretis has called 'double-identification': that is, by aligning herself alternatively with the male viewing position and the women who are the object of the gaze.[25] Any woman reading this poem with gender consciously to the fore must, in my opinion, recognise her historical solidarity with Mary; no matter how much she might 'sympathise' with the plight of the narrator. To this extent, it could be argued that the sections of Clare's poem which feature sympathetic male speakers are no more 'available' to the feminist reader than those that feature the aggressive, misogynistic libertines. The sexual politics of the respective literary traditions always ultimately subsume the formal dynamics of the individual texts. My opinion, in retrospect, is that *all* Clare's speakers in *Child Harold* operate within traditions and discourses that effectively exclude the woman reader – as long, that is, as she retains a sense of her own gendered identity.

CONCLUSION: TRESPASSING

> I dreaded walking where there was no path
> And prest with cautious tread the meadow swath,
> And always turned to look with wary eye,
> And always feared the farmer coming by;
> Yet everything about where I had gone
> Appeared so beautiful I ventured on;
> And when I gained the road where all are free
> I fancied every stranger frowned at me,
> And every kinder look appeared to say,
> 'You've been on trespass in your walk today.'
> I've often thought, the day appeared so fine,
> How beautiful if such a place were mine;
> But having naught I never feel alone
> And cannot use another's as my own.
>   John Clare, 'Trespass'[26]

Writing this essay has caused me to return to a text, author and period of my academic life that I shelved, three years ago, with considerable relief. I did not want to make the journey back and, as I indicated in my preliminary remarks, did so only with reluctance. My feelings, in retrospect, are much the same as those I set out with.

This was not a difficult piece for me to write because Clare's poem, and the ways into it, were still familiar to me. My practice was simply to follow the roads back to the places I had been before, and to reconsider my position there as a woman. As a woman, I felt mostly that I should not have been there in the first place; a feeling similar, perhaps, to that expressed by Clare's speaker in the sonnet 'Trespass' (quoted above) which describes the effects of Enclosure on the peasant community.[27]

Our problem, as women readers and critics, is that none of these texts were ever our 'common-land'. Literary theory has shown us new routes into them, enabled us to tap their mechanisms and subvert their exclusions, but it has not enabled us to also make them our property.

Therefore, although I think we should continue to visit such texts, in the way that we continue to visit all sites of historic interest, we should not delude ourselves that we have come to own them. Rather, I believe it is our duty as feminists to retain a sense of our marginality: any easy appropriation of 'meaning' from a nineteenth-century male-authored text indicates that we have indeed forgotten our place, transcended our gender.

By the same token, we must also question the political value of such activity. Since our resources as readers and scholars are *not* expendable, is it legitimate to devise ever more subtle means of making hostile texts speak to us, when there are so many others – directly addressed to us – requiring to be heard? A socialist may argue that trespassing is, on occasion, a politically useful act: a contravention of existing property laws. To an extent this is true, and as long as we are expected to teach and study 'the canon' in its present form, trespassing will remain a necessary activity.

When it comes to making scholarly choices beyond this, however, I would advise any female students about to embark on postgraduate research to think carefully. Any author or text which causes you to suspend your gendered identity, for whatever theoretical purpose, should be regarded with caution. Trespassing may be fun for the occasional afternoon only, but is it something you want to dedicate your life to?

NOTES

1. *Woman-Image-Text: Readings in Pre-Raphaelite art and literature* (Hemel Hempstead: Harvester Wheatsheaf, forthcoming 1991).
2. I presented this paper, entitled "Jane Eyre eat your heart out": Jeanette Winterson's re-reading of Romantic Love in *Oranges Are Not the Only Fruit*' at the Northern Network meeting in Durham in March 1990. Many of my retrospective thoughts on John Clare's love poetry owe, indirectly, to things I worked out there.
3. See in particular the collection of essays, *Contextualized Stylistics*, ed. M. Toolan (London: Routledge, 1991).
4. Many new books on Bakhtin have appeared in recent years, but still the most comprehensive in its interpretation/analysis is (to my knowledge) Katerina Clark and Michael Holquist's *Mikhail Bakhtin* (Cambridge, Mass. and London: Harvard University Press, 1984). Another useful introduction to the wide cultural applicability of Bakhtinian thought is Robert Stam's *Subversive Pleasures* (Baltimore: Johns Hopkins University Press, 1989).
5. See Marion Shaw, *Alfred Lord Tennyson* (Hemel Hempstead: Harvester Wheatsheaf, 1988). Shaw writes: 'And at times of grief, fragments of *In Memoriam* spring unbidden to mind in ways which I both distrust and am grateful for because they make a (male) artefact of my (female) experience. If I dismiss Tennyson, I dismiss my past; in any case, it cannot be done, I am in possession of this voice from the past' (p. 5).
6. See my Introduction to *Woman-Image-Text*. My line in this book is that although some texts are more available to feminist appropriation than others, the context of their original production/consumption will remain a problem for the Marxist-feminist reader.
7. *Don Juan*, like *Child Harold*, was written by Clare as an 'additional canto' to Byron's poem of the same name. While in technical terms it closely parodies the original, its prurience

exceeds it. A particular obsession is the fantasy of Queen Victoria's orgiastic infidelity (!). The following stanza is a representative sample of the tenor of the whole:

> Children are fond of sucking sugar candy
> & maids of sausages – larger the better
> Shopmen are fond of good sigars [sic] & brandy
> & I of blunt – & if you change the letter
> To C or K it would be quite as handy
> & throw the next away – but I'm your debtor
> For modesty – yet wishing nought between us
> I'd hawl close to a she as vulcan did to venus
> (*Later Poems*, 1, p. 92)

The 'symbiotic' relationship of *Child Harold* and *Don Juan* is dramatically evidenced in MS 8 where the opening stanzas of both poems appear one after the other on the same page. This can be taken as evidence that Clare did, indeed, conceive/compose the two simultaneously.

8. Most of the selections of Clare's work include biographical introductions. For example, *Selected Poems and Prose of John Clare*, ed. Eric Robinson and Geoffrey Summerfield (Oxford: Oxford University Press, 1967); *John Clare*, ed. Eric Robinson and David Powell (Oxford: Oxford University Press, Oxford Authors Series, 1984); *John Clare: Selected poetry and prose*, ed. Merryn and Raymond Williams (London: Methuen, 1987). The best biography is still J.W. and Anne Tibble's *John Clare: His life and poetry* (London: Heinemann, 1956).

9. In my thesis I deal extensively with Clare's literary 'debts': from what Bakhtin called 'stylization', through parody, and including outright forgery. During one period of his life, Clare was successful in presenting newspapers and periodicals with the 'lost' work of sixteenth- and seventeenth-century poets. He even invented a surrogate persona – Percy Green – to be the author of some of these, before he was eventually found out.

10. Clare's own autobiography (see *John Clare's Autobiographical Writings*, ed. Eric Robinson, Oxford: Oxford University Press, 1983) stresses the importance of the ballad tradition in his literary development. His own father sang and played the fiddle, and during one period of his life Clare began collecting local Northamptonshire ballads.

11. Clare was fortunate in that both asylums were enlightened establishments which allowed him considerable personal freedom and encouraged him to pursue his writings.

12. Looking back over MS 19 I was struck by the extensiveness of these lists. On one page, for example, is written: Mary Hobbs, Fanny Broughton, Eliza Jones, Susan Harris, Ann Macpherson, Mary Anne Sweeny, Jane Hobbs. Sometimes the names are followed by a location, for example: 'Maxey', 'Glinton'. Although no proper work has been done on identifying these women, many are known to have existed and were not simply figments of Clare's imagination.

13. From *John Clare: Selected letters*, ed. Mark Storey (Oxford: Clarendon Press, 1988), p. 214. Many of these letters are written in code, emphasising their clandestine nature.

14. *Selected letters*, pp. 200–1.

15. Related material is also to be found in Northampton MSS 7, 49, 57 and Bodleian MSS Don. a. 8 and Don. c. 64.

16. See Chapters One and Two of my thesis, 'John Clare and Mikhail Bakhtin – the dialogic principle: readings from John Clare's manuscripts 1832–45', unpublished Ph.D. thesis (University of Birmingham, 1987).

17. The Journal is reproduced in *John Clare's Autobiographical Writings*.

18. From Mikhail Bakhtin, *Problems of Dostoevsky's Poetics*, trans. Caryl Emerson (Manchester: Manchester University Press, 1984), p. 63.

19. See my article, 'John Clare's "Child Harold": a polyphonic reading', *Criticism* 31 (2), (spring, 1989), 139–57, and, in particular, note 1 (p. 154).

20. The principal literary sources for the 'voices' include: Byron, Philip Sidney (the 'Petrarchan' lover), the ballad (the 'peasant' lover), the Bible, Wordsworth (the Romantic contemplative poem). See my article cited in note 19 above for a full analysis of these.

21. Clark and Holquist, *Mikhail Bakhtin*.
22. The text of *Child Harold* is reproduced from *The Later Poems of John Clare*, ed. Eric Robinson and David Powell (2 vols; Oxford: Oxford University Press, 1984).
23. See, for example, Lynda Nead, *Myths of Sexuality* (Oxford: Basil Blackwell, 1987).
24. For a fuller exposition of this see my article cited in note 19 above.
25. Teresa de Lauretis, *Alice Doesn't: Feminism, semiotics, cinema* (London: Macmillan, 1984). Cited by Mary Anne Douane in *The Desire to Desire: The woman's film in the 1940s* (Bloomington: Indiana University Press, 1987).
26. The reason this early sonnet by Clare is punctuated is that the text has been taken from the Tibbles' 1935 edition, *The Poems of John Clare*, (2 vols, London and New York: Dent, Dutton, 1935). It was the practice of Clare's early editors to 'correct' Clare's work in this way.
27. The village of Helpstone was enclosed when Clare was 16 years old. Many of his poems (e.g. 'The Mores', 'Remembrances', 'The Parish') refer explicitly to the changes this wrought on the countryside and the alienation he suffered as a result.

Elaine Hobby

'Oh Oxford Thou Art Full of Filth': The Prophetical Writings of Hester Biddle, 1629[?]–1696

Essex University, October 1978; 1642 and the Sociology of Literature. She (I?) was in a classroom, surrounded by other students, embarking on the study of what was then a fairly new phenomenon in Britain, something now called Critical Theory. This MA course was intended to focus on 1642, the year of the outbreak of the English Revolution; the students were to read new theory, and work out how to use it in relation to seventeenth-century texts. She (I?) was there to learn about the theory, wanting to use it to study nineteenth-century women novelists, a desire inspired by Elaine Showalter's *A Literature of Their Own*; knowing nothing about 1642 and caring less. The point was to explore how best to study women, how to think about gender in history in a properly theorised way. But no one else there seemed to care about women (I know now that this is not true: but it is how it seemed), and in confusion and anger she (I?) erupted, 'What about women?' 'Don't worry dear, there weren't any then.' And in that moment began the activity that has become central to my life: the rediscovery of seventeenth-century women's writing.

I have told this story many times; so many that it seems both more true and less true than it is. Sitting in Beeston, Nottingham now in October 1990, trying to think back to that time so that I can explain why I do what I do as a feminist critic, I realise I cannot remember the incident at all: all I can recall is some of the times I have told the story, and I am acutely aware that my version of what happened in Essex that year is partial and in some ways unfair. And if even that moment of my own history is now so vague to me, and my understanding of it so radically affected by the stories I have told about it and by changes in my life since (then I was a student, and we were living in the death throes of a Labour Government, now I am a teacher, and there is Thatcherism and all we have lost to contend with); how can I hope to understand a much more distant history, that of Hester Biddle and her allies and enemies? I don't know. But I do know that I was at Essex University in 1978, and that some exchange like the one in my story took place, and catapulted me into this passion which gives me so much joy. And I do know that in 1649 our ancestors – some of them – cut off the king's head, and that for eleven years, until the Restoration of the Monarchy in 1660, radical and reactionary groups engaged in struggles over how the country was to be run, and in whose interests. And I also know that many women were involved in these upheavals, publishing pamphlets and publicly challenging male authority figures such as church ministers and members of parliament. Those things happened, whatever some of the cleverer versions of contemporary critical theory say about the impossibility of writing history because all we have is documents, not actual events, and because we read those documents through the distorting lens of our own culture. On my ruder days, I think that the current theoretical dismissal of history is merely an excuse for not doing 'proper work': you can sit in your bath and play with words; to consider the past as the past you have to spend days, weeks, years trawling through nearly incomprehensible documents trying to make sense of them, trying to stay alert to how they put into question your preconceptions about your material. You have to use theory against history and history against theory. It takes years and years to write a book. On my more sober days, I suspect that this abandoning of archival research is the outcome of something more troubling within academia today: as the pressure to 'publish or perish' has spread from the United States to Britain – and, I suppose, elsewhere – it has become essential for academics to publish, and publish, and publish if they are to get a job, or keep one. We are being refused the time to do research of the kind I think valuable, and some of the apparent theoretical justifications for the abandoning of history are a caving-in under economic pressures, and will in time to come be understood as that. I am worried that if we lose what the study of history is able to teach us – that society has changed, and that oppressed people's insistence that it must change has forced some of those transformations – then we will lose our sense that society can, and must, change again, and that we can change it.

In this essay, I want to examine a short pamphlet by a seventeenth-century radical, Hester Biddle. I know very little about her, except that she died in 1696 and was born about 1629; that she was raised an Anglican but joined the Quakers and travelled around Britain, to Amsterdam, Newfoundland, Barbados, and, in the 1690s to France (meeting Louis XIV), spreading her message; that she was arrested for these activities on more than one occasion and imprisoned. Between 1655 and 1662 she published a number of pamphlets, and between 1663 and 1668 she had four sons with Thomas Biddle, a shoemaker, who died soon thereafter (Rickman, 1955). I have chosen to write about Hester Biddle's *Woe to thee, city of Oxford* because of that pamphlet's formative status in my research. Before I first read it, I thought I was working on seventeenth-century women's poetry. The day Hester Biddle's words arrived on my desk I realised that that simply would not do. By working on poetry alone I was allowing academic convention to dictate what was 'worthy of study' and what was to be used as 'background information' to that study. (I was reading *Woe to thee* to provide a context to the work of women poets.) That academic convention, as I already knew, was male and middle class (later I came to realise that it is also white and heterosexual, though the significance of those aspects did not strike me in 1979 when Biddle's words first arrived in my life). Biddle's pamphlet, which threatens to burn the two university towns to the ground because of their role in reproducing and maintaining social hierarchies, brought me up short, and gave me the courage and compulsion to refuse to be bound by a modern sense of 'literature' in the emphasis I gave my materials.

In choosing to write now about *Woe to thee, city of Oxford* I am faced with another dilemma that my work constantly confronts me with. Here I am, studying the perhaps 300 or more texts that were published by women between 1649 and 1688, and almost none of those writings has been in print since the seventeenth century. If I don't write about them, most people will not even know they exist (though this is changing, as more women are working on this material). But what is the use of my writing about these texts if readers can't look at them for themselves? What is the point of my making analytical remarks about Hester Biddle's work when not one word of it is available to the modern reader? What I have done here, therefore, is what I also do in my working life generally. Part of this essay is given over to a reproduction of Biddle's *Woe to thee, city of Oxford* so that others can read her words too, and perhaps use them in ways quite different from mine. Readers should bear in mind though, that what they have here is Biddle as mediated by me: I have modernised her spelling, and introduced or changed punctuation marks where the original seems so odd as to hinder comprehension. And the footnotes and parenthetical interpolations are also mine, and may include many errors and misdirections that are not intentional, but are the inevitable result of my ideological preoccupations (some of which are invisible to me). Schooled as I am in modern theories, and especially marxist analyses of the relationship between texts and ideologies, I cannot but be aware that seventeenth-century Britain has a foreign culture, one I am trying to understand. Not only is Biddle's reading of her own culture necessarily ideological, but so is mine; and differently so. Constantly, I read things written then that force me to realise that something I had thought or assumed was true of that period is not, and that as a result, something I have said or written about a seventeenth-century text is inaccurate or irrelevant or misleading.

My feminism helps greatly in living with this provisionality, this constant sense of the past changing in front of me, whilst at the same time it gives me courage to acknowledge my mistakes and try again. I do not ever want to become so much the academic that I am too frightened of loss of face to admit when I have got things wrong, or to say what I think simply and clearly so that others can understand and criticise it too. (I don't want to become one of those whom Hester Biddle would burn to the ground in her wrath.)

Woe to thee, city of Oxford was probably published about May 1655. (A copy owned by George Thomason, a seventeenth-century collector, dates it 24 May 1655.) It is a political pamphlet, threatening the university towns with destruction by fire if they do not heed Biddle's message. The copy I edit here is addressed only to Oxford, but there is an almost identical pamphlet, published by Biddle on the same day, addressed to the town of Cambridge. The pamphlet is resonant with echoes of places in scripture where God's prophets accurately foretell the punishment of cities and their people for wrongdoing. In weaving such references into her text, Biddle, like many of her fellow prophets, is claiming for herself the status of male, biblical prophets who asserted that they knew God's will and the meaning of past scriptures. *Woe to thee*, therefore, simultaneously threatens those defined by Biddle as God's enemies, promotes her own importance, and details her own version of Quaker theology.

Publishing prophecies was a popular occupation amongst radicals such as Quakers and Baptists in the 1650s, when many people who had previously been publicly silent claimed that the 'great overturning' prophesied in the Books of Daniel and Revelation was at hand, when

> it shall come to pass in the last days, saith God [that] I will pour out of my Spirit upon all flesh: and your sons and your daughters shall prophesy, and your young men shall see visions, and your old men shall dream dreams: And on my servants and on my handmaidens I will pour out in those days of my Spirit; and they shall prophesy. (Acts 2: 17–18)

Such activities were combined with systematic disruption of church services as Quakers, in particular, refuted the doctrines promoted in more mainstream churches. Barry Reay has estimated (Reay, 1984) that of some 300 Quakers arrested for such behaviour between 1654 and 1659, 34 per cent were women. It is difficult for us, in our secular society with its general separation between church and state, to grasp what was involved in such behaviour, which was then experienced as a fundamental challenge to social hierarchies. By considering the language used by Biddle in *Woe to thee*, I want to indicate here some of the ways in which these politico-religious pamphlets could engage with what she and other women saw as women's issues.

To understand what Biddle is up to in this proclamation, careful comparison needs to be made between the phraseology of her pamphlet and the related messages of the biblical passages she is evoking. (My method of proceeding is to examine what is sometimes called intertextuality.) For Biddle to use the Bible was a profoundly democratising move, since many people in her society would have known the Bible with a thoroughness that is unusual today. She is making reference, therefore, to a collection of stories that were read as both literally true and at the same time symbolically relevant to the affairs of the day. Bearing this in mind, it becomes clear that Biddle's attack on the universities, the training-ground of church ministers and other agents of the ruling hierarchy, is a class-specific one. The university men are described, for instance, as 'greedy dumb-dogs that never have enough, and love greeting in the market-places, and long prayers in the synagogues and the upper seats of feasts, and to be called of men, masters' (see page 165). This passage begins in the same way as the language of Isaiah 56:11, but goes beyond it in two ways: first, Biddle's clergymen are 'dumb' where Isaiah's are not; second, the phrases describing their behaviour have come not from Isaiah but from Christ's condemnation of scribes and Pharisees for their love of social status (Matthew 23:6–14; Luke 20:46–7). Putting these images together, Biddle creates a picture of university men acting like dogs in marketplaces, smelling one another's genitals in an act of mutual recognition, silent on the important social matters they are supposed to be concerned with, obsessed with their own status and power.

The class analysis continues in Biddle's condemnation of enclosures, of those who join 'house to house, and field to field, until there is no place left for the poor' (see page 165). The biblical allusion here is to Isaiah 5:8, but Isaiah makes no mention of the fate of the poor. It is in keeping with this shift of emphasis that Biddle refers (page 166) to 'the corn and wine and oil I gave to feed the poor'. None of the many biblical mentions of these symbolic gifts from God to his people suggests that they are to be used for such a purpose, and indeed in Deuteronomy 18:4 God commands his people to pay a tithe of these gifts to their priests, an instruction that directly contradicts Biddle's politics, and which she chooses to suppress. In addition, in her reference to the story of Esau and Jacob (see page 165), Biddle once more uses a familiar bible story – Esau sells his birthright to his younger twin Jacob, and is unsuccessful in his attempt to trick it back from him (Genesis 27) – to comment on the greed of church ministers who, like Esau, are motivated by material interests rather than spiritual ones.

There is other social analysis at play here: the university men are compared to Cain, who slew his brother Abel and was banished by God as 'a fugitive and a vagabond' (Genesis 4:12; see page 166). Biddle takes up the word 'vagabond' and joins to it 'runagate' (renegade), a word not used, as far as I know, in the Bible, but which was employed in reference to the social outcasts and propertyless who were policed by oppressive laws in seventeenth-century England. The real vagabonds, Biddle is saying, are not the unemployed and homeless, but the university-educated, whose proud hearts are 'full of dirt and filth' (page 165), and who spend their time 'murdering and killing the just in you, and whipping and stocking them that the Lord hath sent to you' (page 165). The poor and uneducated, as is often the case in radical pamphlets of the period, are shown to be those who 'know the mind and will of God', because they are not confused by the 'corrupt language' of university education (page 166).

Biddle's concern is not only with class politics. Many of the biblical condemnations of evil people make symbols of promiscuous women and prostitutes, referring to them as representations of all that is most abhorrent, and Biddle would have encountered such imagery repeatedly in her own reading of the Bible and in other people's use of it. The ubiquity of these images is demonstrated in her reference to Jezebel (page 163), and in her assertion (page 163) that 'the well favoured harlot lodgeth in thee, the mother of witchcraft', which specifically echoes the condemnation of the city of Ninevah in Nahum 3:4. (Her comparison of the sufferings of the wicked to the pain of a woman in labour, page 163, is also a biblical commonplace.) Perhaps to prevent such misogynous images standing unchallenged, Biddle laments 'I have mourned for you as one mourneth for her first-born' (page 163), discretely changing the gender of the mourner, who in Zechariah 12:10 is male. In using the word 'I' to stand both for herself and her God, Biddle is explicitly performing a trick her pamphlet constantly repeats: she is speaking in God's voice, as his prophet, merging his will with hers and naming her enemies as his. And she implies that her prophecy will come to be seen as true and the evil cities destroyed: cities and people wished woe to in the Bible repeatedly end in destruction, often destruction by fire. Through the intertextual construction of her pamphlet, Biddle thus establishes for her female voice an authority and rage that would have been quite unacceptable in other formats.

A great deal more could be said about this tract and the linguistic tricks it performs to political ends, but I do not have the space. What follows is an edited version of *Woe to thee, city of Oxford*. I have inserted into the text in square brackets the location of the biblical passages I believe Biddle is reusing, and added some footnotes to explicate more obscure places. The arrow-shaped brackets indicate my guesses as to the content of parts of the original pamphlet that have been destroyed by a tear in it. My hope is that readers can use these prompts to explore the complex structure of this text, which spirals constantly around a number of biblical passages and Biddle's related political imperatives, to create an argument that becomes ever more complicated, angry and triumphant.

———————————————— * ————————————————

Woe to thee [Numbers 21:29; Jeremiah 48; Isaiah 17:23; Ezekiel 34], city of Oxford, thy wickedness surmounteth the wickedness of Sodom [Genesis 19:23–5; Ezekiel 16:49]; therefore repent whilst ⟨thou⟩ hast time, lest I consume thee with fire, as I have done it; therefore harden not your hearts, lest I con⟨sume⟩ you, and my wrath burn like fire, and I consume you in my fierce anger, and so be brought to nought; for ⟨thou⟩ hast joined hands with thy sister Jerusalem;[1] therefore will I uncover thy nakedness [Nahum 3:5; Ezekiel 16:35–7], and thy shame will I unfo⟨ld th⟩at the beast in thee may be discovered that sitteth on many waters [Revelation 17:1]; for thou art full of wickedness, thy hands are full of deceit, th⟨e we⟩ll favoured harlot lodgeth in thee, the mother of witchcraft [Nahum 3:4]; and now I am raising my swift witness to confound her ways [Malachi 3:5]: I am th⟨e li⟩ght of the world and do enlighten everyone that cometh into the world, saith Christ Jesus.[2] I am the sure foundation, and he that bu⟨ild⟩eth upon me shall have eternal life [Matthew 7:24–7; Luke 6:46–7; 2 Timothy 2:16–20; 1 Timothy 6:17–19]; I have mourned for you as one mourneth for her first-born [Zechariah 12:10], and you would not come unto me that you might live [John 5:40]: I have knocked and called, and none would hear [Revelation 3:20]; therefore will I thunder out my judgements upon this wicked generation which hath not the fear of God; therefore the wicked shall see it and tremble: horror, and terror, and pain shall take hold upon them as upon a woman in travail, and many shall cry, but there shall be none to deliver them; therefore repent whilst I give you a day ⟨l⟩e⟨st⟩ you become as fruitless trees which cumbers the ground [Luke 3:6–9]; for every plant that my heavenly Father hath not planted will be plucked up by the roots [Matthew 15:13], and therefore repent whilst I give you a day, for I gave Jezebel a day [Revelation 2:20–1], and I gave Jerusalem a day, but they would not; therefore mind what I shall say, and where I do speak be still, and low, and wait in silence;[3] and then you shall hear a voice saying, 'This is the way, walk in it,' and if any have any desire to walk in this way, I will be with them, and guide them, and there shall you find sweet paths, and plenteous redemption. Therefore for your souls' health – for it was for the good of your souls that I took upon me the seed of Abraham, and became the likeness of sinful flesh,[4] were it not that I loved the world [John 3:16] – therefore I would not have you go astray as sheep without a shepherd,[5] scattered up and down upon every mountain and valley [Nahum 3:18], and carried away with every wind of doctrine [Ephesians 4:14]; but now am I araising up my own seed which hath been so long under Pharaoh the taskmaster,[6] Oxford thou taskmaster, Pharaoh thou oppressor which oppresseth the just seed within thee, in setting up thy own righteousness and wisdom, which shall grow as ragged as an old garment that moths hath eat, and I will make thee know that my righteousness endureth from generation to generation [Isaiah 50:9, 51:8], and so for ever. And now let hills be removed, and mountains be dashed to pieces, and the stronghold be levelled [Isaiah 40:4]; for a day there is coming that will make the keepers of the house tremble, woeful and terrible will that day be to the wicked, whilst the strong man keeps the house all is at peace [Ecclesiastes 12:3], but when a stronger than he cometh, he then must be turned out;[7] 'I came not to bring peace but war,' saith Christ Jesus [Matthew 10:34], and now turn in your eyes from beholding vanity [Psalm 119:37]; for that eye looketh from Christ,[8] and that nature is accursed from God, for Christ Jesus is pure, and can behold no vain thing:[9] Esau is accursed from God, 'Jacob have I loved and Esau have I hated [Genesis 27; Malachi 1:2–3; Romans 9:13], for out of Abraham shall my name be called'. Death reigneth over all men till they be regenerate and born again: and they that be born again of God sin not, but their sins are forgiven them; therefore repent that your sins may be forgiven you also [Romans 6]; the master hath given you a talent to see how you will improve it, that you may be found faithful stewards, that when the Lord shall call for that which he hath given you, that when the Lord comes, he may say, 'Come ye good and faithful stewards, enter into your Master's joy': but for the wicked, 'Go ye cursed,' and ye that forget God shall be cast into hell.[10] Praises, praises to the Lord, that he is raising up his own saints to judge the earth [1 Corinthians 6:2]: and many now do witness their judgments true; but to the wicked, judgments are terrible: and none but them cometh to see the fresh springs of eternal life, but they that live in the life of them that gave them forth,[11] and there they will come to see the filthiness of these two wicked cities, how they lie wallowing in their blood, and their blood shall be required at their own hands [Ezekiel 33:1–5]; for they that come forth of Oxford and Cambridge, they are such as Isaiah was sent to, to cry woe against, greedy dumb-dogs that never have enough [Isaiah 56:11], and love greeting in the marketplaces, and long prayers in the synagogues and the upper seats at feasts, and be called of men, masters [Matthew 23:6–14; Luke 20:46–7]; they are filthy brute beasts which maketh my people to err, therefore the ground is cursed for your sakes: thorns and thistles shall it bring forth for your sakes until you return to Adam's first estate [Genesis 3:17–18]. And now I have shown you the way that you should walk in, take heed to the light that shineth in a dark place [2 Peter 1:19–21]: light shineth in darkness, and the darkness comprehendeth it not [John 1:5]; therefore repent that the darkness may be taken away, and so become children of the light, and not children of the night, but children of the day [1 Thessalonians 5:5]; for they that walk in the day stumble not, because they have the light with them: but they that walk in the night stumble, because they are in darkness [John 11:8–10]; and now let the light search you, for Christ Jesus is now searching Jerusalem with candles [Zephaniah 1:12], and not one corner of it must go unsearched. Beware of seducers that cometh in sheep's clothing, but inwardly are ravenous wolves; for such Christ Jesus spoke of that should come in the latter days [Matthew 7:15]. Oh Oxford, thou art full of filth, thy priests are all corrupt as brass and iron is corrupt and cankered [Ezekiel 22:17–22; Jeremiah 6:28–9; James 5:1–3], so is this city full of heinous sins; thou art full of pride and covetousness, thou art polluted in thy blood,[12] and joins house to house, and field to field, until there is no place left for the poor [Isaiah 5:8]. God exalteth the poor in spirit, but the rich he sendeth empty away [Matthew 5:3; Luke 6:24]; it is the humble and lowly mind trembles at my word [Isaiah 66:2], that I teach, and now see in you, and search in you whether you are not in Cain's ways, murdering and killing the just in you [Genesis 4], and whipping and stocking them that the Lord hath sen⟨t⟩ to you; therefore repent and do so no more, take heed and do so no more, lest I render my plagues double on thy head; and when the book of conscience[13] is opened, then shalt thou witness this to be true; therefore remember that thou wast forewarned in thy lifetime, therefore wait in silence till the day dawn, and the day-star arise in your hearts [2 Peter 1:19–21], then will you come to witness sweet springs, ⟨fre⟩sh ones of eternal life; but for the wicked they be like the raging sea that tosseth to and fro, that casteth up nothing but mire and ⟨di⟩rt [Isaiah 57:20]: your hearts are full of dirt, and filth, thy pride shall become as filthy rags upon the dunghill; therefore sit down and bethink thee what thou art, thou art but dust and ashes [Job 30:19]: and cannot I kill and make alive [Deuteronomy 32:39], cannot I cast down and raise up [John 6:54], spread abroad and bring together? Yea, my hands have done all these things; I am a-gathering all my sheep together where they have been scattered in this dark and cloudy day, I will bring them from under Pharoah that they may have one Master, one Shepherd, and one sheepfold; the true Shepherd will lay down his life for his sheep: but the hireling will fly when persecution comes; and therefore will I gather my sheep out of their mouths [Ezekiel 34:1–16; John 10:11–16], and he that hath an ear let him hear; and therefore will I pour out my judgments upon them, to cut down and burn up and to destroy; for it is to the cutting down of pride, of filth, of covetousness, voluptuousness, and all wicked ways. And what delight is in the pride of life [1 John 2:16]? If thy conscience accuse thee, what peace canst thou have? Therefore have I sent light into the world, but men love darkness rather than light, and there is their condemnation [John 3:19–20]. Christ Jesus is the eternal life, and they that come to witness him in power and glory, cometh to witness Christ Jesus the substance; and this light will lead thee out of all forms and shadows, and in it will come to see all things have an end but Christ Jesus, and he endureth for ever; and therefore build upon him that endureth for ever; build not upon the sand, for the waves beating to and fro, they bring the sand into the sea, and so the builder loseth his work, and he that waiteth upon me shall not wait in vain, but have eternal life [Matthew 7:24; Luke 6:46–9]: it is them that endureth to the end shall be saved [Matthew 10:24]: it is not him that cryeth Lord, Lord, but them that doth the will of my Father which is in heaven shall be saved [Matthew 7:21]; and see whose will thou art doing, and see if thou be not in thy own will and man in his own will hath never seen God at any time: for Adam when he was in his fallen estate, he was driven out from God, and so alienated from God; and see if you be not vagabonds as Cain was, for Cain was a vagabond and a runagate, he slew the just, and so dost thou [Genesis 4:8–15]: therefore thou hast run after other gods, and hast cast my righteous Law behind thy back [1 Kings 14:9]; and therefore am I coming to rip up all hearts, it is I that tryeth the reins,[14] it is I that knoweth the thoughts long before, and how can you hide yourselves from such a God as I? I will render judgments upon the head of the wicked, and all the world shall see the glory of God; for he is arising in his glory to judge the earth, with righteous judgment and equity will he judge the earth, and the wicked shall see it and tremble [Psalm 98:9–10]; and now am I looking for the corn and wine and oil I gave to feed the poor [Deuteronomy 7:13, 18:4], but you have spent it upon your lusts; the whole creation groans under you [Romans 8:22], for your evil deeds and corrupt language: in Cain's nature you are, and death speaketh of the fame of God. Powerful, powerful is the God of glory in all his works, his ways past finding out [Romans 11:33], and to them that live in Christ Jesus, they know the mind and will of God their guide and keeper; but to the wicked he is a destroyer, to destroy their wicked ways with fire and with a sword to cut down the fruitless branches; for what is the wild grape-tree good for? Men cannot make any instruments of the wood; therefore it is good for nothing but to be cast into the fire: so shall the wicked; for Tophet[15] is prepared of old for them that will not obey God's word, and his servants', but obey sin and Satan: and therefore will I pour out my seven vials upon the seat of the beast [Revelation 15:7, 16]; the wicked beast is in every wicked heart, and therefore sink down and wait and see how thy soul lyeth in death, drowned in filth, smothered in wickedness; therefore repent that that which presseth down thy soul may be taken away, for the soul is mine, and I desire nothing of any but my own, and that with advantage; for he is the slothful servant that improveth not his master's goods; and therefore from him that hath a little, that little he hath shall be taken away and given to him that hath most,[16] and he that hath an ear let him hear: and while you have time prize it. Remember you are warned in your lifetime, and all left without excuse.

Hester Biddle.

NOTES

1. *thy sister Jerusalem*: Ezekiel's prophecy against Jerusalem refers to Sodom and Samaria as her sister cities (Ezekiel 16:46). Biddle is adding the English university towns to this list of condemned, immoral places.
2. *I am the light . . . Jesus*: words spoken by Christ after he had prevented the stoning to death of a woman arrested for adultery, John 8:12; repeated by him before the Last Supper, John 12:46. Quakers interpreted this and other similar passages in scripture, such as 2 Peter 1:19–21, as evidence that the 'light within', the inner certainty that one is listening to God, is a clearer source of knowledge of divine will than either Church or Bible. Biddle takes up this issue again in the middle of this pamphlet, in her images of light and darkness.
3. *wait in silence*: Quakers and other radical sectaries attributed great importance to their belief that those who wished to know God's will should wait in silence for inspiration, rather than heeding Bible or church ministers. Biddle might also, here, be turning against male authorities their frequent use of Paul's command to women to be silent, 1 Corinthians 14:34.
4. *took . . . flesh*: was born a man, making myself into one of Abraham's descendants.
5. *sheep without a shepherd*: God's care for his people is frequently compared in the Bible to that of a shepherd for his sheep. The simile is used at greatest length in John 10:1–18, where Christ compares his own love for his people with the ill-doings of hirelings. Quakers frequently attacked university-trained church ministers, whose wages were paid from tithes (a form of local tax), as 'hireling priests', arguing that they were more interested in their incomes than in the needs of their people.

6. *Pharoah the taskmaster*: the Egyptian ruler of the time of Moses who ill-treated the children of God, and 'did set over them taskmasters' (Exodus 1:10).
7. *strong man . . . turned out*: Luke records how Jesus, when casting out devils, contradicts those who think he is inspired by the evil Beelzebub by pointing out the power of his God who allows him to be successful in this work (Luke 11:21–3).
8. *eye looketh from Christ*: eye looks away from Christ.
9. *vain thing*: 'vain' and 'vanity' are always used in the Bible, as here, with the meaning of worthless(ness), not in the sense of conceited(ness).
10. *the master . . . hell*: alluding to the parable of the talents, Matthew 25:14–30. Christ tells the story of a master giving talents (coins) to three servants, only two of whom make good use of them and are therefore rewarded, to indicate the importance of Christians using their talents to the greater glory of God.
11. *and none . . . forth*: and the only people who will receive eternal life will be those who live their lives according to Christ's teaching (i.e. according to the will of him who gave forth the fresh springs of eternal life).
12. *polluted in thy blood*: filthy because covered with blood, following Ezekiel 16:6, 22.
13. *book of conscience*: perhaps the book of life referred to in Revelation 20:12–15, 'And whoever was not found written in the book of life was cast into the lake of fire.'
14. *tryeth the reins*: God's ability to search out deep motivations and judge them ('try the reins' or kidneys) is frequently alluded to in the Bible, for instance in Psalm 7:9; Jeremiah 17:10.
15. *Tophet*: the 'place of burning' where those who have rejected God were burnt (Jeremiah 7:31, 19:11–13).
16. *with advantage . . . most*: referring again to the parable of the talents, Matthew 25:14–30; see note 10 above.

-- * --

The kind of feminist criticism I do, then, focuses crucially on forgotten women's writing in an endeavour to discover the concerns of women in the past. It is as much a historical concern as a literary one, though I think my preoccupation with language and the structures of dissemination and consumption of texts (matters I have not had space to discuss here) still situate my work within literary criticism. Whilst this activity was inspired by Elaine Showalter's research in the modern period, I think there are crucial differences between the US-based schools of criticism she has developed and my own priorities. I am not interested at all in the 'greatness' of texts, believing that different writings have their own, specific complexities which might not be traditionally literary ones; and I am not seeking a women's tradition. Rather, I believe that the material circumstances of women's lives in the past differed from those of men, and so their work differs from men's, although it has many formative forces in common. This concern with the specifics of history also means I see diversity in women's writing, which varies depending on a number of factors, such as the author's class, sexuality, and political commitments. By no means all of women's forgotten writings are to be celebrated, just as in these days of Thatcherism, it is clear that not all women are our sisters. Their texts are all, none the less, part of the multiple, suppressed history of women's lives and creativity.

I still believe – believe more and more – that there is special value in studying women's writing, rather than in producing gender-conscious readings of work by men. This value is demonstrated to me most clearly in my experience of teaching seventeenth-century women's writing. My students, like myself, are astounded at the inventiveness of these long-dead women, and angered that we live in a world that has robbed us of knowledge of their existence. We do not have to be fooled into the essentialism of thinking that all women everywhere are and were 'the same' to be inspired by their works: indeed, the discovery that women's oppression has operated differently, and been differently fought against, in different cultures, is in itself a useful experience as we form strategies against our current, ever-changing oppression. The creativity of my students in their reworking of these texts is a constant source of energy to me, as are in particular the words of one of them, Pam Linden, when I asked her what she had gained from reading works by seventeenth-century women. Pam replied, 'What I've learned is that if women have been fighting back for 300 years, I'm not putting up with any more of this shit'.

That is good enough for me; perhaps it would have been good enough for Hester Biddle, too. But there is no way of knowing that.

Ruth Evans and Lesley Johnson

The *Assembly of Ladies*: A Maze of Feminist Sign-Reading?

The discussion which follows arises out of a dialogue between us about how we might define our feminist critical practice and how we might read the anonymous fifteenth-century text, the *Assembly of Ladies*. We have decided to work together here and elsewhere because we share a commitment to working out a politically aware approach to medieval culture and enjoy the opportunity to exchange and challenge views, and the respite from the solitary writing self which collaborative ventures offer. Our academic backgrounds are similar: we have both specialised in the study of literary culture in medieval England, were trained in a formalist tradition, and were feminists before we were self-conscious and critical about our critical practice. There has been a time lag between our practice and our theory and, undoubtedly, some aspects of how we read, and how we define that process (though not its aims and ends) will shift again. Along with many other feminists we believe in the value of acknowledging our political stance and our motives for writing; inevitably there will be blind spots in our critical undertaking because there will always be motivations of which we are unaware.

The focus on critical *process* in this piece is important, as important as the eventual 'reading' we offer. The problem of just how to engage with texts from a feminist position can perhaps best be illustrated by modelling for the reader some of that difficult and sometimes inconclusive process. We have tried to demonstrate that the meanings we derive from/devise for the *Assembly of Ladies* are not arbitrary but are the result of certain reading processes, which are determined by our training, by the kind of material we have read which we can bring to bear on the text, and by our particular political agenda. There is no 'formula' for feminist critical practice: all the factors we have mentioned are relevant, and will vary from reader to reader. We have decided to speak as 'we' because we are in agreement here, but we recognise that this use of the collective pronoun is politically suspect because it collapses any sign of difference: as Gillian Beer and others have pointed out,[1] a feminist cannot claim to be a representative woman, representing all women. Our discussion is organised around some general questions which we have taken over from the set devised by Susan Sellers as an aid to contributors to this volume: we begin by looking at the issue of where our contribution might fit into the broad context of current feminist debate; move on to introduce the *Assembly of Ladies* and why we have chosen to focus on it here; then offer an outline of our methodology and theoretical underpinning; and finally consider how the text 'means' and how we go about reading it.

REWRITING THE MIDDLE AGES

In the context of an essay collection such as this it is important to affirm ways in which a feminist critical practice is not limited to the post-medieval periods and, concomitantly, that the engagement with literature of the past is of value for feminist critical practice. Gillian Beer has expressed this point well in her essay 'Representing woman: re-presenting the Past' when she warns against getting caught in the trap of 'presentism' (Belsey and Moore, 1989: 67):

> The encounter with the otherness of earlier literature can allow us to recognise and challenge our own assumptions, and those of the society in which we live. To do so we must take care not to fall into the trap of assuming the evolutional model of literary development, so often taken for granted, in which texts are praised for their 'almost modern awareness' or for being 'ahead of their time'. . . . This means engaging with the *difference* of the past in the present and so making us aware of the trajectory of arrival . . . the study of past writing within the conditions of its production disturbs that autocratic emphasis on the self and the present as if they were stable entities.

We do not claim, of course, that medieval texts in general are more 'other' than those from any other time: all texts require historically informed, self-conscious reading. But the initial difficulty of reading a Middle English text may serve a useful function in jolting assumptions about identification between readers and characters in texts, and (because language functions so powerfully as a sign of cultural difference) in highlighting the need to consider the wider cultural formations in which the work has been produced and read. There are however special problems in gaining access to the conditions in which a work was produced and read in, for example, late fifteenth-century England, the context for the text we have chosen to discuss, the *Assembly of Ladies*. There is some information available on lay literacy and its permeation through the population of late medieval England, and from this we can conclude that the women of the social élite of the time were more likely to participate in the 'literacy of recreation' as consumers of literature rather than as producers.[2] But there is much that we do not know about social formations and communities of readers at this time and there is still much to be done, both in uncovering evidence and in interpreting it.[3]

Having suggested that medieval literary culture might be a fruitful area of engagement for modern feminist readers, we do recognise that medieval studies has not seemed to be as active an arena for feminist literary practices compared with other periods of post-medieval literary culture. However, this situation is changing. The constructions of the medieval period, the construction of the 'Middle Ages' itself, are being investigated by the critics represented, for example, in the collections of essays in *Women and Power in the Middle Ages* (edited by Mary Erler and Maryanne Kowaleski, 1988), in *Medieval Literature* (edited by David Aers, 1986), in the new journal *Exemplaria* (1–2, 1989, 1990) and in the work of feminist historians such as Martha Howell and Judith Bennett, whose researches, as David Aers has argued, offer the basis for examining the threats to 'the traditional sex-gender system and the institutions based on it', so that we can 'begin to unpack changing as well as continuing sources of masculine anxiety and aggression towards women' (Aers, 1988: 236), rather than simply offering up again the old anti-feminist clichés as the only framework for our understanding of women in the Middle Ages.[4] This is not the place for a history of these developments, nor do we have the space for a survey, but it is important to make clear that we are operating in a broader context and are very much indebted to the work of others in this field.

WHAT IS THE *ASSEMBLY OF LADIES*?

The *Assembly of Ladies* is a relatively rare phenomenon: a late medieval poem, dating from the second half of the fifteenth century, in which a female first person narrator is represented as the central protagonist of the narrative and the writing subject of 'this booke' (l.740) which tells her story.[5] The narrative is set in the world of the leisured classes, 'whan al . . . other busynesse was done' (31), in a formal maze garden where a group of five ladies, their four 'gentil wymmen' (8) and many knights and squires are walking. It opens with an exchange between one of the ladies (the narrator) and one of the men (whether he is a knight or a squire is not made clear): she is asked what she is doing in this garden, whom she is seeking, why she is so pale. In response she tells him about a dream she had experienced on an earlier occasion in this garden when she and her female 'felawship' were summoned to the court of Lady Loyalty, at Pleasaunt Regard, to present their complaints about anything 'wherein ye fele your hert is displeased' (125). The household of Lady Loyalty, and the appropriate dress and manners required at her court, are described in some detail. The lady and her fellowship are introduced to the all-female personnel of Loyalty's court (including 'Perseveraunce' the usher, 'Countenaunce' the porter, 'Discrecioun' the chief purveyor) until finally they offer their complaints to Loyalty's secretary, 'Avisenesse' (that is, Prudent Consideration) for formal presentation before Loyalty herself. The narrator herself seems reluctant to take her turn and spell out her complaint, but she does so finally and the formal assembly scene closes with the promise from Lady Loyalty that all the offences will be remedied at the next 'court of parlement' (720).[6] The dream vision frame evaporates as the narrator wakes with a splash of water on her face:

> Al sodainly the water sprang anone
> In my visage and therewithal I woke.
> 'Wher am I now?' thought I, 'al this is goon,'
> Al amased: and up I gan to looke.
> With that anon I went and made this booke,
> Thus symply rehersyng the substaunce
> Because it shuld nat out of remembraunce.
>   (736–42)

The narrative itself closes with a further exchange between the lady and her male 'reader' in which she reveals that the name of the book is 'La Semble de dames'.[7]

WHY HAVE WE CHOSEN THE *ASSEMBLY OF LADIES*?

The equivocal narratorial voice

The *Assembly of Ladies* presents itself as the product of a woman writer, but there is no firm evidence either from outside or within the text which might enable us to identify its author more precisely. It is an anonymous text, extant in three manuscript copies dating from the later fifteenth century.[8]

However, to say that the text is anonymous does not mean that it has always been read in this way. In fact for more than two hundred years (from Thynne's edition of 1532), the *Assembly of Ladies* was included in the collected editions of Chaucer's work and was read in this context. The late-eighteenth-century editor of *The Canterbury Tales*, Thomas Tyrwhitt, expressed considerable scepticism about Chaucer's authorship of the *Assembly of Ladies* (though it continued to be reprinted in some later editions of Chaucer's work as a poem 'imputed' to the poet), and its exclusion from the Chaucerian canon was finally confirmed by W. W. Skeat at the end of the nineteenth century. Skeat, in fact, seems to have been the first to suggest that the *Assembly of Ladies* was written by a woman – possibly the same woman, in his view, who wrote *The Floure and the Leafe* (a text which is often regarded as a companion piece to the *Assembly of Ladies* and which is another of Chaucer's apocryphal works).[9] Although Skeat may have felt that 'surely these descriptions of seams, and collars, and sleeves, are due to a woman' (Skeat, 1897: lxviii), not all subsequent readers have agreed, and the attribution of female authorship of the text remains a subject of some debate: opposed in favour of Sir Richard Roos by Ethel Seaton in 1961; more or less dismissed by Derek Pearsall, its modern editor, in 1962; and periodically revived, most recently – and inconclusively – by Alexandra Barratt in 1987.[10]

This lack of a named, gender-identified author has interesting implications for a feminist reading practice. There is no need to subscribe to crude theories of essentialism to recognise that men and women write from different positions – positions within society, culture, history – which are determined not only by their gender, but also by their class, race and sexuality. Such determinants are not going to be constructed in the same way today as they were in the late fifteenth century; nor is the relationship between the positioning of authors and the subject positions available within their texts ever one of simple continuity or reflection. But the equivocal relationship between the identity of author and narratorial voice of the *Assembly of Ladies* means that it is not amenable to efforts to reclaim it now as a 'lost' woman's work (a strategy which has had spectacular results in the case of the fifteenth-century Franco-Italian writer, Christine de Pisan), nor as the voice of female experience in any simple sense.[11] The *Assembly of Ladies*, then, offers a challenge to those who believe that 'the feminist project of making women visible' (Moi in Belsey and Moore, 1989: 129) is, reductively, a matter of investigating *women* writers. Such projects are, of course, still urgently needed, because of the comparative neglect of many women writers, but they do not displace the simultaneous need for a 'feminist critique', as Elaine

Showalter has called it (Showalter, 1986: 128) – the revisionary reading, from a feminist position, of texts by men (in contrast to 'gynocritics' – the study of writing by women). The practice of 'feminist critique' can be extended to anonymous texts like the *Assembly of Ladies* (the history of whose reception provides the opportunity for feminist revisionary readings), although it is also important to recognise the ways in which the *Assembly of Ladies*, by reason of its anonymity and the construction of its narratorial voice, cannot easily be read with the critical presuppositions assumed by Showalter's two main modes of feminist criticism.

In developing a feminist reading strategy which is appropriate for anonymous texts – which could have been written by men – in which the central voice is a woman's, we need to consider factors such as how the relationship between the representation of the central protagonist and that of the author has been variously interpreted in the course of the work's reception, and how the status, meaning and even form of a text (in the sense of how its central speaker is identified) may change within the historical context of its reception. Chris Weedon has suggested ways in which feminists can make use of deconstructive theory, 'with its critique of the metaphysics of presence, in which the speaking subject's intention guarantees meaning' (Weedon, 1987: 13) and its assumption that 'meaning is constituted within language and is not guaranteed by the subject which speaks it' (p. 22). The radical possibilities of such assumptions are that they free us to talk about the construction of gender identity within the text and to produce new feminist meanings, without making claims for the text based upon a reductive equation between the author and the textual voice. One example of this is Alexandra Barratt's remark that 'it is generally agreed that the *Assembly of Ladies* is not a good poem. Often inept, it is hard to interpret coherently, but presents a number of interesting features if we are prepared seriously to entertain the possibility that a woman wrote it' (Barratt, 1987: 14). For Barratt, it seems, the *Assembly of Ladies* fails to meet some generally accepted norm of literary value, but apparently can be redeemed if we are prepared to accept that it is by a woman. A more fruitful feminist approach to the problem of the equivocal authorial voice in our view is to consider not just poststructuralist views about the production of meaning within language, but also wider theories derived from cultural materialism which have avoided the narrowness of a model of literary production which is simply author-based: art, as Janet Wolff has persuasively argued, is a social product (Wolff, 1981: 1).

Our choice of the *Assembly of Ladies*, then, is partially determined by its use of an unusual narrative voice and the comparatively rare image it offers, for its time in England, of a woman of the élite class as a composer of a book. This is not to say that this image is unique (there is a female writing subject in *The Floure and the Leafe*), nor that the notion of a lay woman participating in the production of a courtly text was otherwise quite inconceivable. Whilst we do not have evidence of the existence of any parallel female figures to the 'aristocratic' poets such as Sir Richard Roos (if he did indeed translate *La Belle Dame sans merci*) or Charles d'Orléans, there is evidence that the work of Christine de Pisan was in circulation in England in the fifteenth century (including the *Cité des dames*).[12] However, from the images of authorship included in comparable courtly texts and from the evidence we have of who was responsible for the courtly material in fifteenth-century England, it seems fair to suggest that the image of the female writer in the *Assembly of Ladies* had some novelty value. We are certainly not going to suggest that this sustained use of a female first person narrator necessarily endows this text with a radical quality: in many ways the values espoused in the *Assembly of Ladies* are highly conservative. It is a work which is indebted to, and in its turn contributes to, a long-standing prestigious courtly literary tradition, which promotes the court as the idealised arena for the illustration of a moral code and legitimates the élite social position of its members. Nevertheless, given the general dominance of both the male voice and male gaze in courtly writing of this period (and of earlier periods), the sustained use of a female voice does open up some interesting differences of view on how ladies and gentlewomen are placed in a courtly frame. It also becomes a source of difference of view in our feminist reading which allows us to reproduce the text in ways that are distinct from prevailing and preceding critical trends.

Revaluing the fifteenth century

Although the *Assembly of Ladies* is accessible in a modern edition it has attracted comparatively little critical interest and, therefore, has not established much of a place within the twentieth-century canon of medieval literature in England. In part, this is the result of a tendency to subordinate the quality and interest of this text to that of *The Floure and the Leafe*, as is the case in Pearsall's single edition of both texts. In turn, this critical preference for *The Floure and the Leafe* may be explained partly by the fact that although *The Floure and the Leafe* also belongs to the category of Chaucerian apocrypha, it was praised as being one of the best of Chaucer's works by influential readers of earlier centuries (including Dryden, Pope and Wordsworth and Elizabeth Barrett Browning).

However, this comparative lack of modern critical interest in the *Assembly of Ladies* (and in *The Floure and the Leafe* too) is also the result of the place of fifteenth-century literary studies within our institutional frames (these institutions include those of higher education and of literary criticism). The fifteenth century still does seem like 'the last, vast terra incognita of English literature' (in contrast to its place in the study of English history), and though some of the writers of this time (perhaps Malory above all) and some of its literary modes (above all the drama) have attracted much more general interest, the literary profile of the fifteenth century is not high, nor are its literary products generally well esteemed.[13] In addition, the *Assembly of Ladies* belongs to a textual grouping that seems to be of especially little interest: the corpus of 'court verse' produced in the fifteenth century (that is several hundred lyric poems and a smaller number of longer love poems) which has generally been regarded as contributing nothing much to the fair field of English letters and as marking something of a vacuum in poetic creativity following Chaucer's work.[14]

Of course this comparative neglect of fifteenth-century literary culture is being challenged now in many ways.[15] Interestingly, however, the particular challenges to the received opinion of fifteenth-century court verse are coming from the revisions of ideas about the receptive milieu of these works based on detailed studies of their manuscript contexts, compilers, scribes and owners and readers.[16] Although R. H. Robbins claimed that the corpus of court verse (including the *Assembly of Ladies*) was composed 'for intellectual and social diversion and amorous dalliance amongst a miniscule élite group' (Robbins, 1979: 245), it seems that if some of the collections may have functioned in this way, the audience for this poetry embodying courtly views 'ultimately extended well beyond such boundaries' to the emergent middle-class reading public (Strohm, 1982: 19). Indeed Paul Strohm suggests that one of the functions of the fifteenth-century literary compilations of courtly verse from Chaucer, Lydgate and other anonymous writers (specifically those associated with the scriptorium of John Shirley – as two of the manuscripts of *Assembly of Ladies* are) might be to lead '"all thoo that beon gentile of birthe or of condicions" . . . in a reassuring way to an already-existing world of taste and gentility which they seek but have not previously known' (p. 22).[17] The fifteenth-century reading context for the *Assembly of Ladies* begins to look a good deal more complex from this perspective, as does the question of whose interests and experiences this work mediates. However, the kind of reassurance offered by the *Assembly of Ladies* as it guides its readers through the social codes of behaviour appropriate to gentlewomen and ladies is, in our view, more equivocal than Strohm's picture of gentle, genteel, induction suggests.

WHAT IS OUR CRITICAL METHOD?

In introducing the *Assembly of Ladies* we have already signalled some of the movements of this work as it has been read and interpreted within a variety of reading formations. But although like any other text its meaning is not fixed, this does not mean that it can mean anything. The kind of materialist feminist critical framework that we are trying to develop is one which seeks to contextualise a work as fully as possible, investigating all known aspects of its production and consumption in order to bring out the text's relation both to material realities and to the 'ideas, language and culture' (the terms are Newton and Rosenfelt's) of which it is a part and which it continues to form part, by its reproduction and rereading by critics and readers who are themselves positioned as gendered social subjects. If the test of a good theory is that it allows the representation of what would otherwise elude understanding (Jacobus, 1986: 107), then we have found it enabling to borrow from cultural materialism the Marxist concept of ideology. In that version of it which derives from Althusser's redefinition, it is 'that system of beliefs and assumptions . . . which represent the imaginary relationship of individuals to their real conditions of existence.' Catherine Belsey offers a further elaboration:

> Ideology obscures the real conditions of existence by presenting partial truths. It is a set of omissions, gaps rather than lies, smoothing over contradictions, appearing to provide answers to questions which in reality it evades and masquerading as coherence in the interests of the social relations generated by and necessary to the reproduction of the existing mode of production. (Belsey, 1980: 57–8)

The process, as Belsey's gloss makes clear, is not a totalising one, but involves contradictions, gaps, doublings over, which allow us to glimpse the working out of this ideology in the representational forms in which it is inscribed. One of the dominant ideologies of the Middle Ages in Western Europe is that reflected in and by the system of 'courtliness' itself: the projection, that is, of an élite social nexus (the economic basis of which is commonly elided), which appears to be founded on, and distinguished by, refinements of inner and outer behavioural codes, and social relationships bound in hierarchies of service. The manifestation of this system of beliefs and assumptions in the sphere of heterosexual relations is conventionally invoked by modern critics under the umbrella term of 'courtly love', in which (to borrow the words of Sarah Beckwith) woman is 'constructed as the other [the static, voiceless lady of *fin'amor*] . . . as the demarcator of [the feudal aristocracy's] own boundaries and so establishing a confirming and legitimising definition of themselves and their own power' (Beckwith, 1986: 35).[18] Ideology works by offering powerfully attractive images – in this case, the projection of women as goddesses to be served and worshipped from afar answers to both male and female fantasy – within particular cultural forms (courtly love is commonly inscribed in a particular poetic register) which makes those same images appear 'natural', and thus serving to keep subordinate groups in their place by masking the real social conditions in which they live (and which they otherwise protest about). The *Assembly of Ladies*, which draws on fifteenth-century court culture and participates in it, is both ideological and has ideology inscribed within it: it is concerned to elaborate on the distinctive qualities required of refined women by men within that court culture in order to legitimise their dominant patriarchal position. Ideology though is never unitary, and our section on critical practice will explore some of the ways in which the use of the female voice and the concentration on a female point of view exposes some of the rifts in this idealised culture and its construction of particular definitions of feminity.

If these are the macro-parameters of our critical approach we should also stress here its micro-features: the importance of paying close attention to specific textual effects. Reading practices are the product of both ideological biases and conscious choice, yet few critics reveal where they get their readings from. Close-focus textual analysis is frequently a 'given' of methods of reading, but can be used for widely differing ends. The New Critical practice, for example, of paying attention to the 'words on the page', aimed to identify and affirm the special 'literary' quality of the text, the meaning of which was held to be singular and exclusive, immobilised in a timeless vacuum. Our own reading practices are the result of years of training in reading texts following just this particular formalist tradition, but it is important to stress how very different is our political project. For we read to pay attention to the text's rhetorical effects, to the way that its discourse is structured, to the metaphors and terms in which it presents itself, since it is only through an analysis of its discursive effects that we can understand its relation to other discourses which exist in culture and which help to determine its meaning. Such techniques allow a radical critique of the ideology of the text, apprehended through its use of language. We read therefore not for aesthetic reasons but in order to examine textual ideology, and to situate the text within wider cultural frameworks.

HOW DOES THE *ASSEMBLY OF LADIES* MEAN?

Sellers' question 'How does the text you have chosen "mean"?' is possibly the most searching one of all. The form of the question – 'how' rather than 'what' – is productive because it suggests that one of the projects of feminist literary criticism is to engage in something other than a hermeneutic exercise – an 'interpretation' of the text. We have already tried to suggest some of the ways in which the text has been made to 'mean' (as, for example, the typical product of a female writer) – how meaning is produced in particular historical and cultural conjunctures, and as the result of particular modes of reading. We will go on now to look more specifically at some of the forms and narrative motifs deployed in the text which are oriented in courtly literary culture and which form a complex generic mix – dream vision, complaint, court allegory, *débat*. The *Assembly of Ladies* 'means', in part, by drawing on and reworking material from a literary repertoire which has been built up in the preceding centuries by writers working in French and in English (notably Chaucer), as Derek Pearsall has indicated (Pearsall, 1962: 52–8). We will not attempt to reproduce Pearsall's detailed work on sources and analogues of the *Assembly of Ladies*: our efforts to unscramble its generic mix and examine some of the traditions behind the text and its mode of representation will be (necessarily) more selective.

Genre and the female voice

The use of a dream-vision frame to explore an inner terrain of sentiment, shaped to illustrate social codes of court behaviour, is one that can be traced back at least to the thirteenth-century archetype of love-vision narratives, the *Roman de la rose*, and is reproduced in the numerous later love-visions which follow the format. The use of an allegorical court to shape the experience of the dreamer (as in the God of Love's court in the *Roman de la rose*) and/or to provide an arena for the expression of formal love complaints (as in, for example, Lydgate's *Temple of Glas* or in the *Parliament of Love*) is also found with many variations in this courtly heritage which provides both the diachronic and synchronic literary context for the *Assembly of Ladies*.[19] However, the sustained use of a female narrator in dream-vision poetry is extremely rare and it is to the corpus of complaint lyrics that we have to turn for comparable exercises in the construction of female voices. In fact, in the view of R. H. Robbins, the complaints voiced by the nine women at

Lady Loyalty's court provide the generic core of the text (Robbins, 1979: 253). He argues that the *Assembly of Ladies*, like most of the longer court poetry of the fifteenth century, is best seen as an elaboration on a basic lyric structure.[20] The issue of whether to name the *Assembly of Ladies* an 'elaborated lyric' text, rather than a love-vision narrative, indicates the element of subjectivity involved in all exercises in generic labelling which we will not pursue here: neither label is mutually exclusive.[21] More important is the recognition of the kinds of precedents for the construction of the female voice that complaint lyrics may provide.[22] Examples of courtly complaints in a female voice are in the minority in the corpus of medieval English and French lyric poems but, as Robbins points out, whereas in the *Assembly of Ladies*, the nine stanzas of the fellowship's complaint in Lady Loyalty's court are distributed across nine voices, in other examples (such as in 'A gentlewoman's lament', attributed to Lydgate, or in the anonymous female complaints in the 'Findern' anthology) the emotional offences are consolidated and articulated through the voice of a single gentlewoman or lady (which is the overall effect of the *Assembly of Ladies*).[23]

These exercises in female complaint may be found 'free standing' in lyric collections, or embedded in narrative contexts and are a particular feature of the literary tradition of representing the stories of betrayed or abandoned female lovers from the world of legendary history. Ovid's collection of complaints from women such as Phyllis, Briseis, Oenone, Dido and Ariadne in the *Heroides*, provides the classical reference point for such a collection of voices (in this context voiced in epistolary form), but more immediate Middle English precedents are to be found in Chaucer's *Legend of Good Women*, or in his fragmentary *Anelida and Arcite*. This complaint tradition, and the larger corpus of narratives about betrayed women, is specifically recalled in the *Assembly of Ladies* in the decoration on the walls of Lady Loyalty's hall where the narrator sees the engraved stories of 'Phillis', 'Thesbe', 'Cleopatra', 'Melusene' and 'Aneleda the quene/Upon Arcite how sore she did complayne' (ll. 456–66).[24]

There are then free-standing complaint lyrics voiced by women; there are complaints by women voiced in larger narrative contexts and in dream-visions, but there are few sustained narratives (outside the corpus of Christine de Pisan's work) which use female first person narrators/dreamers. What we will try to isolate here is some sense of what difference it makes if the dream viewer is a courtly woman. How far is the *Assembly of Ladies* a text with a different agenda which does not reproduce the conventional (or even unconventional) position with regard to courtly women? Our discussion will concentrate on three narrative motifs.

Narrative motifs: I. The maze

One of the unusual details of the *Assembly of Ladies* is the poem's setting in a maze, a setting whose symbolic significance we are alerted to, and which is of interest to feminist readers because of recent critical explorations of medieval mazes as symbols of the female body and of a female textual hermeneutic (Dinshaw, 1989: 77–81; N. Miller, 1986: 286). The *Assembly of Ladies* opens with the narrator and her eight companions (four 'ladyes', four 'gentil wymmen') 'in crosse aleys walkyng'; the narrator, in her conversation with the knight, elaborates at length on the various behaviours of the women in the maze:

> Whan al oure other busynesse was done,
> To passe our tyme in to this mase we went
> [And toke oure weyes yche aftyr other entent:]
> Som went inward and went they had gon oute,
> Som stode amyddis and loked al aboute;
>
> And soth to sey som were ful fer behynde
> And right anon as ferforth as the best;
> Other there were, so mased in theyr mynde,
> Al weys were goode for hem, both est and west.
> Thus went they furth and had but litel rest,
> And som theyr corage dide theym so assaile
> For verray wrath they stept over the rayle.
> (31–42)

The narrator identifies the maze as a place of leisure, somewhere to 'passe our tyme'. Earlier she had described her companions as 'disportyng hem' in the 'crosse aleys' (9–10); the verb disarmingly suggests an activity of pleasurable amusement, but there are disturbing elements in the opening section which unsettle the apparently calm evocation of an aristocratic society at play. Despite the presence of 'knyghtis and squyers many one', some of the women choose to walk alone – 'som alone *after theyr fantasyes*' (11) [our italics: the phrase suggests an element of self-sufficiency about this particular community of women]. When questioned about her activity by one of the knights, the narrator's almost dismissive claim that she walks about the maze 'as a womman that nothyng rought' (18) is undercut by the knight's subsequent pressing of her to reveal more and to explain her pallor. The sense of tension is further heightened in the passage quoted above, in which the women's behaviour is often severely at variance with the mood of play. Some are 'mased in theyr mynde', and some are so carried away by impetuosity that 'for verray *wrath* they stept over the rayle'. This lingering over the inner and outer behaviour of the women, linked by the use of 'mase' both as a verb and a noun ('(a)masen' [to be confused]; 'mase' [labyrinth]), suggests that the formal garden signifies more than just late fifteenth-century fashions in gardening history, which is how Pearsall interprets it (Pearsall, 1962: 153–5).

According to a study by Penelope Doob, contradictory meanings existed within medieval culture for the figure of the maze or labyrinth, which was derived from classical history and myth, and then reinterpreted within a Christian frame: simultaneously symbol of duplicity and moral confusion – 'an architect's delight and a wanderer's downfall' – and also of ordered ritual and 'the value of persistence' (Doob, 1982: 214). Doob's analysis stresses the classical and religious significances of the maze as a medieval trope, but her argument, though useful for alerting us to the paradoxical range of meanings attributed to the maze in medieval culture, also shows that this meaning depends on specific contexts: it does not offer a key to the maze here. However, Caroline Dinshaw suggests a gender-specific reading of the maze in medieval literary culture, proposing the labyrinth as text, and woman's body as the truth of the text: according to her reading (Dinshaw, 1989: 77–81) it is associated with negative images of female sexuality. This does not however offer us a 'clewe' into the particular maze of the *Assembly of Ladies*, which is not susceptible to Dinshaw's reading model – and here we are interested in why it is possible to read texts in certain ways and not in others. While the maze in the *Assembly of Ladies* clearly belongs to the negative medieval tradition, the symbolic terms in which it is introduced do not have specific sexual resonance (unlike, for example, those in *The Legend of Good Women*, upon which Dinshaw largely bases her analysis), and furthermore the narrative movement of the poem – the dream itself – enlarges on this opening section and provides a gloss which makes its meaning more explicit: the maze articulates a set of social codes governing the behaviour of women. We would argue then that the maze in the *Assembly of Ladies* has a principally *social*, not psychological/libidinal, significance. Moreover, this derives added force from the operations of the dream itself, for it is really through this that the meaning of the maze is elaborated.

The boundaries between inner and outer terrains are already merged before the narrator finds the inner garden within the maze, decorated with the flowers of sentiment, including 'n'oublie-mies' and 'sovenez' (forget-me-nots) and above all 'poore penses' (pansies, i.e. thoughts), which are in profusion everywhere (61–3), where she awaits her companions and falls asleep. But the boundaries between inner and outer landscapes continue to be elided within the dream experience itself, and this is where we find the gloss on the significance of the mazey setting of the poem. This movement inwards via the dream is not represented as a highly private and individualised experience. In fact in moving 'inwards' in the dream, the narrator is given a better vantage point from which to survey the structures determining courtly behaviour for ladies and gentlewomen, as well as an opportunity to publicly air some of the sentiments behind the signs of female discontent glimpsed in the garden. Although the narrator falls asleep alone (albeit 'Remembryng of many dyvers cace / Of tymes past', 75–6) her whole fellowship is summoned to the court at Plesaunt Regard and catch up with her there: the continuity of personnel, inside and outside the dream frame, suggests that this dream experience is itself an elaboration on the garden setting and its collective, female dissatisfactions. The notable absentees from the dreamscape are the knights and squires who are present in the garden. Just why this is to be an assembly 'de *Dames*' is not made clear. When the narrator asks Diligence, her guide to the court, if she or any of her 'felawes' may summon any men, she is told 'Nat one . . . may come among yow alle', and her attempts to pursue the issue draw an official blank:

> 'Nat one?' quod I, 'ey, benedicite!
> What have they don? I pray yow, telle me that.'
> 'Now, be my lif, I trowe but wele,' quod she,
> 'But evere I can beleve ther is somwhat,
> And for to sey yow trowth, more can I nat;
> In questions nothyng may I be large,
> I medle me no further than is my charge'.
>   (148–54)

Evidently, this presentation of complaints is not going to be a specifically 'ad hominem' exercise. Diligence protests that she cannot spell out what offence men have caused. Her vagueness (if not archness) about the offences and the offenders is echoed in the later sequence of complaints made by the female fellowship at Lady Loyalty's court. Here, too, there is no move to complain 'ad hominem', although the women are given the chance to speak within an officially sanctioned environment – in the space, that is, of an all-female court.

Narrative motifs: II. The court
The handling of the dream experience at the court of Lady Loyalty is the focus for much of the modern-day critical dissatisfaction with the *Assembly of Ladies*. One of the problems seems to be that this text does not offer such readers what they expect from a love-vision which uses the allegorical device of personification as an analytical tool. C. S. Lewis's judgement on the text

(Lewis, 1958: 249–50) may be taken as exemplary here since his views have been endorsed by others, including Pearsall, and thus have provided an influential modern frame for reading the narrative:

> What the writer really wants to describe is no inner drama with loyalty as its heroine, but the stir and bustle of an actual court, the whispered consultations, the putting on of clothes, the important comings and goings. She is moved . . . to present the detail of everyday life; and if her poem were not hampered by being still attached . . . to the allegorical form, it would still be an admirable picture of manners. Indeed, if only the first four stanzas survived we might now be lamenting the lost Jane Austen of the fifteenth century.

We could spend the whole essay unpacking the manifold assumptions about 'women's writing' built into this confident identification of what a woman (writer) really wants to do (and then elaborate on the kind of domestic reasoning behind Skeat's argument for the female authorship of the text), but let us concentrate on what Lewis perceives as being out of joint with this major sequence of the text. What Lewis suggests here is that there is a displacement of interest and of appropriate tone: the allegorical form requires a serious dramatic psychomachia (that is, a dramatised struggle of inner qualities or faculties), but what we are given (in his view) is animated by an interest in the small-scale exchanges which characterise 'real' court life. Thus for Pearsall too the allegory of the *Assembly of Ladies* has 'little vitality . . . the personifications drop dead from the pen' (Pearsall, 1962: 57). There seems little point in pursuing the issue in these oppositional terms, in which 'live' and 'real' bits of the poem are contrasted with 'dead' ones; but there is more to say about the effects of personification in the creation of an all-female court in this sequence.

In the *Assembly of Ladies*, as commonly in medieval texts, personification is used to explore codes of behaviour through the representation of abstract qualities in systems of socialised relations. Notions of gender-identity are necessarily implicated in such dramatised sequences, although there have been very few studies of medieval personification allegory which have explored these issues in any depth: the decision to embody an abstract quality in a female or a male form is not an arbitrary one. Indeed, in Marina Warner's view, the choice of a female body to represent a moral ideal frequently works to point up the distinction between the idealised realm of the symbolic order and the actual order of society since it 'depends on the unlikelihood of women practising the concepts they represent' (Warner, 1985: xx). We see the operations of engendering abstract qualities as being more complex than this: in fact in the *Assembly of Ladies* we consider the effect of the court sequence as deriving both from the likelihood and from the unlikelihood of women practising what they are made to represent in the official structure of Loyalty's court.

The personifications of Lady Loyalty's court look two ways. The concentration on *women* (or rather, ladies and gentlewomen) at this court as plaintiffs and as office-holders, suggests that the qualities personified have a gender-specific application. They encode the qualities that ladies and gentlewomen must embody if they are to gain entrance to 'Plesaunt Regard' (170) and be judged true loyal 'dames' ('Perseveraunce', 'Diligence', 'Countenaunce', 'Discrecioun', 'Aqueyntaunce – a womman of right graciouse maner' (270), 'Bealchiere', 'Remembraunce', 'Avisenesse'). But the personifications also anatomise the qualities of an idealised court since each is named after the appropriate quality for their professional job ('Perseveraunce' is the usher; 'Countenaunce' is the porter; 'Discresioun' is the chief purveyor; 'Avisenesse' is the secretary, etc). This idealised structure does stand at some remove from any actual practice: it is hardly likely that women would be allowed to serve in these official capacities (as usher, chief purveyor, lodgings-warden, porter, marshall, chamberlain, secretary, judge) in any fifteenth-century social context. The sequence suggests at the same time how 'courtly' women should be (through this dramatised conduct-book), and how male-dominated courts should be (through the personifications in female form which signal that this is an idealised representation, at some remove from actual practice). We see incongruities in this court sequence, but they do not arise from any disparity between the tone of the small-scale exchanges and the nature of the court allegory (as Pearsall and Lewis have indicated), but rather from the double function of the personifications which suggests both the worthiness of courtly women and their essential redundancy in official court structures (where they have no such legislative or executive functions). Some impression of dissonance arises too from the fact that the 'dames' who evidently embody the behavioural ideals of genteel women (and who make it to Lady Loyalty's court) have found little satisfaction in doing so: they come to make their complaints, but the remedies are deferred to another 'parlement' (717–28).

Narrative motifs: III. Transgression
In the maze garden the narrator noted how some of her companions overstep the mark and the maze path 'for verray wrath' (42). Verbal complaints about dissatisfactions (albeit in generalised, non-personalised terms) are voiced in the court sequence. In this context, where some genteel challenges to social norms do appear to be registered, the characterisation of the narrator as a

lady who follows, but also transgresses, courtly codes is interesting. She wears the blue dress (signifying constancy) as is required of her at the court, but she calmly refuses to wear a motto, although it is expected of her:

'Yowre [worde],' quod she [i.e. Contenaunce], 'fayne
      wold I that I knewe.'
'Forsoth,' quod I, 'ye shal wele know and se:
And for my word, I have none, this is trewe;
It is inough that my clothyng be blew
As here before I had comaundement,
And so to do I am right wele content.'

(310–15)

There is a similar emblematic refusal at l.413. The use of mottoes as part of the symbolic register of a court is not extraordinary in itself: they contribute to the display of material wealth and refinement which identifies these women as members of a privileged and superior group (also signalled in the language of their expression – French, a marker of cultural prestige). But the function of the mottoes is also ideological, in that they emblematise, in stark terms, the codes of conduct which shape these women's lives and the limited positions available to aristocratic women in a dominant male culture – those of endurance, submission ('*entierment vostre*'; '*sanz que jamais*') (to male desire?), faithfulness ('*Une sans changier*')), and underpinned by Christian values (in what is otherwise a secular fantasy world) ('*En dieu est*'). The subjectivity of the narrator, then, becomes a focus for the (mild) questioning of a particular form of late medieval femininity which is simultaneously constructed within the text and exposed as a construction.

CONCLUSION

In Derek Pearsall's view, the *Assembly of Ladies* 'seems to be in general an echo of the feminist controversy which preoccupied the later Middle Ages' (Pearsall, 1962: 53). What Pearsall seems to be invoking here are both the long-standing satirical traditions of representing women's nature and value indexed by the material sources of a text like the *Wife of Bath's Prologue*, and, more particularly, the debate stimulated at the end of the fourteenth century in France (and to some extent in England) about the perceived misogyny of the *Roman de la rose*, which is often referred to as the 'querelle de la rose'. Christine de Pisan played an active part in this debate to which several of her works (such as her *Epistre au Dieu amors* and the *Cité des* dames) contribute.[25] Something of this background certainly seems to inform the Assembly of Ladies (and indeed The Floure and the Leafe): it offers a defence of female loyalty which could function as a compensatory response to attacks on female inconstancy and failure to live up to definitions of 'true' femininity; it is preserved in manuscripts which contain copies of other works also associated with this literary debate about the value and representation of women (such as Hoccleve's version of Christine de Pisan's Letter of Cupid, and the English version of Alain Chartier's La Belle Dame sans merci). However, this is a 'background' phenomenon, which requires much more investigation and analysis than either Pearsall supplies or we can offer here, or indeed has been offered by anyone else. The term 'querelle de la rose', or the more general 'querelle des femmes' (which subsumes the specific 'querelle de la rose') are convenient shorthand phrases which invoke texts, traditions and social practices which require much more historically and culturally specific discussion.[26] We do know that a public debate about the Roman de la rose took place in the late fourteenth/early fifteenth century in Paris and that further debates about the representation of women in courtly contexts were sparked by more contemporary works such as Chartier's La Belle Dame sans merci, but just whether these debates constitute a single identifiable phenomenon, how they are echoed on the other side of the channel, and how they are connected to other kinds of élite social practices and social formations are questions which have yet to be answered. Derek Pearsall more or less dismisses the 'querelle des femmes' as an elaborate literary game (Pearsall, 1962: 53), but if it is such, then it may still offer a way of focusing and channeling expressions of discontent with the organisation of literary life and its representation of what it is to be a woman in society. In Gynesis Alice Jardine has asked whether the coming into discourse of women in the late medieval period (which she sees in the so-called 'querelle des femmes') and in the late eighteenth and nineteenth centuries mark the two major transitions in the Western tradition of thought (Jardine, 1985: 96). Given the current state of studies on the 'querelle des femmes', we would agree with Janet Todd's observation that although 'this is a wonderful question to ask, raising many other questions – as well as doubts about the activity of postulating such immense historical abstraction . . . We should wait a considerable time before answering it' (Todd, 1988: 95).

There is still much that we do not know about the cultural contexts of the Assembly of Ladies: what we have tried to do here is to explore the ways in which there is room for us as feminist readers to reproduce this text as a rather more complex product of its historical and class environment, in which specific female protest is encoded – both overtly (the complaints) and covertly (the various forms of transgression, the lack of narrative resolution). The representation of the maze is unusual: it images the social system in which these women are caught up, and can be interpreted as a set of social rules directed at women, some of whom have the boldness to survey that social landscape critically, some of whom are thrown into confusion by it, some of whom have a lot of catching up to do and yet others who rebel against the rules by cheating and stepping over the dividing rails. The lightness of touch is comic, yet there is a serious relationship between the framing maze and the inner dream, in which these same women progress through the densely peopled court of Lady Loyalty as if through a labyrinth, in order to present serious grievances about their fate in a culture which decreed that their supreme self-definition was that of being loved, yet which continually cheated them of the possibility of fulfilment. The maze functions as an image both of social rules and of the pattern of desire, revealed not as romantic longing but as a condition of frustration, caught up inevitably in a social structure, and enacted in the narrative of the *Assembly of Ladies* by the poem's failure to offer the women any resolution for their grievances. The image of the court in this text may be both an expression of nostalgia for 'old world' literary and social values and of some new dissatisfaction with its boundaries and limitations: it may have a resonance for those on the inside of genteel society and those who aspire to gentle status.

We argue here that attention to the historical contexts of the *Assembly of Ladies* – to its writers, readers, literary traditions, shaping circumstances – realigns the text and offers us a work which hovers on the edge of critique, which is cautious, not to say unclear, about its position but which opens up a distinctively female space for the exploration of gender relations. The equivocal authorial voice allows for the deconstruction of historical and ideological categories, revealing the possibility that courtly women are not 'naturally' submissive, uncomplaining or incapable of protest at the strictures of their social world: the woman in the text questions social norms for women within a context in which we would not expect this to happen. We can speculate that these elements might have been part of an emergent structure of feeling in the fifteenth century, part of the phenomenon of the so-called 'querelle des femmes', which was reshaping, in more political forms, the construction of female subjectivity. The *Assembly of Ladies* indicates some sense of genteel women's dissatisfaction with the straightened terms of their symbolic/literary worlds and their lack of official power. Whether or not the author of the work was a man, the choice of a female narrator would suggest the need to take those dissatisfactions seriously. The *Assembly of Ladies* is no utopian venture, no privileged expression of authentic female experience outside the boundaries of social construction, but it does offer an 'unexpected' view of its pleasures and constraints.[27]

NOTES

1. Gillian Beer, 'Representing women: re-presenting the past', in Catherine Belsey and Jane Moore (eds), *The Feminist Reader: Essays in gender and the politics of literary criticism* (Basingstoke and London: Macmillan, 1989), p. 64.

2. For a general survey of lay literacy see Malcolm Parkes, 'The literacy of the laity', in *The Medieval World*, ed. D. Daiches and A. Thorlby (London: Aldus Books, 1973), pp. 555–77. Parkes distinguishes the 'literacy of recreation' (p. 555) from other kinds of professional literacies (i.e. that required of those in holy orders and that required by one who has to read or write in the course of transacting business). Access to literate skills for women is determined by social status and/or religious vocation (though it should be noted that an ability to read does not necessarily signal an ability to write). See Joan Ferrante, 'The education of women in the Middle Ages in theory, fact and fantasy', in *Beyond Their Sex: Learned women of the European past* ed. Patricia Labalme (New York: New York University Press, 1980), pp. 9–42; Nicholas Orme, *From Childhood to Chivalry* (London: Methuen, 1984), pp. 156–3. For a general survey of noblewomen's participation in religious and secular literary culture of the medieval period see Susan Groag Bell, 'Medieval woman book owners: arbiters of lay piety and ambassadors of culture', in *Women and Power in the Middle Ages*, ed. Mary Erler and Maryanne Kowaleski (Athens and London: University of Georgia Press, 1988), pp. 149–87. Katherine Wilson provides examples of the work of fifteen women writers (the majority are members of religious communities and/or are writing on spiritual or mystical subjects) in *Medieval Women Writers* (Athens, Georgia: University of Georgia Press, 1984). There are two women from this collection (which spans eight centuries) who come from late fourteenth-century/early fifteenth-century England: Julian of Norwich and Margery Kempe (the latter, though apparently illiterate, still, exceptionally, contrives to record the history of her spiritual life). Two notable lay-noblewomen who contribute to the field of religious letters in fifteenth-century England are Eleanor Hull and, of course, Lady Margaret Beaufort. For further discussion of Eleanor Hull see Alexandra Barratt, 'Dame Eleanor Hull: a fifteenth-century translator', in *The Medieval Translator: The theory and practice of translation in the Middle Ages*, ed. Roger Ellis (Woodbridge: D. S. Brewer, 1989), pp. 87–102; for Lady Margaret Beaufort see the biographical information and further bibliography in 'Women writers, 1485–1603' by Elizabeth Hageman in *English Literary Renaissance* 14 (1984), 409–25 (especially pp. 413, 423).

3. Although there are some useful general surveys available on the subject, more detailed, historically specific studies which attend to gender variables are very much needed. The nature of the evidence which may be used to reconstruct patterns of book ownership and readership is often very limited and partial and thus poses interpretative problems as several of the contributors to the recent collection of essays on *Book Production and Publishing in Britain 1375–1475* ed. J. Griffiths and Derek Pearsall (Cambridge: Cambridge University Press, 1989) have pointed out (see the essays by Kate Harris and Carol Meale in particular). The issue is further complicated by the question of which of the literary vernaculars of England (English or French) we are considering. Most of the evidence of women owning secular books in the fourteenth and fifteenth centuries derives from the wills of noblewomen and suggests that their preferred language for their literature of recreation was still French. However, there is some evidence, particularly from signatures in manuscripts, which suggests that some women from the gentry (such as those whose names are recorded in the 'Findern' anthology – Cambridge University Library MS Ff 16 –) did form part of the

reading community for secular works in English in the fifteenth century. Where evidence of identifiable female readers is lacking (in the present state of studies) is from the expanding group of recreational readers from the mercantile sector who formed 'a much more literate and educated section of society than has often been supposed' (Julia Boffey, *Manuscripts of English Courtly Love Lyrics in the Later Middle Ages*, Woodbridge: D. S. Brewer, 1985, p. 125). Carol Meale has surveyed the evidence for ownership of books by women from the aristocratic and gentry sectors in an essay which is to be published in the proceedings of the 1990 Conference on 'Medieval women', organised by Felicity Riddy, Jeremy North, Peter Biller and Amanda Lillie (at the University of York). We are very grateful to Carol Meale for allowing us to read an earlier version of this essay. For an accessible, brief discussion of the social stratification of late-medieval English society, see Christopher Dyer, *Standards of Living in the Later Middle Ages: Social change in England c. 1200–1520* (Cambridge: Cambridge University Press, 1989), pp. 10–26.

4. See Martha Howell, *Women, Production and Patriarchy in Late Medieval Cities* (Chicago and London: The University of Chicago Press, 1986); Judith Bennett, *Women in the Medieval English Countryside* (Oxford: Oxford University Press, 1986). Further information about feminist studies of medieval culture can be found in the bibliographical sections of *The Medieval Feminist Newsletter* (currently edited by Roberta Kreuger, Hamilton College USA).

5. The modern edition is by Derek Pearsall: *The Floure and the Leafe and the Assembly of Ladies* (Manchester: Manchester University Press, 1980). All our quotations will be taken from this edition and cited by line number. There is one section of Pearsall's edition which needs some emendation. He suggests that at line 680 Lady Loyalty intervenes to encourage the narrator to spell out her complaint at last. In our view it is far more likely that the narrator's male interlocutor intervenes at this point in the narrative to chivy the narrator (and thus breaks the autonomy of the dream narrative). For further discussion of this point see Alexandra Barratt, 'The Flower and the Leaf and the Assembly of Ladies: is there a (sexual) difference?', *Philological Quarterly* 66 (1987), 1–21 (especially pp. 19–20).

6. The use of formal legal procedures to provide a frame for the exploration of emotional grievances was a commonplace technique in 'courtly' texts in French and English by the fifteenth century. However, the technical precision of legal terms in the *Assembly of Ladies* gives this text a distinctive quality, as Derek Pearsall has observed (see especially pp. 161–3 of his edition).

7. The title now used to refer to the text, the *Assembly of Ladies*, derives from that provided in William Thynne's copy of the narrative printed in his 1532 edition of 'The workes of Geffray Chaucer newly printed with dyvers workes whiche were never in print before'. The French title given in the narrative has the advantage of referring to a category of women 'Dames' which includes both the ladies and the 'gentil wymmen' who wander in the garden whereas the conventional English title singles out the ladies only. There is a distinction made between the ladies and the gentlewomen in the narrative (the gentlewomen serve the ladies), but in other respects they appear to share values, aspirations and emotional experiences, and, indeed, a common court culture. So though the women of the garden are of different social rankings, they still form a collective court élite (as do the ladies and gentlewomen who serve Lady Loyalty). For further discussion of the growing numbers of 'gentle' members of English society in the fifteenth century see Dyer, *Standards of Living*; D. A. L. Morgan, 'The individual style of the English gentleman', in M. Jones (ed.), *Gentry and Lesser Nobility in Late Medieval Europe* (Gloucester: Sutton, 1986) and Rosemary Horrox, 'The urban gentry in the fifteenth century', in *Towns and Townspeople in the Fifteenth Century*, ed. John Thompson (Gloucester: Sutton, 1988) pp. 22–44.

8. The three later fifteenth-century manuscripts which contain copies of the *Assembly of Ladies* are Cambridge, Trinity College MS R.3.19; Longleat House, Library of the Marquis of Bath, MS 258; London, British Library, MS Additional 34360. In general terms these manuscripts reflect the 'growing taste' for anthologies of 'Chaucerian and neo-Chaucerian poetry which concentrate particularly on works with secular, usually amorous themes' which is noted by Julia Boffey and John J. Thompson in their discussion of 'Anthologies

and miscellanies: production and choice of texts' in *Book Production and Publishing in Britain*, ed. Griffiths and Pearsall, pp. 279–315, especially pp. 270–91. Since Pearsall discusses these manuscripts and provides further bibliographical information in his edition (pp. 7–8) we will offer only a brief account of each and cite more recent bibliography here. MS Additional 34360, a paper manuscript produced by a London-based scribe, contains several moralising works by Lydgate, but also, in addition to the *Assembly of Ladies*, some short complaint poems in English (including Chaucer's *Pity*) and French and a copy of the *Craft of Lovers*. MS Longleat 258 is, like MS Additional 34360, another of the 'major anthologies of writing which attempted to distil a Chaucerian or Lydgatian tone' according to Julia Boffey, *Manuscripts of English Courtly Love Lyrics*, p. 17. In addition to the *Assembly of Ladies*, this manuscript contains copies of Lydgate's love vision poem the *Temple of Glass*, Chaucer's *Anelida and Arcite* and his *Parlement of Foules*, a copy of the English version of Alain Chartier's *La Belle Dame sans merci* and may originally have contained a copy of the *Flower and the Leaf*. This is very likely to have been the manuscript used as a copy by William Thynne for his 1532 edition of the works of Chaucer. See Eleanor Hammond, 'MS Longleat 258 – A Chaucerian Codex', *MLN*, 20 (1905), pp. 77–9; Julia Boffey, *Manuscripts of English Courtly Love Lyrics*, pp. 117–18; Ethel Seaton, *Sir Richard Roos* (London: Rupert Hart-Davis, 1961), pp. 92–3 (for a brief discussion of its later ownership by Thynne's nephew, Sir John Thynne). Trinity College Cambridge MS R.3.19 is a fascicular manuscript (a collection made up from a number of discrete booklets) and contains a wide variety of texts, some by Chaucer (including the *Legend of Good Women* and the *Parlement of Foules*), Lydgate and George Ashby, and several of the lyrics and short narratives which were later attributed to Chaucer in Speght's edition of the works of Chaucer in 1598. Julia Boffey discusses this manuscript on pp. 17–19 of *Manuscripts of Courtly Love Lyrics* and speculates on its possible ownership by a London merchant in the late fifteenth/early sixteenth century on pp. 126–7.

9. Skeat's 'evidence' for the common female authorship of *The Floure and the Leafe* and the *Assembly of Ladies* is set out in *Academy* 35 (1889), 448–9; 41 (1892), 592; *Modern Language Quarterly* 3 (1900), 111–12; *Atheneum* (1903), i, 340. Skeat's summary, discussion and edition of the *Assembly of Ladies* is in the supplementary volume (vol. VII) to his edition of *The Works of Geoffrey Chaucer*, W. W. Skeat, *Chaucerian and Other Pieces*, (Oxford: Oxford University Press, 1897), pp. lvii–lxx (which includes discussion of the *Floure and the Leafe*), pp. 380–404.

10. See Seaton, *Sir Richard Roos*, pp. 294–308; Pearsall, *The Floure and the Leafe and the Assembly of Ladies*, pp. 14–15 and 'The *Assembly of Ladies* and *Generydes*', in *Review of English Studies* 12 (1961), 227–37. In the latter article Pearsall argues that there is sufficient textual evidence to suggest a common author behind both the *Assembly of Ladies* and *Generydes* (an exotic romance, which does not experiment with narratorial voice in a comparable way). Pearsall concludes that 'of the two poems, *Generydes* would be the earlier; it is not likely to have been written by a woman' (p. 237) without fully explaining why. Nevertheless Pearsall indentifies the approach of both texts as being 'ladylike' and suggests that they were written for a 'predominantly female audience in some noble or manorial household' (p. 235). See also John Stephens, 'The questioning of love in the *Assembly of Ladies*', *Review of English Studies*, New Series 24 (1973), ll. 129–140. See also Alexandra Barratt (1987: 1–21) who begins with an interesting discussion of how both of these poems test some of the assumptions behind modern critical approaches to reading texts, but does not sustain this kind of analysis in her own discussion of the texts. It should be noted that medieval audiences did not necessarily expect works to be ascribed to a named author: there are *named* fifteenth-century writers, but there are many anonymous texts. There are also sophisticated and well-established traditions of constructing fictional first-person narrators or personas in medieval literature, including the use of 'female' voices by male poets. One of the most notorious examples of an exercise in ventriloquism of this kind is in the construction of the Wife of Bath's performance in the *Canterbury Tales*, but Pearsall cites other examples in the introduction to his edition, pp. 14; 54.

11. Ann McMillan's study, '"Fayre Sisters Al": *The Flower and the Leaf* and the *Assembly of*

Ladies', *Tulsa Studies in Women's Literature* 1 (1982), 27–42 does not sufficiently emphasise the problems in reading the texts as reflections of the 'concerns of fifteenth-century women' (p. 27). For a cautionary appraisal of the reclaiming strategy as it has been manifested in the recent growth of interest in studies of Christine de Pisan, see Sheila Delany, ' "Mothers to think back through": who are they? The ambiguous example of Christine de Pizan', in her *Medieval Literary Politics: Shapes of ideology* (Manchester: Manchester University Press, 1990), pp. 88–103. In this essay Sheila Delany challenges the idea that 'the act of writing by itself suffices to qualify an early writer as a feminist, a radical, a revolutionary, or a model for us' (p. 89).

12. See Charity C. Willard, *Christine de Pizan: Her life and works* (New York: Persea Books, 1984) for a general discussion of the milieu and literary production of this writer and further bibliography. Christine de Pisan's *Cité des dames*, a literary defence for women, was translated into English by Brian Anslay (*The Boke of the Cyte of Ladyes*) in 1521; the most recent translation was by Earl Jeffrey Richards (London, 1982). For the circulation of Christine de Pisan's work in fifteenth-century/sixteenth-century England see P. G. C. Campbell, 'Christine de Pisan en Angleterre', *Revue de littérature comparée* 5 (1925), 659–70 and the emendations to this piece in A. J. Kennedy, *Christine de Pizan: A bibliographical guide* (London: Grant and Cutler, 1984). Carol Meale also provides a very helpful discussion of the evidence for the ownership and circulation of de Pizan's work in French in 'Patrons, buyers and owners' (cited above note 3), p. 208. As Carol Meale notes, Christine de Pisan's work also circulated (in attributed and unattributed form) in English translations from the early fifteenth century onwards. See Kennedy's bibliographical guide for a list of these translations.

13. For an overview of the poor critical reputation of fifteenth-century literary production in English see *Fifteenth-Century Studies*, ed. Robert Yeager (Hamden, Connecticut: Archon Books, 1984), pp. vi–ix. In the field of historical studies, in contrast, 'the last twenty years have witnessed a remarkable revival of interest in the history of late medieval England. The fifteenth century in particular, from being the "Cinderella" [sic] of the centuries of English "history", has become the most intensively studied of the entire Middle Ages' (Edward Powell, *Kinship, Law and Society*, Oxford: Clarendon Press, 1989, p. 1). Powell provides a useful listing of the most important studies to appear in the 1980s in f. 3 and 4, p. 1.

14. R. H. Robbins comments that 'these court love poems are often dull, often uninspired' in 'The structure of longer Middle English court poems', in *Chaucerian Problems and Perspectives*, ed. E. Vasta and Z. Thundy (Notre Dame: University of Notre Dame Press, 1979), pp. 244–58 (p. 244).

15. In 'Chaucer's influence on fifteenth-century poetry', *Companion to Chaucer Studies*, ed. Beryl Rowland (1st edn, Oxford: Oxford University Press, 1968), pp. 385–402, Denton Fox remarks that it is 'already clear that the traditional notions of fifteenth-century poetry, and its relationship to Chaucer will have to be drastically revised' (p. 385). Douglas Gray's recent anthology, *Late Medieval Verse and Prose* (Oxford: Clarendon Press, 1988) represents an attempt to 'give a sense of the variety and complexity of this long period' (p. iii) and to show the 'absurdity of viewing this period as a dull one'. See also David Lawton, 'Dullness and the fifteenth century', *English Literary Review* 54 (1987), 761–99.

16. As represented in the work of Julia Boffey, Carol Meale and that of the other contributors in the volume on *Book Production and Publishing in Britain 1375–1475*.

17. John Shirley (born sometime in the 1360s and who died in 1456) and who was for some years in the service of Richard Beauchamp, Earl of Warwick, appears to have had a pervasive influence on 'manuscript production and compilation, particularly in London, and particularly in connection with large-format verse anthologies' (Boffey, *Manuscripts of English Courtly Love Lyrics*, pp. 17–19). Both MS Additional 34360 and the Trinity College Cambridge MS R.3.19 which contain the *Assembly of Ladies* have links with Shirley exemplars, though the evidence for this is too complex to set out in detail here. See Julia Boffey and John J. Thompson's discussion of the circulation of exemplars for *La Belle Dame sans merci* (which is copied in the Longleat and Trinity College manuscripts of the *Assembly*

of Ladies), and the interconnections between scribes with links to some kind of commercial milieu in 'Anthologies and miscellanies: production and choice of texts', in *Book Production and Publishing in Britain, 1375–1475*, pp. 283–7 and also Ian Doyle 'English books in and out of court', *English Court Culture in the Later Middle Ages*, ed. V. J. Scattergood and J. W. Sherborne (London: Duckworth, 1983) pp. 163–81, especially pp. 176–8, in addition to the references cited by Strohm (1982).

18. The usefulness of the term 'courtly love' has been much contested. See Toril Moi, 'Desire in language: Andreas Capellanus and the controversy of courtly love', *Medieval Literature*, ed. David Aers (Hemel Hempstead: Harvester Wheatsheaf, 1986), pp. 11–31; Arlyn Diamond, 'Engendering criticism', *Thought* 64 (1989), 298–309.

19. For the *Temple of Glas* (which offers a sympathetic representation of a lady's plight in being married to a man she does not love) see *John Lydgate: Poems*, ed. John Norton-Smith (Oxford: Clarendon Press, 1966). For the text of the *Parliament of Love* (anonymous) preserved in Cambridge University Library MS Ff 16 see F. Furnivall's edition in *Political, Religious and Love Poems*, EETS OS 15 (London, 1866), pp. 48–51. This representation of a court of love through the eyes of a male mentor is of special interest because it appears to reflect the expanding audience for genteel literature in the fifteenth century. In this court of love there are not only ladies and 'gentyll wymmen of lower degree' but also 'marchauntz wyfes'. The codification of genteel behaviour in conduct-book form in circulation in the fifteenth century, offers another important literary context for the *Assembly of Ladies* which has yet to be investigated. For the most detailed study of the sources of the *Assembly of Ladies* see Ruth Fisher's unpublished Ph.D. thesis, 'The Flower and the Leaf and the *Assembly of Ladies*: a study of two love-visions in the fifteenth century' (University of Columbia, 1955).

20. Robbins has a reductive view of the function of the frame for these complaints which we do not share. He suggests that 'the 83 preceding stanzas and the seven concluding are simply devices in yet another effort to give a new format to this old form' (1979: 257).

21. Attempting to recreate the 'horizons of expectation' of a medieval audience by discussing the system of literary genres and their uses is a common first recourse in modern criticism of medieval literature (and obviously a factor which we are attentive to here). But many subjective judgements about form and meaning are inevitably built into this seemingly objective exercise in description and analysis. Hans Robert Jauss has done most on a theoretical level to promote the reconstruction of the medieval audience's 'horizons of expectation' as a modern critical technique and for further details of his work and a critique of its fundamental premisses see Lee Patterson, *Negotiating the Past* (Wisconsin: The University of Wisconsin Press, 1987), pp. 7–8, n.9 and Ardis Butterfield, 'Medieval genres and modern genre theory', *Paragraph* 13 (1990), 184–201.

22. For the construction of women's voices in a broad range of lyric traditions from several countries, including works which do not operate within a courtly verse register, see the collection, *Vox Feminae: Studies in medieval woman's songs*, ed. John Plummer (Kalamazoo, Michigan: Medieval Institute Publications, 1981).

23. For Lydgate's 'A gentlewoman's lament', see *The Minor Poems of John Lydgate, Part II: The secular poems*, EETS OS 192 (London, 1934), pp. 418–20. For the complaint lyrics voiced by women in the 'Findern' anthology (that is Cambridge University Library MS Ff 16) see R. H. Robbins, 'The Findern Anthology', *PMLA* 69 (1954) 610–642. The presence of 'gentlewomen's' names/signatures (?) in this manuscript has led to some interesting speculations about the possible copying, if not composition, of texts in this manuscript by women from families which may be associated with the Findern family itself, though the evidence and its interpretation has been disputed. For more information about this manuscript see the introduction to the facsimile by R. Beadle and A. E. B. Owen (London: Scolar Press, 1977) and K. D. Harris, 'The origins and make-up of Cambridge University Library MS Ff 16', *Transactions of the Cambridge Bibliographical Society*, 8 (1983), 299–333. The existence of lyric complaints voiced by ladies and gentlewomen has not been given enough attention in general surveys and medieval English lyric collections. For some other examples see R. H. Robbins, *Secular Lyrics of the Fourteenth and Fifteenth Centuries* (Oxford: Clarendon Press, 1952), pp. 214–19.

24. See Pearsall (1962: 164) for further account of this tradition of wall decorations from the stories of love's martyrs and details of further examples (the list of which could be considerably amplified). However, the decorations on the walls of Lady Loyalty's court do have a singular quality which has no parallel to our knowledge: the paintings are so bright that they have to be covered by a veil (ll. 470–4) which still allows the stories to be read. This resonant image of the filter through which the narratives of betrayed women are read deserves further discussion.

25. The 'querelle' over the moral worth of the *Roman de la rose* and Jean de Meun's representation of his women protagonists had diverse informal origins but the formal debate is manifested in a series of letters between critics and defenders of Jean de Meun written in the early years of the fifteenth century. Christine de Pisan and Jean Gerson were the foremost critics; on the other side the defenders included Jean de Montreuil, Provost of Lille and Gontier Col (first secretary to the King) and his brother Pierre Col (Canon of Paris and Tournay). But de Pizan both anticipated and continued her critique of Jean de Meun's anti-feminism in other of her literary works as we have noted. See Willard, *Christine de Pizan*, pp. 73–8; *La Querelle de la rose: Letters and documents*, trans. Joseph Baird and John Kane (Chapel Hill: University of North Carolina, Dept of Romance Languages, 1978). For a survey and listing of material which features 'arguments about women in English and Scots literature to 1568' see Francis Lee Utley, *The Crooked Rib* (Ohio: Farrar, Straus and Giroux, 1944). For a résumé of the medieval background to the sixteenth-century 'querelle des femmes' in England, see Katherine Henderson and Barbara McManus, *Half Human Kind: Contexts and texts of the controversy about women in England 1540–1640* (Urbana and Chicago: University of Illinois Press, 1985), especially pp. 4–11.

26. Joan Kelly's pioneering article, 'Early feminist theory and the "querelle des femmes"', *Women, History and Theory: The essays of Joan Kelly* (Chicago and London: University of Chicago Press, 1984), pp. 65–109, tries to define the phenomenon of the 'querelle' more precisely but reveals just how imprecise current notions of the parameters and subjects of the 'querelle' are. There seem to be slippages of usage from critic to critic and a general uncertainty about how the specific 'querelle de la rose' contributes to (or is subsumed by) the 'querelle des femmes' (and whether this latter phenomenon really emerges or peaks in the sixteenth century). The parameters, and consequences of, the debate about the representation of women stimulated by *La Belle Dame sans merci* (and its reverberations amongst readers and writers in England) has yet to be investigated in detail. The 'counterblasts' to Chartier's text are not easily available. See *The Poetical Works of Alain Chartier*, ed. J. C. Laidlaw (Cambridge: Cambridge University Press, 1974), especially pp. 7–8, 39–40.

27. See Alexandra Barratt's comments on the significance of the dream-vision frame in the *Assembly of Ladies* (in which the narrator is prompted by and draws validation from a male audience) as offering a 'paradigm of women's writing' (Barratt, 1982: 14–15).

Penny Boumelha

'The Rattling of her Discourse and the Flapping of her Dress': Meredith Writing the 'Women of the Future'

'The happiest women, like the happiest nations, have no history.'
George Eliot, *The Mill on the Floss*, VI, 3

In *The Egoist*, George Meredith poses the question, 'Can a woman have an inner life apart from him she is yoked to?'[1] I want to propose that his novel of six years later, *Diana of the Crossways*, is in part an extended meditation on the same question; not, of course, on the question of whether actual, historical women had inner lives (then as now, the answer could be taken for granted, though the *nature* of those lives and the relation between them and questions of gender has remained just as contentious), but rather, a meditation on the possibility and desirability of writing such an 'inner life'. According to Peter Brooks, 'if [our] secret lives are to be narratable, they must in some sense be plotted',[2] and it is to this point that I want primarily to address myself here: to the ways in which the writing of 'woman' is formed and constrained by the continuing necessity of *plot* at least as much as by the widely noted treadmill of repetition of stereotypes.

The period of early modernism is one in which a lack of confidence in history as a readily perspicuous mode of explanation becomes apparent, and with it a concomitant suspicion of individual history, of the bibliographical form so characteristic of realism. The ease and readability of realist plotting betrays what has been called its 'desire for continuous re-affirmation of the commonality of experience',[3] and in this it calls upon and calls up a consensual agreement of reader and text that the individual life is comprehensible and meaningful on the basis of a shared narrative structure. And yet, at the very moment of its greatest discursive dominance, the explanatory power of serial structure comes simultaneously to be thrown into doubt; evolutions and causalities are undermined, arguably by that irruption of the feminine that contemporaries felt marked the *fin de siècle* period as a whole. Women writers, New Women, the Woman as Hero: the unplottable and disorderly force of feminine desire could no longer be abandoned to illegibility, and with it came a wider play of narrative and formal possibilities. A self-conscious, interrogative mode of plotting marks many of the novels-of-women (as writer or as heroine) in which the period abounds.

In Diana Merion/Warwick/Redworth, Meredith writes a woman who is, variously, 'yoked' to no one and to a series of men, and in this he poses himself the difficulty of writing an inner life which will not be a mirror, a reflection, an echo, of the male, as the 'inner lives' of heroines have so frequently been. But he further compounds the problem by setting himself the necessity of a plot which can render this, in Brooks' words, 'secret life . . . narratable'. It is this that underlies the novel's concern with the telling and evasion of stories, its rhetoric of true and false representation, its discussion of a fiction informed by 'brainstuff' as against the 'rose-pink' and 'dirty-drab' of contemporary practice.[4] *Diana of the Crossways* focuses pre-cisely upon the gap, or alternatively the bridge, between inner life and social plot: its central narrative motivation might be said to be the publication of the private life. In the virtually literal anatomy of fiction that occurs early in the novel, it is, we are told, only the presence of 'internal history' that can give a novel 'brainstuff' (p. 15), and the all but unreadable first chapter doubly explores the process by which such 'internal history' may become fiction. The novel begins, that is to say, not with narration in the indicative, but with a series of partial accounts of its heroine, ostensibly published from the private writings – diaries, journals – of named but insignificant charac-ters, as a way of making public the private life of Diana Warwick. This motif continues in the gossip and speculation by which events and feelings are so often represented to the reader, and in the recurring metaphor of the woman stripped by baying hounds. Diana's own fiction – taken within the novel to be either retrospectively or presciently autobiographical – suggests the possibility or exploration in another mode of writing (the romantic) of what Meredith here investigates in the taut and interrogative writing of early modernism. And the novel is itself in part a making public of actual private lives, since, as is well known, it adapts the career of the Hon. Caroline Norton (herself a public figure by virtue, initially, of her personal relation-ships) and, in addition, refers to Meredith's own first wife, Mary Ellen Peacock. The story and figure of Diana, then, mark the historic shift within English culture, at this period, in the position of at least middle-class women, from the apparently 'private' sphere of home and domesticity to the public domain of politics.

So, in all these ways, the dialectic of private and public, inner and social, is fundamental to the novel. But the most flamboyant instance of the publication of the private is, surely, Diana's selling of the Cabinet secret confided in her by her lover, Percy Dacier. It is an act upon which the romantic plot of the novel hinges; and it is, crucially, an act susceptible of only constructed explanations. No narrative comment gives us a definite motive. By attending to the placing of the episode within the novel (following immediately upon Dacier's *failure* to recognise her wishes and desires), it is possible to see it as an act of revenge, or, less pejoratively, as a reciprocal betrayal. But the perfunctory naïvety of the account Diana gives to Dacier – '"I had not a suspicion of doing harm, Percy"' (p. 324) – sets up an oscillation which leaves both explanations unsatisfactory, inadequate. The sale of the secret, if viewed in terms of character, must seem almost an *acte gratuit*. The letter of what might, in another novel, one assumes, be motives explained and feelings declared is burned unopened by Dacier, and with it, the reader is faced with the full opacity of the deed.

However, it is noticeable that Diana's 'betrayal' occurs in the narrative context of a rather different kind of rendering public and social what is seemingly private and individual: that is, the interrogation of the trope by which 'a woman', *this* woman, comes to stand for 'woman'. 'Man', as we know, can be individually or species-specific, but 'woman' is invariably sex-specific; it is always summoned as a mode of representing and explaining difference from a norm which is posited, however implicitly, as masculine. The persistence of this mode of linguistic and social organisation constrains the ways in which it is possible, thus far, to speak of what is not man. Hence the discursive and ideological effectivity of the trope; and it is, for these same reasons, a trope which feminist criticism must find itself replaying, as I do here, sometimes to positive effect, in so far as it enables some crucial revaluings, but always, none the less, at the risk of reconfirming the apparent naturalness of the class. Just this relationship between particular and generic is at the heart of many other novels of the 1880s and 1890s; *Tess of the d'Urbervilles*, with its perfectly ambiguous 'pure woman', is an instance that comes readily to mind. It is quite explicitly remarked in *The Egoist*, where Laetitia Dale notes that '"The generic woman appears to have an extraordinary faculty for swallowing the individual"' (p. 181). But whereas in that novel the point is primarily an ethical one, one of the many reflections upon the egoism of the protagonist, in *Diana of the Crossways*, the incident of the betrayed secret brings the trope itself under self-conscious scrutiny. So, Dacier has pursued Diana in 'serious pursuit of a woman's character' although 'she bore no resemblance to the bundle of women' (p. 149). Diana's particularly acute sense of humiliation when he tries to impose his will on hers, in the form of sexual attentions, is partly because 'clearly he took her for the same as other women consenting to receive a privileged visitor' (p. 312). When she goes, with a sense of some importance, to the newspaper office – place of work and publication – she finds that with the denial of generic identity goes the loss of all human status:

> Men passed her, hither and yonder, cursorily noticing the presence of a woman. She lost, very strangely to her, the sense of her sex and became an object – a disregarded object. Things of more importance were about. . . . Here was manifestly a spot where women had dropped from the secondary to the cancelled stage of their extraordinary career in a world either blowing them aloft like soap-bubbles or quietly shelving them as supernumeraries. (p. 314)

After the newspaper appears, Dacier too is ready to dissolve the specific woman into the category as a whole: 'He set his mind on the consequences of the act of folly – the trusting a secret to a woman. All were possibly not so bad: none should be trusted' (p. 328).

Here in little, then, we have the crux of the novel: the difficulty of writing a woman and writing woman, of writing an 'inner life' which will not, as soon as it touches upon the social plot of the public sphere, resolve itself once more into the collection of generalities, ideologies and repetitions by which the category 'woman' constructs, reproduces and transforms itself. Diana's selling of the secret can only indicate, for Dacier, that she is 'like a woman' (and we know that women cannot keep secrets) or else, for herself, that she is not to be treated 'like a woman' (that she is a special case). But by allowing the act to retain its resistant opacity, Meredith places the double bind before us, and in the process makes evident the extent to which *both* possible explanations are implicated in the patriarchal discourses of gender.

And it is here – by way of the novel's throwing into question story, or plot – that *Diana of the Crossways* is most susceptible of feminist interpretation. The framing effect of the opening diary quotations is only the first among numerous ways of staving off those well-established conventions of closure (death or marriage) to which the highly self-conscious conclusion – called 'The Nuptial chapter' (p. 377) – at last accedes. For one of the ways in which the multi-named Diana is at the crossroads is in the novel's explicit project of moving on from a fiction in which women are variously named puppets, blocks of marble, heroines of romance, or 'pedestalled woman' (p. 232) into at least an investigation of the possibility of what Diana calls '"a sketch of the women of the future – don't be afraid! – the far future. What a different earth you will see!"' (p. 276). Hence, I think, the significance of the yacht *Clarissa*, named for the founding English text of the woman as violated body and consciousness. Diana skirts this plot, in the various sexual advances which drive her from one story to the next and in the period of self-starvation which brings her almost to the point of death. By the end of the novel, however, she has departed with her new husband on their unimaginable voyage of transformation on the schooner *Diana*, named (with an astute ambiguity) perhaps only for herself or perhaps for the persisting cultural myths and ideologies from which the 'women of the future' may yet be composed.

But the novel avoids structuring itself upon that over-simple opposition of reality and stereotype, and likewise steers clear of the narrative tactic that would make of its heroine an allegory of truth or nature in a corrupt social world.[5] Certainly, she is by the end the 'flecked heroine of Reality' (p. 335) as opposed to the 'puppet-woman, mother of Fiction and darling of the multitude!' (p. 377). However, I would argue that these very terms are themselves to be read within a context in which Diana is from the first recognised as the product of writing, and *that* not in the most straightforward metafictional sense. The novel is in part a notation of the myths and metaphors, ideologies and discourses, out of which the writing of 'woman' is born. Perhaps it is to underline this sense of assemblage that a kind of Frankenstein's monster of writing emerges through continued images of body parts: fiction without philosophy, for example, is a 'skeleton anatomy' (p. 16); fact to which stories may refer is a 'naked body' (p. 3); once give it 'internal history' and it acquires 'brainstuff' (p. 15). But when this fiction is animated through the account of a woman, or of woman, the body of writing simultaneously hides and accentuates the organs of its generation by recourse to the 'fallen' language of figure which Meredith, like Rousseau, seems to associate with the feminine:[6] 'Metaphors were her refuge. Metaphorically she could allow her mind to distinguish the struggle she was undergoing, sinking under it. The banished of Eden had to put on metaphors . . .' (p. 231). The 'brainstuff' of fiction speaks, that is to say, no more loudly than the clothing of its heroine, as when Diana attempts to understand and make herself understood through 'the rattling of her discourse and the flapping of her dress' (p. 382).

Beneath the figures of 'outlaw' and 'alien', chaste goddess of the moon and fearful Hecate, author of romances and entry in the diary of another, we are to discern no 'naked body' of 'fact' in the representation of Diana. There are other female figures, conceived differently: Lady Wathin, for example, or Constance Asper, whose drawings appeal to her fiancé as '"taken from my favourite point of view"' (p. 333). They are among those figures that the novel calls 'women of waxwork', 'women of happy marriages', 'women of holy nunneries', 'women lucky in their arts' (p. 7): in short, they are 'the idol women of imperishable type, who are never for a twinkle the prey of the blood' (p. 322). But what marks them off from Diana is not the difference between, say, stereotype and reality; it is, rather, that they fall easily into the familiar plots of the nineteenth century precisely by virtue of the simplicity of their stories. There is a predictable, unilinear progression from one socially authorised category to another: from virgin to wife (Miss Asper, Lady Wathin) or to fallen women (Miss Paynham). Diana, on the other hand, is a woman with a history who exists for the greater part of the novel in a vertiginous state of sexual-categorical suspension: 'wife and no wife' (p. 160), '"neither maid nor wife, neither woman nor stockfish"' (p. 238), 'maid again' (p. 374) and widow, she is allowed – or forced – to escape those categories that had encompassed the narratives of femininity in the mid-century. But to stand outside the categories is not to be free, and in *Diana of the Crossways* Meredith tests the possibilities of writing a heroine outside the plots of death and desire.

This evasion of the same old story produces instead a string of mutually interrupting plots, some allusively (the sexually threatened and self-starving plot of a Clarissa), some only adumbrated (the damning story of 'the woman Warwick', p. 114), some symbolic (the romanticised union of dependent Celt and masterful Saxon). A series of crucial events is not recounted directly: they occur in the interstices of the narrative (like the night visits from Lord Dannisburgh); or they are displaced from Diana herself onto another character (like the surrogate version of Redworth's wooing and proposals which are given to his scenes with Emma); or else they are so densely figurative as to refuse narrative explication (like the quasi-rape of Diana by Dacier). There is, then, no (as it were) 'true' story of Diana which the reader is invited to reconstruct. Caught among the multiplying stories and the displacement of event by figure, the reader can only share in the final pathetic symptom of Diana's estranged husband: '"I hear reports"' (p. 284).

'Reports', here, is something of a pun, for one of Diana's most potent (if not fully controllable) weapons in that duel or war that in this novel represents relations between women and men is the explosive nature of the proliferating plots in which she figures; her marriage to Warwick fires 'its shot like a cannon' (p. 54); her planned elopement situates her '"like a cartridge rammed into a gun"' (p. 240); and she undertakes the journey to the newspaper office where she sells her lover's Cabinet secret '"like a bullet"' (p. 327). '"If we take to activity, with the best intentions"', she cautions, '"we conjugate a frightful disturbance"' (p. 64). Diana's figure for the role of women is, famously, linguistic: '"We women are the verbs passive of the alliance"' (p. 64). But there is, I think, a sense in which Meredith and Diana are engaged in a joint enterprise to use linguistic profusion to forestall the narrative implications of this linguistic metaphor, by obscuring the unequivocal progress of conventional plot through the multiple directions of self-generating figuration.

Allon White has drawn attention to the prominence of the idea of gossip in Meredith's fiction;[7] and gossip, I suppose, might reasonably be seen as the production of story without grounding reference to any specific 'naked body' of facts. Culturally, it is associated with the speech of women together. In *Diana of the Crossways*, we are told that gossip renders those who indulge in it 'Oriental' (p. 338). Taken together, these two associations serve to introduce what might be called a Scheherezade motif in the novel. What has sometimes been called its 'Chinese boxes' structure might more productively be seen as a structure like that of the *Arabian Nights*, that interleaved fiction *par excellence*.

But the Thousand Nights and a Night of Baghdad do not only constitute an interleaved fiction: they are also an instance of a female speaker, generating plots as a way of prising apart the identical twin endings of the narrated woman, marriage and death. The *Arabian Nights* is set in motion, in the frame narration of the Prologue, by sexual jealousy on the part of a powerful man, and this sexual jealousy is compounded by racial difference: King Shahzaman finds his wife in the arms of a black slave, on his unexpected return to his palace. This mode of narrative motivation is then twice repeated: replicated in the precisely similar infidelity of his brother Shahriyar's wife with a second black slave, and then tripled in the forcible seduction of the two kings themselves by the wife of the sleeping jinnee. It is in response to this – all women having proved themselves to be as one, to be 'woman' – that Shahriyar establishes his custom of taking a virgin in marriage each night and having her killed the next morning, thus merging the expected endings (marriage and death) so closely in one another that there remains no space at all for the woman's story. But with Scheherezade, there comes a break: the initiation of the woman as teller of stories (not, we might note, autobiographies). And in this she is put to the test at once as individual – as *unlike* woman – and as defender, representative of her sex. Thereafter, it is by means of an unceasing, always beginning generation of plot and language that she is able to postpone the narrative death that falls upon the woman sexually possessed in marriage.

But what finally brings to an end the proliferating stories of Scheherezade is, of course, not marriage, nor even her sexualisation thereby, but motherhood: in the Epilogue, she is saved because she has proved herself to be, in the words of the king-husband, '"chaste, wise, and eloquent"',[8] and the evidence of these qualities lies in her stories and her sons – sons whose existence she has hitherto kept secret from the king. But with the evidence of motherhood comes the end of speech, and it is the husband who comes at last to speak for his wife.

In *Diana of the Crossways* too, each of a number of apparently imminent endings – the marriage with Warwick, the planned elopement with Dacier, the near-suicidal self-starvation – is postponed by the generation of new story. And Diana too uses language to stave off those double closures, union and death, which have so often constituted the narratives of femininity (as her occasionally rather frantic conversations with the inflamed Percy illustrate). Now Meredith argues, in his *Essay on Comedy*, that comedy lifts women to a station offering them free play for their wit, and praises the comic heroines of Congreve and Molière for being 'so copious and so choice of speech', for what he calls their 'freedom of action' and, in a nice phrase, 'fencing dialectic'. He uses the *Arabian Nights* as his example of a culture without comedy:

> Eastward you have total silence of Comedy among a people intensely susceptible to laughter, as the Arabian Nights will testify. Where the veil is over women's faces, you cannot have society. . . . There has been fun in Bagdad. But there never will be civilization where Comedy is not possible; and that comes of some degree of social equality of the sexes.[9]

It is particularly striking, then, that he has made Diana not merely an intelligent woman, not merely a woman 'copious . . . of speech', but a *witty* woman: of all kinds, according to the underlying premises of the *Essay on Comedy*, the most threatening to the patriarchal social order. 'A quick-witted woman exercising her wit is both a foreigner and potentially a criminal', the novel tells us (p. 103), and of course the metaphor is made literal in Diana's situation as both Irish woman in English society, and the object of a law-suit brought by her jealous husband. As foreigner and criminal, outcast and outlaw, Diana stands outside the narrative of the 'women of waxwork' and 'women of happy marriage'. Finally, however, Meredith's heroine, like Scheherezade, will surrender language in exchange for motherhood. First, though, she must be brought to the point of marriage.

The role of Emma Dunstane is important here, for it is the relation of the two women which constitutes the novel's most intense emotional focus and its only continuous narrative thread. Tess Cosslett has drawn attention to the way in which, in the nineteenth-century novel, relationships between women tend to fall outside the events of the story; they are often, she suggests, perceived as static, whereas male figures are 'thought to be needed to create tensions and initiate significant action'.[10] To a degree, this is true of *Diana of the Crossways*; certainly, the physical inertia of the sickly Emma helps to make her a fixed point of return for Diana in between the romantic plots, and consequently the point from which new stories are embarked on. Emma is a more conventional figure of Victorian womanhood than her friend: she suffers, she is patient, she is an invalid, though the operation to which she must submit provides a somewhat gruesome figure for the amputation or mutilation that the process of such an invalidisation of women entails; and Sir Lukin's outburst that '"women *are* the bravest creatures afloat"' (p. 247) suggests a revaluation of the apparent passivity that she represents. In this female friendship, it is possible to see the tension and the attempt at reconciliation between the exceptionality of Diana and the community of 'ordinary' women of the period.[11] But there is more to it than this: Emma, after all, plays a somewhat ambiguous role in the development of Diana's career as a heroine. On the one hand, she is a force for restraint, rescuing the protagonist from extremes of conduct (elopement, self-starvation) and, above all, acting as Redworth's agent, conducting his wooing and relaying his proposals for him. In this, she is in part the means by which the strong heroine comes to be recuperated into the marriage plot, assimilated to the narrative and social status quo. Meredith noted in a letter to a friend the difficulties of bringing about such a resolution:

> Diana of the Crossways keeps me still on her sad last way to wedlock. I could have killed her merrily, with my compliments to the public; and that was my intention. But the marrying of her, sets me traversing feminine labyrinths . . .[12]

The traversing of such 'feminine labyrinths' is precisely the role to which he has suited the frail and delicate Emma.

Yet, on the other hand, the friendship of the two women turns aside or pre-empts the endings of romance, and, most significantly, offers a framing narrative for the succession of apparently self-substituting males in the book. Although Emma is clearly a *restraint* upon the more extreme plot options into which the heroine at times seems set to dash, she is equally the agent of disruption of the romantic plots. From this slightly different angle, it is possible to note, for example, that it is for Emma that Diana leaves Dacier waiting, if not at the church, then at least at the station. And when Emma coaxes Diana back to life after her period of anorexic withdrawal – warming her, kissing her, feeding her 'as a child' (p. 346) from a spoon – it is by the assertion of the primacy of what looks very like mother love over the conjugal. Marriage comes to be validated at the end of the novel, it is true; but the final episode, with the two women embracing and planning what seems almost a joint motherhood, constitutes one last, ironic evasion of the

'Nuptial chapter'. '"Banality, thy name is marriage!"' (p. 402), as Diana puts it, and even the eventual union with Redworth is no wholehearted capitulation to romance.

Amongst Redworth's characteristics throughout have been his inability to understand Diana's jokes and his imperviousness to figuration. '"Similes applied to him,"' says Emma, '"will strike you as incongruous"' (p. 399). Like Warwick, whose savage mockery kills Diana's 'bright laugh . . . dead' (p. 6), his 'bluntness' kills 'the flying metaphors' (p. 352) which she shares with her fellow-countryman Sullivan Smith, and which are themselves a linguistic analogue of the categorical disordering found in Diana's lawless plots. It is not only stories, plots, that proliferate in the no end of gossip in *Diana of the Crossways*. The notorious copiousness and difficulty of Meredith's early modernist style are here enlisted in the rhetorical dilation (to borrow Patricia Parker's term)[13] that expands and delays narrative as a means of postponing collapse into that 'Nuptial chapter'. The heaps of obscuring figures for which Meredith is sometimes castigated, the often rather recondite aphorisms which constitute the reader's first Diana, the 'flying metaphors' of the feminised Celt, all of these are amongst that 'fraternity of old lamps for lighting our abysmal darkness' that, drawing on another reference to the *Arabian Nights*, Meredith tells us 'have to be rubbed' if we are to see our way.[14] '"She's the Arabian Nights in person, that's sure"', remarks Sullivan Smith of Diana (p. 350), and this focuses at once the way in which 'Diana' embodies the interweaving of stories, and the way in which the generation of language – aphorisms, novels, newspaper stories, and what are called the '"men's phrases"' (p. 132) of public discourse – is explored as a safeguard against sexual threat, financial disaster, reduction to indistinguishability from 'the bundle of women' (p. 149). It is, Meredith remarks, especially the 'pedestalled woman' who needs metaphor (p. 232) and with it, I think, the possibility of evading being swallowed up or crushed by the 'clumsy machinery of civilisation' (p. 136) here associated with men: railways, printing presses, the public spheres of politics and the law that serve only either to pedestal or to cancel the woman, to render her 'soap-bubble' or 'supernumerary'. To say this, though, is not to imply a version of that familiar ideological structure in which women equal nature and men culture. In any case, Meredith's somewhat Arnoldian mapping of ideologies of race, of Celt and Saxon, onto gender, would cut across any such view. Rather, Diana (like, in different ways, a number of women in the novel) is associated with the production of language, figure, story. But such a strategy of infinite deferral fails in the end, as it must in any narrative – it is not only all good things that must come to an end. Or to put it more formally, in Parker's words, 'Dilation . . . is always something to be kept within the horizon of ending, mastery, and control.'[15] And Diana's venture into the 'men's phrases' of the public world proves to be the very thing that brings about collapse into the generic fate of narrated woman. By the conclusion of the book, Diana the novelist has disappeared,[16] Diana the wit has come to recognise in the plain-speaking Redworth a mate and master. Early in the novel, the 'governing country', England, trusts those who would speak of Ireland to take up one of only two options: to 'be silent or discourse humorously' (p. 37). Diana the Irishwoman, in the final pages, relinquishes the role of discoursing humorously that has so marked her, in favour, not, certainly, of silence, but of what is called 'the language of her sex' (p. 414). For Diana at the close, as for Emma, to be 'deeply a woman' is to be only 'dumbly a poet' (p. 414). She comes to speak primarily by means of mute kisses, dumb embraces and all the language of the body – 'an involuntary little twitch of Tony's fingers' (p. 415) is her last communication of the novel. The metaphors that the pedestalled woman must embrace for their civilising power (p. 232) are recuperated at last by such a sense of an ending. It is perhaps most in its acceding to this particular version of such necessity that *Diana of the Crossways* explores the limits and enacts the problems of writing that '"sketch of the women of the future"' (p. 276).

NOTES

1. George Meredith, *The Egoist* (1879; Harmondsworth: Penguin, 1968; rpt. 1985), p. 250. Further references to this edition will be given in the text.
2. Peter Brooks, *Reading for the Plot: Design and intention in narrative* (Oxford: Clarendon Press, 1984), p. 5.
3. Tim Dolin, '"A long familiar inscription": *The Lifted Veil* and the perception of plot in George Eliot', unpub. dissertation, University of Western Australia, 1987, p. 6.
4. George Meredith, *Diana of the Crossways* (1885; London: Virago, 1980), pp. 13–15. Further references to this edition will be given in the text.
5. cf. Allon White, *The Uses of Obscurity: The fiction of early modernism* (London: Routledge, 1981), p. 93, citing Alexander Welsh, 'The allegory of truth in English fiction,' *Victorian Studies* 9 (1965), 7–27.
6. On this point, see Jacqueline Rose, *The Case of Peter Pan, or The Impossibility of Children's Fiction, Language, Discourse, Society* (London: Macmillan, 1984), pp. 47–9.
7. White, *The Uses of Obscurity*, pp. 95–8.
8. *Aladdin and Other Tales from the Thousand and One Nights*, trans. N. J. Dawood (Harmondsworth: Penguin, 1957), p. 211.
9. George Meredith, 'On the idea of comedy and of the uses of the comic spirit,' in *Essays*, vol. XXXII of *The Works of George Meredith* (Westminster: Archibald Constable & Co., 1898), pp. 20, 35 and 45–6 respectively.

10. Tess Cosslett, *Woman to Woman: Female friendship in Victorian fiction* (Brighton: Harvester Press, 1988), p. 11.
11. cf. Cosslett, *Woman to Woman*, pp. 4–6.
12. George Meredith, 'To Mrs Leslie Stephen', 19 May 1884, in *The Letters of George Meredith*, ed. C. L. Cline (3 vols, Oxford: Clarendon Press, 1970), II, p. 737.
13. Patricia Parker, *Literary Fat Ladies: Rhetoric, gender, property* (New York: Methuen, 1987), *passim*.
14. George Meredith, *One of Our Conquerors* (1891), ed. Margaret Harris, Victorian Texts III (St Lucia: University of Queensland Press, 1975), p. 314.
15. Parker, *Literary Fat Ladies*, p. 14.
16. cf. Judith Wilt, 'Meredith's Diana: freedom, fiction, and the female', *Texas Studies in Literature and Language* 18 (1976), 42–62.

Isobel Armstrong

Postscript

Feminist criticism now has its own classics. Susan Sellers in her introduction and many other writers in this volume look back to and salute writers such as Kate Millet, whose *Sexual Politics* (1970) might be considered the founding text of a new wave of feminist criticism. Her kind of feminist triumphalism – the zealously aggressive exposure of misogyny – was consolidated by Sandra Gilbert and Susan Gubar in their *Madwoman in the Attic* (1979), who looked at the other side of misogyny: the women writers who suffered from its painful oppression. But this task was scarcely begun before it was subjected to criticism. In America Elaine Showalter, for instance, began to think more positively about a substantive women's tradition, and this early feminism began to look inadequately historicised. In England there was a surge of interest in the French feminists' appropriation of psychoanalysis and an attempt to read Lacan for feminism, and early feminism began to look inadequately theorised. Julia Kristeva, Hélène Cixous and Luce Irigaray (the latter rather later than the others) began to be closely read. Early feminism began to look like the parodies of the feminist which have begun to enter novels – in to A. S. Byatt's *Possession* (1990), or Carol Shields's *Mary Swann* (1990, UK; 1987, Canada), to name recent British and North American examples of the genre.

But if feminist triumphalism now seems naïve, its extraordinary energy initiated a new awareness and a continuing project which is still going on in this book – the re-reading of male texts and the archaeological recovery of hitherto 'invisible' texts by women. Here Lynne Pearce re-reads John Clare and Elaine Hobby rescues the work of Hester Biddle. But feminist triumphalism generated a reactive debate which meant that the projects it began would be pursued with a new awareness and sophistication. What is a historical reading for feminism? How does theory – psychoanalytical, Marxist, poststructuralist – shape a reading? These are questions which dominate the essays in this book. They are questions requiring answers which need to be both meticulous and speculative.

These are timely questions. For one thing, there has always been a tendency for the discussion of theory and text to bifurcate, suggesting a wholly untenable dichotomy between the autonomous *jouissance* of theory and the theory-neutral critical or empirical discussion which is grounded either in fact or in common sense. For another, and rather different reason, the assurance and knowingness with which theoretical ideas are used at present in critical writing, whether they are derived from psychoanalysis, Marxism or poststructuralism, can lead to a kind of eclectic melt-down of ideas, which lacks a sharp sense of their origin and significance. So it is salutary to be returned to first principles and important to ask exacting questions of theory and text.

In this brief summing up I shall suggest what is important about the relation between theory and practice, what new questions it has enabled the writers of these essays to ask, and whether they suggest a further agenda for feminist criticism.

The use of theory in critical writing has never been a question of holding a theory and 'applying' it as an 'approach' to a text, as if a theory could become a kind of technology. In his essay 'Society', Theodore Adorno insisted on the founding importance of speculative theory: though society as a concept could not be logically defined or empirically demonstrated, social phenoma nevertheless called out for 'some kind of conceptualisation'. The proper order for understanding phenomena and conceptualising them was 'speculative *theory*'. He meant that, far from existing in the realm of abstraction, theory actually grounds discussion. It does so because it accounts for the aggregation of discrete facts and empirical data in a way that the continued aggregation of data cannot do, however exhaustive it is: and it does this by providing a speculative *category* by means of which data is ordered, shaped, interpreted, given meaning. It is by means of speculative theory that we can elicit relationships and formulate questions hitherto unknown to us. It can also generate further categories. Thus theory becomes a genuine form of knowledge welded to practice, not a set of postulates we can abstract from what we know. It is genuinely 'critical' because it *is theory*; that is, we are aware of its speculative nature and do not confuse it with beliefs or naturalised ideas which have become 'facts'. Thus 'women are the weaker sex' is theory, but not speculative theory. Feminist theory, in introducing the crucial category of gender and sexual difference, and in trying to account for it and the way it operates in texts, has opened a field of speculative knowledge which has revolutionised our reading of texts. A new set of relationships involving gender and text – to history, social analysis, psychoanalysis – and a new set of *questions* have emerged. These now have their own history and their own continuing debates.

The essays in this book are distinctive for their self-conscious alertness to theoretical difficulties and for their close interrogation of speculative positions. They divide roughly into those discussions which concentrate on feminist strategies of reading, and gendered strategies of writing. In other words, how do we construct or read gender in texts? How do texts construct gender at any particular time? It is the same question approached from opposite directions, and though these often overlap, they produce different kinds of emphasis. The difference is evident in Rebecca O'Rourke's discussion of the resources she would bring to a lesbian reading and Paulina Palmer's attempt to find and define lesbian desire *in* a text. Both writers are aware of a refinement in the essentialism debate, which opens up the problem of essentialist lesbian readings, but both solve the problem rather differently. The emergence of lesbian criticism is itself a consequence of the work of theory, which has enabled an area of experience to be discussed.

What questions can we ask about feminist strategies of reading which we could not ask but for an engagement with theory? Jane Aaron and Janet Todd both consider texts which demand an analysis beyond the comprehension of an individual writer – Mary Shelley and Jane Austen respectively. Both find ways of grasping and describing a historical situation which was gender marked but could not be conceptualised by the writer precisely because she was in it. Mary Shelley's reticence about her writing gains a historical dimension rather than a purely psychological interpretation when her 'modesty' is seen to be not just a product of new, restricted accounts of women's role or the anti-Godwin lobby, but the result of new accounts of the division of labour. The repressions engineered by this division return to haunt the text, as repressed female power returns in the diseased fertility of the plague in *The Last Man*. Similarly, Janet Todd disentangles the question of 'sexual' politics and 'political' politics in Jane Austen's novels, often conflated by critics. If we have trouble in determining empirically whether Austen was a conservative or a radical in nineteenth-century terms rather than ours, we can take the matter further when it *can* be seen that she could mount a radical critique of the novel of sensibility and its collusion in a certain kind of affective femininity: and genre and gender become linked in a new configuration which transforms empirical fact.

Ann Thompson is also concerned with the status of the redescribing which theory makes possible. What kind of historically specific feminist reading of *The Tempest* can emerge when there *is* no empirical evidence in the play – or none to speak of – because Miranda is the only woman in it? There is nothing for it but to read speculatively in the most disciplined way, looking at contradictory inscriptions of the feminine in the language of the text, eliciting a discourse of the feminine from the text at the level of linguistic rather than logical or overt connections, and relating these to the known contemporary context of the royal marriage it celebrates. Interestingly, empirical history, a dynastic, 'patriarchal' marriage, is rendered problematical, its security as simple interpretable fact undone; it is changed, transformed, its significance remade, by the complexities and ambiguities of the play, and its dark response to questions of gender and race. Linda R. Williams, in an important essay, takes the strategies of redescribing availed by theory even further in her discussion of Henry Miller by showing that a critique of Miller which does not reduplicate his own violence and return it to the text, precisely cannot afford to be historical in the simple sense of repeating the categories of the text in critical analysis. For this means one is forever trapped inside it and its violence. It is necessary – and she uses the Lyotardian metaphor of guerilla warfare – to surprise the text into a revelation of its contradictions and vulnerabilities by seizing on those moments when it does not seem in control of its discourse or when, as in the discourse of sado-masochism, its pretentions to control become pathological.

All these strategies, whether they use the discourse of Marxism, psychoanalysis or poststructuralism depend on opening up a split between the manifest and latent text which enables the category of gender to enter and redefine and release its meanings. But what of the text which we are approaching less in terms of the analytical strategy of the critic than in terms of the struggle with meaning in the writing? The problem to be dealt with here is the way in which texts construct and position femininity and the constraints and possibilities with which they work. The category of gender makes visible and problematical complexities and textual strategies which we might elide with other conventions or simply not notice. An example is the way Ruth Evans and Lesley Johnson show that the figure of the maze in the *Assembly of Ladies* is gendered as well as being seen in terms of other medieval signifying patterns. In a similar way, Penny Boumelha shows how Meredith attempts to shift and transform a Victorian discourse of femininity so that it subverts expectations and offers an alternative account of the feminine.

As well as exploring how texts produce alternative readings of gender, speculative theory has no hesitation in using forms of thought to which the text's author may not have had access and relating them to the work, often fusing conventional textual and historical data and scholarship with theoretical writing to elicit meaning, or meanings. The aim of this process is not to flout history by imposing an alien master discourse on a text: nor is the aim to map theory to text and force a fit; rather theoretical work, running parallel to the text rather than being imposed on it, becomes a structural and conceptual analogue which illuminates the struggles of the text, eliciting meaning through its very difference rather than pointing up affinities. It is used for a kind of calibrating function rather than being the equivalent of a source the author did not know instead of one she did. Thus Rebecca Ferguson discloses the slave narrative material in Toni Morrison's *Beloved* and calibrates this with psychoanalytical material concerned with motherhood. And Claire Buck, in her bold and meticulous essay on H.D., brings Irigaray's meditations on the phallic same, a critique of Freud H.D. could not have known, to bear on *Helen in Egypt*. She points out that H.D. was also making a critique of Freud, having undergone Freudian analysis and even putting him into her poem in disguise. But the literal parallel between the texts is less important than the fact that Irigaray provides a clue to the structure of thought in the poem and its verbal complexities.

These essays suggest how diverse and varied feminist theoretical practice can be – and how energetic. This is partly because a meeting of theory and text involves an imaginative reinvention of both as, with each particular text, the discipline of speculative theory encounters different problems, which involve recourse to a range of skills and forms of thought – textual scholarship, political history, sociocultural analysis, Marxist thought, psychoanalysis, poststructuralist theories of language. But theoretical writing always generates new problems. What new problems have emerged from this volume? And what, in the meticulous consideration of the implications of theory and practice, has been left out of consideration? Several kinds of questions can be asked and further explored. One is strategic: should feminist critics exclude male texts from discussion, as Lynne Pearce argues? Another is political: how can feminist critics write about violence without being implicated in it? Freud's later work is startlingly relevant here and needs to be further explored. There seems to be a pact in this volume between psychoanalysis and Marxist analysis which many would regard as problematical. Perhaps this pact and the problem of violence could both be explored further through Freud's later sociopsychic work. Hovering at the edges of everyone's discussions is a philosophical problem. This collection seems to have made another pact between what might be called the empirical and the theoretical: the terms of this distinction need to be more carefully thought out, and might be through an exploration of the possibility of a feminist epistemology, a feminist knowledge. Lastly, *écriture féminine*, a special women's language, language of the body, of *jouissance*, seems to have disappeared as a central concern, discredited, it seems, by its rejection of the symbolic order. It is not altogether frivolous, in this connection, to ask about the function of jokes in feminist criticism (Miller's comparison of his unbeatable sexual power with that of Rudolf Valentino, quoted by Linda R. Williams, is irresistibly comic – it could do with a semiotic guffaw). But surely questions of language and representation must be addressed again. To end with a question asked by a colleague: what would it mean, she asked, *not* to write a language of the body?

Notes on Contributors

Jane Aaron is a Lecturer in English at the University College of Wales, Aberystwyth, where she teaches courses on Romanticism, women's writing, and psychoanalytic and feminist criticism. Her book, *A Double Singleness: Gender and the writings of Charles and Mary Lamb*, is to be published by Oxford University Press in 1991. She is currently working on a more general study of gender and Romanticism for the Open University Press. With Sylvia Walby, she has also edited the proceedings of the 1989 and 1990 Women's Studies Network conferences: the volume, entitled *Out of the Margins: Women's studies in the nineties*, will be published by Falmer Press in 1991.

Isobel Armstrong is professor of English at Birbeck College, London. She is author of a number of books on nineteenth-century and Victorian poetry, and on Jane Austen. She is editing for Oxford University Press a collection of nineteenth-century women's poetry. She is co-editor of *Women: A cultural review*.

Penny Boumelha is Jury Professor of English Language and Literature at the University of Adelaide, where she teaches courses on 'Gender and narrative' and 'Decadence'. She is the author of *Thomas Hardy and Women: Sexual ideology and narrative form* (Harvester Press, 1982) and of *Charlotte Brontë* (Key Women Writers, Harvester Wheatsheaf, 1990), as well as of articles on nineteenth-century fiction and eighteenth-century literary manuscripts.

Claire Buck lectures in English and Film at the Polytechnic of North London. Her forthcoming book, to be published by Harvster Wheatsheaf, is *H.D. and Freud: Bisexuality and a feminine discourse*. She is currently editing *The Bloomsbury International Guide to Women's Writing*.

Ruth Evans is a lecturer in Medieval English Literature at University College of Wales, Cardiff. She has written on both Old and Middle English didactic literature, and on women and lollardy. She is the co-editor, with Lesley Johnson, of a forthcoming collection of essays which are feminist rereadings of Middle English literary texts, *The Wife of Bath and All Her Sect* (Routledge, 1991).

Rebecca Ferguson has been Lecturer in English at Saint David's University College (University of Wales) since 1979, teaching courses on eighteenth-century literature, modern and contemporary drama, theories of representation in relation to literature and the visual arts, and American black women writers. In 1988–9 she was a Fulbright Exchange lecturer at Southeastern Massachusetts University. Her publications include: *The Unbalanced Mind: Pope and the rule of passion* (Harvester Wheatsheaf, 1986), a study guide on Pope's *Rape of the Lock* and *Epistle to Dr Arbuthnot*, and an article on 'Intestine wars: body and text in Pope's *Epistle to Dr Arbuthnot* and *The Dunciad*' for David Fairer (ed.), *Pope: New contexts* (Harvester Wheatsheaf, 1990).

Elaine Hobby is a socialist and a lesbian who has been actively involved in the women's movement since the mid-1970s. She teaches at Loughborough University, where she is Lecturer in Women's Studies in the Department of English and Drama, a position which, thanks to the support of her students and colleagues, allows her to do everything (almost) she has ever dreamed of. She has published *Virtue of Necessity: English women's writing 1646–88* (Virago, 1988; University of Michigan Press, 1989), and co-edited with Elspeth Graham, Hilary Hinds and Helen Wilcox, *Her Own Life: Autobiographical writings by seventeenth-century Englishwomen* (Routledge, 1989). Her current projects include co-editing with her lover, Chris White, an anthology of lesbian literary criticism, *What Lesbians Do In Books*, and with Hilary Hinds, a teaching anthology of seventeenth-century women's writings. She is also trying to make progress with a long-promised study of seventeenth-century women's sexuality.

Lesley Johnson is a lecturer in the School of English at the University of Leeds. She has written on subjects including Old French Fabliaux, Anglo-Norman historiography, and Henryson's *Testament of Cresseid*. She is co-editor (with Ruth Evans) of *The Wife of Bath and All Her Sect* (Routledge, 1991).

Rebecca O'Rourke is a writer and adult education tutor. She teaches 'Second chance to learn' courses for Camden and Hackney Adult Education Institutes and has taught Lesbian Studies for Hackney Workers' Educational Association. She writes fiction as well as criticism and has been a long-time member of the Federation of Worker-Writers and Community Publishers. Her most recent critical publications are *Reflecting on The Well of Loneliness* (Routledge, 1989) and, with Jean Milloy, *The Woman Reader: Teaching women's literature* (Routledge, forthcoming). She is currently completing a short story collection, *Dead Men Don't Rape*.

Paulina Palmer teaches an undergraduate course in 'Feminist approaches to literature' in the English Department at the University of Warwick and contributes to the Women's Studies MA. Her publications include *Contemporary Women's Fiction: Narrative practice and feminist theory* (Harvester Wheatsheaf, 1989), a study of the fiction of Angela Carter, in Sue Roe (ed.), *Women Reading Women's Writing* (Harvester Wheatsheaf, 1987), and an essay on 'Contemporary lesbian fiction' in Linda Anderson (ed.), *Plotting Change: Contemporary women's fiction* (Arnold, 1990). Her essay on 'The lesbian feminist thriller' will appear in Elaine Hobby and Chris White (eds), *What Lesbians Do in Books* (Women's Press, forthcoming). She is currently working on a book on *Contemporary Lesbian Writing* for the Open University Press.

Lynne Pearce studied for her Ph.D. (a Bakhtinian reading of John Clare) at the University of Birmingham. After six years of part-time/temporary teaching in Higher and Adult Education, she has just begun her first permanent job as Lecturer in English at the University of Lancaster. She co-authored *Feminist Readings/Feminists Reading* (Harvester Wheatsheaf, 1989) and her book on the Pre-Raphaelites, *Woman/Image/Text: Readings in Pre-Raphaelite art and literature* (Harvester Wheatsheaf) will appear in 1991. She has now turned her attention away from 'feminist critique' and is looking forward to future projects on contemporary women's writing.

Susan Sellers teaches in the English Department at the École Normale Supérieure and University of Paris VIII. She has published widely in the areas of feminist and critical theory, and is the author of *Language and Sexual Difference: Feminist writing in France*, an exploration of French feminist theory in the context of French philosophical, poststructural and psychoanalytic debate and contemporary French women's writing (Macmillan, 1991).

Ann Thompson is a Reader in English at the University of Liverpool. She has edited *The Taming of the Shrew* (Cambridge University Press, 1984), and is co-editor with Helen Wilcox of *Teaching Women: Feminism and English studies* (Manchester University Press, 1989). She is author of *Shakespeare's Chaucer* (Liverpool University Press, 1978), and *The Critics Debate: 'King Lear'* (Macmillan, 1988), and co-author with John O. Thompson of *Shakespeare, Meaning and Metaphor* (Harvester Wheatsheaf, 1987). Currently she is General Editor of a six-volume series of feminist readings of Shakespeare.

Janet Todd is Professor of English Literature at the University of East Anglia. Recent books include *Feminist Literary History* (Polity Press, 1988) and *The Sign of Angellica: Women, writing and fiction 1660–1800* (Virago, 1989). She is currently working on an edition of Aphra Behn.

Linda R. Williams is Lecturer in English at the University of Liverpool. She is co-editor of *The Body and the Text: Hélène Cixous, reading and teaching* (Harvester Wheatsheaf, 1990), and her other publications and current research include work on feminist theory, D. H. Lawrence, Nietzsche and psychoanalysis.

Bibliography

(The following bibliography of works relevant to feminist criticism has been compiled by the editor and contributors. A number of further references are listed in the Notes accompanying each essay.)

Abel, Elizabeth (ed.), *Writing and Sexual Difference*, Chicago, 1982.

Abel, Elizabeth, *The Voyage In: Fictions of female development*, New England, 1983.

Aers, David, 'Rewriting the Middle Ages: some suggestions', *Journal of Medieval and Renaissance Studies* 18, 2, 1988.

Alexander, Meena, *Women in Romanticism*, London, 1989.

Allen, Mary, *The Necessary Blankness: Women in major American fiction of the sixties*, Illinois, 1976.

Anzaldua, G. and C. Moraga (eds), *This Bridge Called My Back: Writing by radical women of color*, New York, 1981.

Babb, Valerie, '*The Color Purple*: writing to undo what writing has done', *Phylon* 47, 2, 1986.

Barratt, Alexandra, ' The *Flower and the Leaf* and the *Assembly of Ladies*: is there a (sexual) difference?', *Philological Quarterly* 66, 1987.

Barrett, Michèle, *Women's Oppression Today: Problems in Marxist feminist analysis*, London, 1980.

Barrett, Michèle, 'Ideology and the cultural production of gender', reprinted in Judith Newton and Deborah Rosenfelt (eds), *Feminism Criticism and Social Change* , London, 1985.

Bartkowski, Frances, *Feminist Utopias*, London, 1989.

Basch, Françoise, *Relative Creatures: Victorian women in society and the novel*, New York, 1974.

Batsleer, Janet, Tony Davies, Rebecca O'Rourke and Chris Weedon, *Rewriting English: Cultural politics of gender and class*, London, 1985.

Baym, Nina, *Women's Fiction: A guide to novels by and about women in America 1820–1870*, New York, 1978.

Beaumann, Nicola, *A Very Great Profession: The woman's novel 1914–1939*, London, 1983.

Beckwith, Sarah, 'A very material mysticism: the medieval mysticism of

Margery Kempe', in *Medieval Literature*, ed. David Aers, Hemel Hempstead, 1986.

Bell, Roseann P., Bettye J. Perker and Beverly Guy-Sheftall (eds), *Sturdy Black Bridges: Visions of black women in literature*, New York, 1979.

Belsey, Catherine, *Critical Practice*, London, 1980.

Belsey, Catherine and Jane Moore (eds), *The Feminist Reader: Essays in gender and the politics of literary criticism*, London, 1989.

Bernheimer, Charles and Claire Kahane (eds), *In Dora's Case: Freud–hysteria–feminism*, New York, 1985.

Bernikow, Louise, *The World Split Open: Four centuries of women poets in England and America 1552–1950*, New York, 1974.

Betterton, Rosemary (ed.), *Looking On: Images of femininity in the visual arts and media*, London, 1987.

Boose, Lynda E., 'The family in Shakespeare studies; or – studies in the family of Shakespeareans; or – the politics of politics', *Renaissance Quarterly* 40, 1987.

Brown, Cheryl and Karen Olsen (eds), *Feminist Criticism: Essays on theory, poetry and prose*, New Jersey, 1978.

Brunt, Rosalind and Caroline Rowan (eds), *Feminism, Culture, Politics*, London, 1982.

Bunch, Charlotte et al. (eds), *Building Feminist Theory: Essays from Quest, a feminist quarterly*, New York, 1981.

Butler-Evans, Elliott, *Race, Gender and Desire: Narrative strategies in the fiction of Toni Cade Bambara, Toni Morrison and Alice Walker*, Philadelphia, 1989.

Cameron, Deborah, *Feminism and Linguistic Theory*, London, 1985.

Carby, Hazel V., *Reconstructing Womanhood: The emergence of the Afro-American woman novelist*, New York, 1987.

Chodorow, Nancy, *The Reproduction of Mothering: Psychoanalysis and the sociology of gender*, Berkeley, 1978.

Christian, Barbara, *Black Feminist Criticism: Perspectives on black women writers*, New York, 1985.

Cixous, Hélène, *The Newly Born Woman*, trans. Betsy Wing, Manchester, 1986.

Cornillon, Susan Koppelman (ed.), *Images of Women in Fiction: Feminist perspectives*, Ohio, 1972.

Coward, Rosalind and John Ellis, *Language and Materialism: Developments in semiology and the theory of the subject*, London, 1977.

Coward, Rosalind, '"This novel changes lives": are women's novels feminist novels?' *Feminist Review* 5, 1980.

Coward, Rosalind, *Female Desire: Women's sexuality today*, London 1984.

Cunningham, Gail, *The New Woman and the Victorian Novel*, London, 1978.

Daims, Diva, *Toward a Feminist Tradition: An annotated bibliography of novels in English by women, 1891–1920*, New York, 1982.

Daly, Mary, *Beyond God The Father: Towards a philosophy of women's liberation*, Boston, 1973.

Daly, Mary, *Gyn/Ecology: The metaethics of radical feminism*, Boston, 1979.

Davidson, C. N. and E. H. Broner, *The Lost Tradition: Mother and daughters in literature*, New York, 1980.

Davis, Angela Y., *Women, Race and Class*, New York, 1983.

Delaney, Sheila, *Writing Women: Women writers and women in literature, medieval to modern*, New York, 1983.

DeShazer, Mary K., *Inspiring Women: Reimagining the muse*, Oxford, 1986.

Diamond, Arlene, and Lee Edwards (eds), *The Authority of Experience: Essays in feminist criticism*, Amherst, 1977.

Dinshaw, Caroline, *Chaucer's Sexual Poetics*, Wisconsin, 1989.

Dixon, Marlene, *Women in Class Struggle*, San Francisco, 1980.

Donovan, Josephine (ed.), *Feminist Literary Criticism: Explorations in Theory*, Kentucky, 1975.

Doob, Penelope, 'The labyrinth in medieval culture: explorations of an image', *University of Ottawa Quarterly* 52, 1982.

DuPlessis, Rachel Blau, *Writing Beyond the Ending*, Bloomington, 1985.

Dworkin, Andrea, *Our Blood: Prophecies and discourses on sexual politics*, New York, 1976.

Eagleton, Mary, *Feminist Literary Theory: A reader*, Oxford, 1986.

Eagleton, Terry, *Literary Theory: An Introduction*, Oxford, 1983.

Edwards, Lee R., *Psyche as Hero: Female heroism and fictional form*, Middleton, CT., 1984.

Eisenstein, Hester, *Contemporary Feminist Thought*, Boston, 1983.

Eisenstein, Hester and Alice Jardine (eds), *The Future of Difference*, Boston, 1980.

Eisenstein, Zillah (ed.), *Capitalist Patriarchy and the Case for Socialist Feminism*, New York, 1979.

Ellmann, Mary, *Thinking About Women*, New York, 1968.

Erikson, Peter, *Patriarchal Structures in Shakespeare's Drama*, Berkeley, 1985.

Evans, Mari (ed.), *Black Women Writers: Arguments and interviews*, New York, 1984.

Evans, Mari (ed.), *Black Women Writers 1950–1980: A critical evaluation*, New York, 1984.

Evans, Mary (ed.), *The Woman Question: Readings on the subordination of women*, London, 1982.

Faderman, Lillian, *Surpassing the Love of Men: Romantic friendship and love between women from the Renaissance to the present*, New York, 1981.

Ferguson, Margaret, Maureen Quilligan and Nancy J. Vickers (eds), *Rewriting the Renaissance: The discourses of sexual difference in early modern Europe*, Chicago, 1986.

Ferguson, Mary Anne, *Images of Women in Literature*, Boston, 1973.

Fetterley, Judith, *The Resisting Reader: A feminist approach to American fiction*, Bloomington, 1978.

Figes, Eva, *Sex and Subterfuge: Women writers to 1850*, London, 1982.

Firestone, Shulamith, *The Dialectic of Sex*, New York, 1971.

Fisher, Dexter (ed.), *The Third Woman: Minority women writers of the United States*, Boston, 1980.

Franklin, Sarah and Jackie Stacey, 'Dyke tactics for difficult times', in Christian McEwan and Sue O'Sullivan (eds), *Out the Other Side: Contemporary lesbian writing*, London, 1988.

Freedman, E. B. and B. C. Gelpi (eds), *The Lesbian Issue*, Chicago, 1985.

Gallop, Jane, *Feminism and Psychoanalysis: The daughter's seduction*, London, 1982.

Gamman, Lorraine and Margaret Marshment (eds), *The Female Gaze: Women as viewers of popular culture*, London, 1988.

Gardiner, Judith Kegan, 'Self psychology as feminist theory', *Signs* 12, 4, 1987.

Garner, Shirley Nelson, et al. (eds), *The (M)other Tongue: Essays in feminist psychoanalytic interpretations*, New York, 1985.

Giddings, Paula, *When and Where I Enter: The impact of black women on race and sex in America*, New York, 1985.

Gilbert, Sandra and Susan Gubar, *The Madwoman in the Attic: The woman writer and the nineteenth-century literary imagination*, New Haven, 1979.

Gilbert, Sandra and Susan Gubar, *Shakespeare's Sisters: Feminist essays on women poets*, Bloomington, 1979.

Gilbert, Sandra and Susan Gubar, *No Man's Land: The place of the woman writer in the twentieth century*, vol. 1, *The War of the Words*, New Haven, 1988.

Gilbert, Sandra and Susan Gubar, 'Sexual linguistics: gender, language, sexuality', *New Literary History*, 16, 1985.

Graham, Elspeth, Hilary Hinds, Elaine Hobby and Helen Wilcox (eds), *Her Own Life: Autobiographical writings by seventeenth century Englishwomen*, London, 1989.

Green, Richard Firth, 'Women in Chaucer's audience', *The Chaucer Review* 18, 2, 1983.

Greene, Gayle, Carolyn Ruth Swift Lenz and Carole Thomas Neely (eds), *The Woman's Part: Feminist criticism of Shakespeare*, Illinois, 1980.

Greene, Gayle and Coppélia Kahn (eds), *Making a Difference: Feminist literary criticism*, London, 1985.

Greer, Germaine, *The Female Eunuch*, London, 1970.

Heath, Stephen, *The Sexual Fix*, London, 1982.

Heilbrun, Carolyn, *Re-Inventing Womanhood* , New York, 1979.

Heilbrun, Carolyn and M. Higonnet (eds), *The Representation of Women in Fiction*, Baltimore, 1982.

Hennegan, Alison, 'On becoming a lesbian reader', in Suzannah Radstone (ed.), Sweet Dreams: Sexuality and popular fiction, London, 1988.

Herrmann, Ann, *The Dialogic and Difference: 'An/other woman' in Virginia Woolf and Christa Wolf*, New York, 1989.

Hirsch, Marianne, *The Mother/Daughter Plot: Narrative, psychoanalysis, feminism*, Bloomington, 1989.

Hobby, Elaine, *Virtue of Necessity: English Women's Writing 1646–88*, London, 1988.

Homans, Margaret, *Women Writers and Poetic Identity: Dorothy Wordsworth, Emily Brontë and Emily Dickinson*, Princeton, 1980.

Homans, Margaret, '"Her very own howl": the ambiguities of representation in recent women's fiction', *Signs* 9, 2, 1983.

Homans, Margaret, *Bearing the Word: Language and female experience in nineteenth century women's writing*, Chicago, 1986.

Hooks, Bell, *Ain't I A Woman: Black women and feminism*, Boston, 1982.

Humm, Maggie, *Feminist Criticism: Women as contemporary critics*, Hemel Hempstead, 1986.

Humm, Maggie, *An Annotated Critical Bibliography of Feminist Criticism*, Hemel Hempstead, 1987.

Irigaray, Luce, *Speculum of the Other Woman*, 1974, trans. Gillian C. Gill, New York, 1985.

Irigaray, Luce, *This Sex Which Is Not One*, 1977, trans. Catherine Porter, New York, 1985.

Jacobus, Mary (ed.), *Women Writing and Writing About Women*, London, 1979.

Jacobus, Mary, 'Is there a woman in this text?', in Jacobus (ed.), *Reading Woman: Essays in feminist criticism*, New York, 1986.

Jardine, Alice, *Gynesis: Configurations of woman and modernity*, New York, 1985.

Jehlen, Myra, 'Archimedes and the paradox of feminist criticism', *Signs* 6, 1981.

Jelinek, Estelle (ed.), *Women's Autobiography: Essays in criticism*, Bloomington, 1980.

Johnson, Barbara, *The Critical Difference*, Baltimore, 1980.

Joseph, Gloria I. and Jill Lewis, *Common Differences: Conflicts in black and white feminist perspectives*, New York, 1981.

Juhasz, Suzanne, *Naked and Fiery Forms; Modern American Poetry by Women: A new tradition*, New York, 1976.

Kaplan, Cora, 'Language and gender', *Papers on Patriarchy*, London, 1978.

Kaplan, Cora, 'Pandora's Box: subjectivity, class and sexuality in socialist feminist criticism', in Gayle Greene and Coppélia Kahn (eds), *Making A Difference*, London, 1985.

Kaplan, Cora, *Sea Changes: Culture and feminism*, London, 1986.

Kaplan, Sydney, *Feminist Consciousness in the Modern British Novel*, Illinois, 1975.

Kauffman, Linda (ed.), *Gender and Theory: Dialogues on feminist criticism*, Oxford, 1989.

King, Deborah A., 'Multiple jeopardy, multiple consciousness: the context of a black feminist ideology', *Signs* 14, 1, 1988.

Klaich, Dolores, *Woman Plus Woman: Attitudes towards lesbianism*, New York, 1974.

Kolodny, Annette, *The Lay of the Land: Metaphor as experience and history in American life and letters*, North Carolina, 1975.

Kolodny, Annette, 'Some notes on defining a feminist literary criticism', *Critical Enquiry* 2, 1975.

Kolodny, Annette, 'Dancing through the minefield: some observations on the theory, practice, and politics of a feminist literary criticism', *Feminist Studies* 6, 1, 1980.

Kristeva, Julia, *Revolution in Poetic Language*, 1974, trans. Margaret Waller, New York, 1984.

Kristeva, Julia, *Desire In Language: A semiotic approach to literature and art*, trans. Thomas Gora, Alice Jardine and Leon S. Roudiez, New York, 1982.

Kristeva, Julia, *The Kristeva Reader*, ed. Toril Moi, Oxford, 1986.

Kuhn, Annette, *Women's Pictures: Feminism and cinema*, London, 1982.

Lakoff, Robin, *Language and Woman's Place*, New York, 1975.

Lerner, Gerda, (ed.), *Black Women in White America: A documentary history*, New York, 1972.

Lipshitz, Susan (ed.), *Tearing the Veil: Essays on femininity*, Boston, 1978.

Loomba, Ania, *Gender, Race, Renaissance Drama*, Manchester, 1989.

Lorde, Audre, *Uses of the Erotic: The erotic as power*, New York, 1978.

Lorde, Audre, *Sister Outsider: Essays and speeches*, New York, 1984.

McLuskie, Kathleen, *Renaissance Dramatists*, Hemel Hempstead, 1989.

McMillan, Ann, '"Fayre sisters al": the *Flower and the Leaf* and the *Assembly of Ladies*', *Tulsa Studies in Women's Literature* 1, 1982.

Marcus, Jane (ed.), *Feminist Essays on Virginia Woolf*, London, 1981.

Marks, Elaine and G. Stamboulian (eds), *Homosexualities and French Literature: Cultural contexts/critical texts*, New York, 1979.

Marks, Elaine and Isabelle de Courtivron (eds), *New French Feminisms: An anthology*, Hemel Hempstead, 1980.

Marxist Feminist Literature Collective, 'Women's writing', *Ideology and Consciousness* 1, 3, 1978.

Mellor, Anne K. (ed.), *Romanticism and Feminism*, Bloomington, 1988.

Miles, Rosalind, *The Fiction of Sex*, London, 1974.

Millard, Elaine, Sara Mills, Lynne Pearce and Sue Spaull (eds), *Feminist Readings/Feminists Reading*, Hemel Hempstead, 1989.

Miller, Jane, *Women Writing About Men*, London, 1986.

Miller, Nancy K. (ed.), *The Poetics of Gender*, New York, 1986.

Millett, Kate, *Sexual Politics*, New York, 1970.

Mitchell, Juliet, *Women's Estate*, Harmondsworth, 1971.

Mitchell, Juliet, *Psychoanalysis and Feminism*, London, 1974.

Mitchell, Juliet, *Women, The Longest Revolution*, London, 1984.

Mitchell, Sally, *The Fallen Angel: Chastity, class and women's reading 1835–1880*, Ohio, 1981.

Moers, Ellen, *Literary Women: The great writers*, New York, 1976.

Moi, Toril, *Sexual/Textual Politics: Feminist literary theory*, London, 1985.

Montefiore, Jan, *Feminism and Poetry: Language, experience, identity in women's writing*, London, 1987.

Monteith, Moira (ed.), *Women's Writing: A challenge to theory*, Hemel Hempstead, 1986.

Mulford, Wendy, 'Socialist-feminist criticism: a case study: women's suffrage and literature 1906–1914', *Re-Reading English*, ed. Peter Widdowson London, 1982.

Myers, Carole Fairbanks (ed.), *Women in Literature: Criticism of the seventies*, New Jersey, 1976.

Neely, Carol Thomas, 'Constructing the subject: feminist practice and the new Renaissance discourses', *English Literary Renaissance*, 18, 1988.

Newton, Judith, *Women, Power and Subversion: Social strategies in British fiction, 1778–1869*, Georgia, 1981.

Newton, Judith and Deborah Rosenfelt (eds), *Feminist Criticism and Social Change*, New York, 1985.

Novy, Marianne (ed.), *Women's Re-Visions of Shakespeare*, Illinois, 1990.

Olsen, Tillie, *Silences*, London, 1980.

Ostriker, Alicia, 'Body language: imagery of the body in women's poetry', in Leonard Michaels and Christopher Ricks (eds), *The State of the Language*, Berkeley, 1980.

Ostriker, Alicia, *Writing Like a Woman*, Michigan, 1983.

Palmer, Paulina, *Contemporary Women's Fiction: Narrative practice and feminist theory*, Hemel Hempstead, 1989.

Parker, Patricia, *Literary Fat Ladies: Rhetoric, gender, property*, London, 1987.

Pearson, Carol and Catherine Pope, *The Female Hero in American and British Literature*, New York, 1981.

Penley, Constance (ed.), *Feminism and Film Theory*, New York, 1988.

Person, E. S. and Catherine Stimpson (eds), *Women and Sexuality*, Chicago, 1980.

Poovey, Mary, *The Proper Lady and the Woman Writer: Ideology as style in the works of Mary Wollstonecraft, Mary Shelley and Jane Austen*, Chicago, 1984.

Pratt, Annis, *Archetypal Patterns in Women's Fiction*, Bloomington, 1981.

Radway, Janice A., *Reading the Romance: Women, patriarchy and popular literature*, London, 1984.

Reay, Barry, 'Quakerism and society', in B. Reay and J. F. McGregor (eds), *Radical Religion in the English Revolution*, Oxford, 1984.

Rich, Adrienne, *Of Woman Born: Motherhood as experience and institution*, New York, 1976.

Rich, Adrienne, 'Compulsory heterosexuality and lesbian existence', *Signs* 5, 1980.

Rich, Adrienne, *On Lies, Secrets, and Silences: Selected prose 1966–1978*, London, 1980.

Rickman, Lydia, 'Esther Biddle and her mission to Louis XIV', *Friends Historical Society Journal* 47, 1955.

Roberts, J. R., *Black Lesbians: An annotated bibliography*, Florida, 1981.

Robinson, Lillian, *Sex, Class and Culture*, Bloomington, 1978.

Roe, Sue (ed.), *Women Reading Women's Writing*, Hemel Hempstead, 1987.

Rogers, Katherine, *The Troublesome Helpmeet: A history of misogyny in literature*, Seattle, 1966.

Rogers, Katherine, *Feminism in Eighteenth Century England*, Illinois, 1982.

Rowbotham, Sheila, *Women, Resistance and Revolution*, Harmondsworth, 1972.

Rowbotham, Sheila, *Woman's Consciousness, Man's World*, Harmondsworth, 1973.

Rowbotham, Sheila (ed.), *Beyond the Fragments: Feminism and the making of socialism*, London, 1979.

Rubenstein, Roberta, *Boundaries of the Self: Gender, culture and fiction*, Urbana, 1987.

Rule, Jane, *Lesbian Images*, New York, 1975.

Ruthven, K. K., *Feminist Literary Studies: An introduction*, Cambridge, 1984.

Russ, Joanna, *How to Suppress Women's Writing*, Texas, 1983.

Sage, Lorna, *Contemporary Women Novelists*, London, 1985.

Sellers, Susan (ed.), *Writing Differences: Readings from the seminar of Hélène Cixous*, Milton Keynes, 1988.

Showalter, Elaine, *A Literature of Their Own: British women novelists from Brontë to Lessing*, London, 1978.

Showalter, Elaine (ed.), *The New Feminist Criticism: Essays on women, literature and theory*, New York, 1985.

Showalter, Elaine, 'Toward a feminist poetics', in Mary Jacobus (ed.), *Women Writing and Writing About Women*, London, 1979.

Showalter, Elaine, *Speaking of Gender: Essays on women, literature and theory*, London, 1989.

Skeat, W. W., *Chaucerian and Other Pieces*, Oxford, 1897.

Smith, Barbara, *Toward a Black Feminist Criticism*, New York, 1977.

Smith, Barbara, *Home Girls: A black feminist anthology*, New York, 1983.

Spacks, P. M., *The Female Imagination*, New York, 1975.

Spencer, Jane, *The Rise of the Woman Novelist: From Aphra Behn to Jane Austen*, Oxford, 1986.

Spender, Dale, *Man Made Language*, London, 1980.

Spivak, Gayatri Chakravorty, 'Displacement and the discourse of women', in M. Krupnik (ed.), *Displacement, Derrida and After*, Bloomington, 1983.

Spivak, Gayatri Chakravorty, *In Other Worlds: Essays in cultural politics*, London, 1987.

Springer, Marlene (ed.), *What Manner of Woman: Essays on English and American life and literature*, New York, 1977.

Sternburg, Janet (ed.), *The Writer on her Work: Contemporary women writers reflect on their art and situation*, New York, 1980.

Stetson, Erlene, *Black Sister: Poetry by black American women 1764–1980*, Bloomington, 1981.

Stimpson, Catherine R., *Where the Meanings Are: Feminism and cultural spaces*, London, 1988.

Stubbs, Patricia, *Women and Fiction: Feminism and the novel 1880–1920*, London, 1979.

Tate, Claudia (ed.), *Black Women Writers at Work*, New York, 1983.

Taylor, Helen, 'Class and gender in Charlotte Brontë's *Shirley*', *Feminist Review* 1, 1979.

Taylor, Helen (ed.), *Literature Teaching Politics 1985 Conference Papers* 6, Bristol Polytechnic Department of Humanities.

Thompson, Ann, '"The warrant of womanhood": Shakespeare and feminist criticism', in Graham Holderness (ed.), *The Shakespeare Myth*, Manchester, 1988.

Thompson, Ann and Helen Wilcox (eds), *Teaching Women: Feminism and English studies*, Manchester, 1989.

Todd, Janet, *Feminist Literary History*, Oxford, 1988.

Todd, Janet, *A Dictionary of British and American Women Writers 1660–1800*, London, 1984.

Vetterling-Braggin et al. (eds), *Feminism and Philosophy*, New Jersey, 1977.

Walker, Alice, *In Search of Our Mothers' Gardens*, New York, 1983.

Wandor, Michelene, *On Gender and Writing*, London, 1983.

Ward Jouve, Nicole, *White Woman Speaks with Forked Tongue: Criticism autobiography*, London, 1991.

Warner, Marina, *Monuments and Maidens*, London, 1985.

Weedon, Chris, *Feminist Practice and Post-Structuralist Theory*, Oxford, 1987.

Williamson, Judith, *Decoding Advertisements: Ideology and meaning in advertising*, London, 1978.

Williamson, Marilyn L., *The Patriarchy of Shakespeare's Comedies*, Detroit, 1986.

Willis, Susan, *Specifying: Black women writing the American experience*, Madison, 1987.

Wolff, Janet, *The Social Production of Art*, London, 1981.

Woolf, Virginia, *A Room of One's Own*, 1928, London, 1963.

Woolf, Virginia, *Women and Writing*, ed. Michèle Barrett, London, 1979.

Zimmerman, Bonnie, 'What has never been: an overview of lesbian feminist criticism', in Gayle Greene and Coppélia Kahn (eds), *Making a Difference: Feminist literary criticism*, London, 1985.